CW00495753

NATIONAL SECURITY CINEMA

The Shocking New Evidence of Government Control in Hollywood

~

Matthew Alford and Tom Secker

National Security Cinema

Copyright © 2017 by Matthew Alford and Tom Secker in association with Drum Roll Books. All rights reserved.

No part of this book may be reproduced, copied, or used in any form or manner whatsoever without written permission, except in the case of brief quotations in reviews and critical articles.

Legal Notice:

This book contains copyrighted material, the use of which has not always been specifically authorized by the copyright owner. We are making such material available in our efforts to advance understanding of issues of critical significance. We believe this constitutes a 'fair use' of any such copyrighted material as provided for in section 107 of the US Copyright Law.

For information, contact m.alford@bath.ac.uk

Cover Image: Michael Bay
Cover Production: Tom Secker

Paperback   ISBN 978-1548084981

Non-Fiction / Censorship / Propaganda / Cinema / Hollywood

CONTENTS

~

Oliver Stone: Thirty Years on the Front Line
Paul Verhoeven: Robocop, Total Recall, Starship Troopers

BREAK THIS MATRIX

APPENDICES

INDEX

ENDNOTES

ABOUT THE AUTHORS

~

Dr. Matthew Alford is a Teaching Fellow at the University of Bath in England. His doctoral thesis applied Ed Herman and Noam Chomsky's Propaganda Model to the contemporary Hollywood film industry. His first book, *Reel Power: Hollywood Cinema and American Supremacy*, was published by Pluto Press in 2010 and has since been translated into Chinese. In 2014, Dr. Alford produced a documentary film of his research, *The Writer with No Hands*, which premiered at Hot Docs in Toronto and won the Tablet of Honor at the Ammar Popular Film Festival in Tehran.

Tom Secker is a private researcher who runs spyculture.com— the world's premier online archive about government involvement in the entertainment industry. He has used the Freedom of Information Act to obtain unique government documents since 2010, which has been reported on by *Russia Today, Salon, Techdirt, The Mirror, The Express* and other outlets. He has authored and co-authored articles for *Critical Sociology* and the *American Journal of Economics and Sociology* and hosts the popular ClandesTime podcast.

ACKNOWLEDGEMENTS

~

Our closest, long-term research colleagues have been Tricia Jenkins, Robbie Graham, and Pearse Redmond. This book is broadly reflective of their considerable research, counsel, and analysis over the past decade and we thank them very much.

We are aware that the data used in this book warrants more years of study and that by compiling this manuscript in just two years there will inevitably be some errors and omissions. However, we feel an obligation to put this information out into the public domain swiftly, clearly, and affordably. Consequently, alongside this book, we have begun an ongoing process of submitting adapted sections of the manuscript for peer review and we are releasing all our source data freely on spyculture.com. In the endnotes, unless otherwise stated, documentation is provided on this site.

Our latest articles are published by the *American Journal of Economics and Sociology*, *Critical Sociology*, *Westminster Papers in Communications and Culture*, and the *Quarterly Review of Film and Video*, which are accessible through university libraries.

We consider the contribution made by each author to this project as equal, with the names on the cover arranged alphabetically.

ACRONYMS

~

BBC	British Broadcasting Corporation
CIA	Central Intelligence Agency
DOD	United States' Department of Defense, aka the Pentagon
ELO	Entertainment Liaison Office/Officer
FBI	Federal Bureau of Investigations
MCU	Marvel Cinematic Universe
MPAA	Motion Picture Association of America
NGO	Non-Governmental Organisation
NSA	National Security Agency
NSC	National Security Council
OSS	Office of Strategic Services (forerunner to CIA)
OIG	Office of the Inspector General
OPA	Office of Public Affairs (public relations at CIA)
PCA	Production Code Administration
POW	PrisonerofWar

PREFACE

~

The content of film and television is directly, regularly, and secretly determined by the US government, led by the CIA and Pentagon. More visible since the 1980s is what we identify as a distinct genre: 'national security cinema'—namely, those films that follow self-serving official histories and exalt in the righteousness of US foreign policy.

And yet the reality of a slick and extensive military PR machine in the entertainment industry only became apparent to us, as long-standing researchers in this field, quite recently. When we first looked at the relationship between politics and motion pictures around the turn of the Twenty-First century, we accepted the consensus opinion that a small office at the Pentagon had assisted the production of around 200 films throughout the history of modern media.

How ignorant we were.

More appropriately, how misled we had been—by those who sought to plug the leak of censored scripts or discussion about them, as we shall see.

It gradually became apparent to us that the relationship between the US government and Hollywood is—or rather always was—more political than acknowledged. The files we have received through the Freedom of Information Act indicate that between 1911 and 2017 eight-hundred and fourteen films received DOD support.

If we include the 1,133 TV titles in our count, the number of screen entertainment products supported by the DOD leaps to 1,947. If we are to include the individual episodes for each title on long-running shows like *24*, *Homeland*, and *NCIS*, as well as the influence of other major organisation like the FBI, CIA and White House then it becomes clear that the national security state has supported thousands of products.

National security entertainment promotes violent, self-regarding, American-centric solutions to international problems based on twisted readings of history. However, even those products that don't meet such a lamentable yardstick are still to some degree designed to recruit personnel and, in doing so, must adhere to the desired self-image of the national security state.

Furthermore, we found that the government has been the decisive factor in both the creation and termination of projects, and has manipulated content in much more serious ways than has ever been known.

We also ask a crucial question, though: if the entertainment industry is essentially trapped in a kind of ideological straitjacket, as our books and articles have increasingly suggested, how can we account for the release of what appear to be genuinely subversive products by directors like Paul Verhoeven, Oliver Stone and Michael Moore? Our answer, we think, will confound critics who consider, for example, that Hollywood is biased towards left-wing liberalism.

First, though, let's get back to the scale of the national security state's operation in Hollywood.

THE PENTAGON: THE STRONG ARM IN HOLLYWOOD

For over a century, filmmakers in America have received production assistance in the form of men, advice, locations, and equipment from the US military to cut costs and create authentic-seeming films. The Pentagon is, and has been since its creation, the most important governmental force shaping Hollywood movies.

One of the earliest examples of Hollywood-military cooperation was when the Home Guard provided tanks for the infamous feature film *Birth of a Nation* (1915), in which black slaves revolt against their masters, before the Ku Klux Klan ride in on horseback to save the day. This was severe race hate propaganda, which came with government backing.

It was following the Second World War, with the founding of the Pentagon in 1947, that the US military formalised its operations in Hollywood. In 1948, it set up Entertainment Liaison Offices (ELOs) under the authority of Donald Baruch. Phil Strub took over in 1989.[1]

If the DOD deems that script changes need to be made for it to authorise support, then the producers must adhere to these requests and sign a production assistance agreement (see Appendix D). A technical adviser ensures that the agreed-upon script is the one that is actually used when shooting. The DOD requires a post-production viewing to certify that there is nothing in the film that contravenes the agreement and may make further suggestions at this stage.[2] Where cooperation is more limited, the written agreement may be unnecessary.

The official documentation trail of DOD script changes dries up around the year 2004. Vast amounts of annotated scripts and DOD-Hollywood correspondence had been either taken by or donated to a single historian—Lawrence Suid—from 1976 to 2005, possibly beyond.[3] Suid continues to keep his material in a private archive in a public library in Georgetown, Washington DC, and his apparent unwillingness to share the material represents a substantial and unnecessary loss to the research community.

In the early 2000s, the Los Angeles-based journalist David Robb temporarily gained access to Suid's collection and published the explosive 2004 book, *Operation Hollywood: How the Pentagon Shapes and Censors the Movies*. Since Robb's archival raid we know of no researcher who has been granted access to Suid's collection, with the exception of Texas Christian University professor Tricia Jenkins, who asked for access but was offered just a pitiful handful of material from the early Vietnam War era. Under such conditions, Jenkins was unable to complete the article she was working on, and instead collaborated on an early draft of a 2016 paper with Matthew Alford that established how Suid has, despite his impressive marshalling of data, in some ways choked this field of study.[4]

The DOD's post-2004 papers on Hollywood cooperation— acquired primarily by the authors via the FOIA—do not contain any annotated scripts and there is very little by way of correspondence and script notes. Almost all the officially available material is anodyne diary-like entries which simply log the ongoing activities of the ELOs. We have analysed what little relevant documentation is available along with draft scripts, leaks, interviews and other sources to trace the Pentagon's Twenty-First century influence over movie content.[5]

What does the DOD want to avoid revealing to the public? Read on.

The Key to Production

On a large proportion of film and TV products, the DOD's support is not decisive to content or tone. Most products would be made without its involvement.

However, there are numerous high-profile examples like *Top Gun* (1986) and *Battleship* (2012), which are so dependent on the Pentagon that it is inconceivable they would exist without its assistance. The film *Act of Valor* (2012) even made much of its use of real life Marines as lead actors.

While filmmakers usually have to submit drafts of their screenplays to the military along with their requests for support, the DOD waived these rules for Michael Bay's *Transformers*. In exchange for very early influence over the scripts, the *Transformers* producers secured more military assistance than any other franchise in movie history. We obtained production assistance agreements for the second and third *Transformers* films that show that the screenplays were not even finished by the time that these contracts were signed.

Reports from both the US Army and Marine Corps ELOs show their enthusiasm for assisting the *Transformers* franchise. For *Transformers II: Revenge of the Fallen* they held a joint planning meeting with the producers, 'to discuss the military's role in the sequel' while the script was still in development.[6] Likewise, they provided script assistance throughout the development process for *Transformers: Dark of the Moon*, recording how Bay was 'very receptive to our notes and expressed his desire for us to "help (him) make it better."'[7] A few weeks into pre-production, the Army facilitated a meeting between Paramount Pictures Worldwide Marketing Partnerships and the US Army Accessions Command advertising agency McCann Worldwide. The purpose was to 'discuss opportunities for the US Army to leverage the success of the *Transformers* franchise.'[8] Noting how the second film was the most commercially successful of 2009, the DOD saw the third instalment as an 'opportunity to showcase the bravery and values of our soldiers and the excellent technology of today's Army to a global audience, in an apolitical blockbuster.'[9]

The first *Transformers* film received a record amount of aid from the military, featuring twelve types of Air Force aircraft and troops from four different bases. Bay's military wish list for the second film ran to over 50 items (each item being access to a location or use of vehicles or military extras) with an estimated cost of over $600,000. To borrow a phrase from the Pentagon, this investment was 'force multiplied' by the inclusion of technology such as the $150m F-22 fighters, which had never appeared on screen prior to the first *Transformers* movie. Who else but the Pentagon high command could provide a billion-dollars-worth of unique vehicles and shooting locations, along with trained and uniformed extras, all for only a few hundred-thousand dollars? As producer Ian Bryce put it, 'We would never have been able to make this movie without the willingness of the DOD to embrace this project.'[10]

The Pentagon's influence on *Transformers* extended into the production phase. During the shooting of one scene in the first movie where American troops have been attacked by the Decepticons, Jon Voight, playing the Secretary of Defense, approached Bay to tell him that the scene needed an extra line. Voight felt that he needed to 'express his concern for the troops' safety' so Voight, Bay, Strub and others went into a huddle. Strub suggested, 'Bring 'em home' and 'murmurs of agreement moved through the circle.' The line appears in the finished movie, followed by a shot of 'an approaching helicopter with soldiers silhouetted against swirling red dust.'[11]

[Above] 'Bring 'em home'—but only so we can regroup before taking our revenge.

Of course, despite the claims to the contrary, the *Transformers* franchise is not apolitical. While in the first film almost all of the action happens within the US, in the second and third instalments the fighting takes place all over the world. Despite this, it is only the American (and to a lesser extent the British) military who are shown joining forces with the Autobots to defeat the evil Decepticons, including during a mission in Shanghai. It does so with astounding weapons, in a display of what is often called war pornography. The implicit message is that we should be thrilled that only the Pentagon is up to the task of fighting a global war against an external threat. Plus, of course, we are to trust in officialdom to 'bring 'em home.'

[Above] On the set of Transformers: the US military is in the thick of the action.

The Key to Prevention

That the DOD plays a vital role in generating some movies is one thing. It is quite another if it can actually prevent a film being made. Here we document clear cases where the military's refusal to cooperate seemingly prevented the creation of a film that would otherwise have gone ahead.

Fields of Fire was a prospective film under the direction of James Webb in 1993. Webb was a distinguished Vietnam War veteran, who also went on to serve as Secretary of the Navy and as State Senator for Virginia. The screenplay was based on Webb's eponymous semi-autobiographical novel, which was set in the Vietnam War and so widely praised for its realism that it still appears as a core text at Marine training facilities. As such, *Fields of Fire* seemed like a shoe-in for military support. It was accurate, right? Right, but the DOD denied Webb's request for support.

The Pentagon found representations of some of the Marines objectionable in *Fields of Fire*. These included: fragging (assassination of an officer by their own troops); a Marine posing for a photo with his arm around an enemy POW who has just been burned by napalm; one of the principle characters setting a village hut ablaze; a Marine casually firing his M16 into the bodies of Vietnamese troops to ensure they were dead; and Marines torturing and murdering a man and woman they suspect of doing the same to two other Marines.

In a letter to Webb, Strub wrote that the fact that these kinds of criminal activities actually took place is a matter of record but that by providing official support to the film, the Marines and the DOD would be 'tacitly accepting them as every day, yet regrettable acts of combat.' The movie was never made.

In 1994, Touchstone had scripted *Countermeasures*, to star Sigourney Weaver as a Navy psychiatrist who uncovers a murderous crime ring on board a nuclear aircraft carrier during the Persian Gulf War. In the screenplay, Weaver finds out that her patient was part of a White House cover-up to ship jet parts to Iran, in a plot that echoed the real-world 1980s Iran-Contra scandal, in which the US created a slush fund through illegal arms sales to Iran, some of which ended up arming the Contra fascists in Nicaragua.[12]

The DOD refused to cooperate on *Countermeasures*. The filmmakers needed an aircraft carrier, so the Pentagon's decision effectively terminated the production. Strub assessed that 'fundamental aspects' of the script 'prevent it from reaching the [DOD] criteria.' He commented:

[Navy personnel are] completely unrealistic and negative. They're unprofessional, blatantly focused on personal agenda, and unapologetically sexist if not guilty of outright sexual harassment or assault. ...The astonished reaction of crew members to the presence of a woman aboard the ship is quite unrealistic... Making the principle villain an agent of the (then) Naval Investigative Service fosters a negative perception of the service, implicates all agents by association, and reinforces the allegations of a lack of professionalism that was widely reported by the media over the last few years.

Strub also commented of *Countermeasures*, 'There's no need for us to denigrate the White House, or remind the public of the Iran-Contra affair,' which is again an explicit rejection of a script based on a proven political scandal.

Top Gun II was proposed in the early 1990s. The Navy refused to cooperate with the film because of an infamous scandal just prior. In 1991, a series of incidents had taken place in which more than 100 US Navy and Marine Corps aviation officers were alleged to have sexually assaulted at least 83 women and 7 men or otherwise engaged in 'improper and indecent' conduct at the 35th Annual Tailhook Association Symposium at the Las Vegas Hilton. The scandal—usually abbreviated to 'Tailhook'—led to a damning internal report which cited the original *Top Gun* film by name for contributing to such a regressive military culture.[13] Now, in 2017, press reports suggest the long-planned sequel is finally going ahead, with military support, since the Tailhook scandal has been largely forgotten—thanks, in no small part, to the military's efforts in Hollywood on films like *Countermeasures*.

There are likely many more such cases where the Pentagon has been decisive in a film not being produced, which we have not included in our tally. Just in reference to the Marine Corps' film office in Los Angeles, David Robb refers to a 'floor-to-ceiling shelf of files on films that asked for assistance but were never made.' He remarks that 'some of these probably couldn't get financing, but many weren't made because they would have been impossible—or prohibitively expensive—to make without military assistance.'[14]

The Pentagon as Key to the Politics of Film

Primarily, the Pentagon's role is not to be a decisive force in making movies, nor in short-circuiting their creation, but rather to manipulate existing scripts. This book uses a series of case studies to illustrate the kind of influence that can be implemented by the DOD, along with other agencies, and we will elucidate some briefer examples in this chapter too.

It is important to emphasise at this stage that the DOD is conscious of its propaganda role, even though its defenders hide behind absurd statements to the effect that their changes are 'inadvertent' and 'not intentional.'[15]

Let's begin with the classic case of US military film propaganda. In *The Green Berets* (1968), Western star John Wayne convinces sceptical news reporters that the Vietnam War is necessary and leads a team of Green Berets (US Special Forces) and Army of the Republic of Vietnam (ARVN) soldiers on a successful mission to capture a top North Vietnamese field commander.

During production of *Green Berets*, the DOD requested that the scriptwriter delete any mention of the soldiers entering Laos because it 'raises sensitive questions.'[16] Presumably, these questions revolved around the fact that in the real world the US had been secretly bombing a neutral country for the past three years.

In a scene that explains the purpose of the war at the start of the film, Francis Tully, Speech Review Staff for the Department of State, also suggested that the scriptwriters insert the following language:

We do not see this as a civil war, and it is not. South Vietnam is an independent country, seeking to maintain its independence in the face of aggression by a neighbouring country. Our goal is to help the South Vietnamese retain their freedom, and to develop in the way they want to, without interference from outside the country.[17]

These lines do not appear in the final film, but Tully's suggestion indicates that he hoped to simplify the war in Vietnam in a way that Americans could support, and this simplification occurs though in the final version of the scene, as military leaders explain to reporters that the war boils down to stopping 'Communist domination of the world.   '

[Above] Fresh from winning World War II, John Wayne turns his sights on Vietnam.

Green Berets was partly based on the non-fiction work of Robin Moore, who described the torture of prisoners by real-life Green Berets in Vietnam. The DOD wanted violent scenes to be tempered. In an early script, a prisoner is brutalised by a South Vietnamese officer, whose actions are approved by the Americans. In the final film, John Wayne intervenes to prevent the violence further than a slap, and then the presumed torture of the prisoner takes place off-screen outside the company of American soldiers.

Charles Hinkle, Director of Security Review for the Assistant Secretary of Defense also objected to how the film 'accentuates terms of contempt, such as "maggots," for the Viet Cong.' According to Tully, the scene was 'grist for the opponents of US policy in Viet-Nam' because they support 'some of the accusations of these opponents against the US, and is of course a clear violation of the Articles of War.'[18]

John Wayne also acceded to a DOD request that the film omit its standard 'thank you' credit. The producer wrote to the Pentagon: 'We all agree with the DOD suggestion that such a credit could conceivably categorize the picture as a US propaganda film—rather than an exciting piece of motion picture entertainment. With that in mind, we will delete the DOD credit.'[19]

The whole *Green Berets* project had begun life with Wayne writing to President Johnson to ask for his support in making a film to support US efforts in Vietnam.[20]

Not intentional, eh?

Just like it was presumably 'unintentional' when the Pentagon altered James Bond scripts. On *Goldeneye* (1995), Strub required a change to the nationality of the American admiral who is duped and murdered by Xenia Onatopp.[21] In the finished film he is Canadian. On *Tomorrow Never Dies* (1997), in the scene where Bond is about to parachute jump into Vietnamese waters, Strub successfully requested that a CIA agent not warn Bond: 'You know what will happen. It will be war, and maybe this time we'll win.'[22] Peculiarly, Strub emailed us to say there was no DOD cooperation on *Tomorrow Never Dies* but we checked the credits and even obtained a Production Assistance Agreement between the DOD and the filmmakers (see Appendix D), confirming that Strub is simply wrong about this.[23]

In an illustrative instance of academia soft-balling this topic, Suid categories *Tomorrow Never Dies* in a section called "Films with Unseen Military Assistance", alongside *Birth of a Nation* and

```
>
>> Mr. Alford,
>>
>> The only information that we maintain on these productions (if any)
>> would be a brief entry in an incomplete data base. We didn't have
>> any involvement with "Three Kings" or "Tomorrow Never Dies." You can
>> submit a FOIA request for this information, but I can also provide it
>> without one, and you might even receive it sooner, depending on my
>> work load.
>>
>> Best,
>>
>>
>> Philip M. Strub
>> Director of Entertainment Media
>> Department of Defense
>> The Pentagon, Room 2E966
>> Washington, DC 20301-1400
```

nine others, as though secret (and officially denied) government work on film scripts should just be accepted as par for the course.[24]

[Above] The Pentagon's denial that it worked on Tomorrow Never Dies.

The Producers gratefully acknowledge the cooperation of the
U.S. DEPARTMENT OF DEFENSE AND THE U.S. AIR FORCE
THE MINISTRY OF DEFENCE, LONDON
DIRECTORATE OF PUBLIC RELATIONS, ROYAL NAVY
HMS WESTMINSTER   HMS DRYAD
U.S. AIR FORCES IN EUROPE
U.S. AIR FORCE SPECIAL OPERATIONS COMMAND
48TH FIGHTER WING, RAF LAKENHEATH U.K.
100TH AIR REFUELING WING, RAF MILDENHALL U.K.
352ND SPECIAL OPERATIONS GROUP, RAF MILDENHALL U.K.

[Above] End credits from Tomorrow Never Dies thanking the Pentagon. Note the role played by Britain's Ministry of Defence here, too—the script influence unknown.

The DOD negotiated for weeks with the producers of the Nicholas Cage World War II movie, *Windtalkers* (2002). The film was about Cage's character protecting an important code known only by

Navaho Indian recruits, based on a true story. The Pentagon was keen to ensure that the film did not explicitly say that the Marine command had ordered its men to kill the Navajo if captured, even though this was established as a fact by Congress. They were successful, although the filmmakers used a suggestively lingering shot of the commander's face to indicate that the order was implicit.

Other elements were removed from the original *Windtalkers* script following DOD pressure. Firstly, a scene in which a Marine stabs a dead Japanese soldier in the mouth to retrieve a gold filling. 'The activity is unMarine,' said the DOD, insisting on its removal and trying to pin the blame for such activities on conscripts.[25] Secondly, the original script has Cage's character kill an injured Japanese soldier who is attempting to surrender by blasting him with a flame-thrower. The DOD complained; the scene was eliminated.[26]

On the Bruce Willis movie *Tears of the Sun* (2003) the DOD had a decisive impact. In fact, *Tears of the Sun* was the first movie to be allowed to shoot aboard the USS *Harry S Truman* and the production was loaned SH-60 Seahawk helicopters and F/A-18 Hornet jet fighters. Internal DOD documents explain that, 'After lengthy script negotiations,' they managed, 'to increase military realism [and] to prevent the depiction of the US government as complicit in nasty conspiracies overseas.'[27]

The 'nasty conspiracies' in question presumably relate to *Cry Freetown* about Sierra Leone, and *Delta Force* about Nigeria—the actual country depicted in *Tears of the Sun*. Both documentaries were watched enthusiastically by director Antoine Fuqua. The latter film focuses on the role of Shell Oil—the corporation behind half the wealth of the Nigerian dictatorship—in polluting the land of the country's poorest citizens. When peaceful protests erupted in response, the government responded violently and, at times, fatally. One scene in the *Delta Force* documentary draws on eye witness accounts to indicate that the government had used heavy weaponry on some communities and then blamed it all on local ethnic in-fighting.[28] Fuqua carried a book about African genocide with him on the set of *Tears of the Sun*. Ironically given the declawing of the film he was making at that very moment, it was called *The Silence*.[29]

The filmmakers of *Jurassic Park III* (2001) approached the Pentagon about borrowing some A-10 Thunderbolts for a scene where they would battle mid-air against a flock of pterosaurs. This request was refused, as Strub told them, 'They're tank killers. A flying dinosaur is no match for an A-10. It would only cause the audience to feel pity for the dinosaur.'[30] It is probable that this decision was made due to audience responses to the ending of the DOD-sponsored *Godzilla* (1998), where the monster is shot dead with missiles by Marine Corps jets.

In discussions with the producers of *Jurassic Park III* Strub managed to leverage two other major changes to the script. He suggested a 'nice military rescue' at the end of the film, and the production was loaned soldiers and vehicles from the Marine Corps for this sequence. Strub also said to the producers, 'But tell me this: You've got this major running around the world with the authority that the president can only dream about, so if you don't care, would you change his character, make him like the president's science adviser or something like that? Just get him out of the uniform.' The filmmakers obliged.[31]

[Above] The DOD's 'nice military rescue' at the end of Jurassic Park III.

The DOD also granted some support to *Tropic Thunder* (2008), a comedy that lampoons the story of the problems producing *Apocalypse Now*, portraying a film crew trying to make a Vietnam war film and everything goes wrong.[32] In contrast to the military's reaction to *Apocalypse Now,* though, a special promotional screening of *Tropic Thunder* took place at the Marine Corps base at Camp Pendleton alongside a visit by the stars Robert Downey Jr, Ben Stiller and Jack Black.[33] One line that appears in an earlier draft and was likely removed at the DOD's request is a joke that, 'At a reported budget north of $200 million, Tropic Thunder could end up costing almost as much as the real war!'[34] This is the only reference to the real war that appears in the draft, whereas the final film remains firmly in a fictional world.

Another film set, in parts, in the Vietnam War was *Forrest Gump* (1994), which the Pentagon managed to wield some influence over even though they refused to provide any production support. The Army rejected an early script because of the 'nihilistic view of military & Vietnam experience.' While a later script was 'much better' the Army were 'still not interested in assisting,' but 'the filmmakers did make one very important change suggested by the Army: Original script had an entire company of men like Forrest and Bubba; Army pointed out that the actual program distributed soldiers like Forrest among "normal" soldiers in many companies. The final script made this important change.'[35]

An episode of *NCIS* titled 'Toxic' featured a storyline involving, 'military personnel making bio-weapons illegally' leading to 'significant storyline changes requested by DoD.'[36] The finished episode changed the storyline so the military scientists believe they are trying to cure 'Afghanistan War Syndrome' and the Army has been duped into making the bio-weapon without realising it. Similarly, when CBS rebooted the popular TV series *Hawaii Five-0* they depended on significant military support. Army script notes show how the pilot episode was crafted with close co-operation from the ELOs who had a lot of input when it came to moulding the protagonist Steve McGarrett, including his background as a former Navy SEAL.

The opening scene was rewritten to make the US military appear 'more capable and lethal' and to address the Pentagon's concern that, 'the bad guys in the opening assault scene are not foreign military and therefore their equipment need not be specifically Chinese, etc.' The notes also object to another scene later in the pilot episode where one of McGarrett's colleagues attacks a criminal, 'Although not a military issue per se, we think that it's way too heavy-handed for Chin to torture Sang Min by beating him with an ashtray, but, more to the point, we can't go along with McGarrett turning a blind eye to it.' In the finished scene, Chin only hits Sang Min once and apologises as soon as McGarrett walks in and sees him.[37] These changes helped shape not just the pilot episode but the central character, tone and 'moral compass' of the rebooted series, which is now in its 7th season.

[Above] Katy Perry joins the Marine Corps for Part of Me.

Likewise in exchange for allowing the pop star Cher to film aboard the battleship Missouri for the music video for *If I Could Turn Back Time*, the DOD reviewed the storyboard. They removed one shot where, 'A chief rips a pin-up photo from the inside of a sailor's locker.' Though the DOD were concerned about Cher's 'vulgar black leather thong-type of outfit' ultimately there were 'no official complaints, and app[roximately] $8 million of free MTV advertising.'[38] The DOD has worked on music videos for Katy Perry's *Part of Me* (where she joins the Marine Corps), Hootie and the Blowfish's *Musical Chairs* and Mariah Carey's *I Still Believe*, among many more.

~

As we will see in the upcoming case studies, Pentagon manipulation of film scripts for political ends is widespread, so we will leave the examples for now.

It is also worth noting here that the military has also sometimes operated a PR team out of the White House, most recently on Kathryn Bigelow's *Zero Dark Thirty*, which we examine in more depth later. In 2000, *Salon* magazine discovered that the White House's drug war officers, under the leadership of General Barry Macaffery, had spent over $20m paying the major

US networks to inject 'war on drugs' plots into the scripts of prime-time series such as: *ER*; *Beverly Hills 90210*; *Chicago Hope*; *The Drew Carey Show*; *7th Heaven; The Practice*, and *Sabrina the Teenage Witch*.[39] This had decisive effects. A script for *Chicago Hope* was produced solely because it had anti-drug theme. In the episode, ravers endured drug-induced death, rape, psychosis, a two-car wreck, a broken nose and a doctor's threat to skip life-saving surgery unless the patient agreed to an incriminating urine test.

Let's say you consider tough media messages to be useful or even essential to curb the use of drugs in society. Okay, but should this be done secretly? Should these messages single out certain illegal drugs as being more harmful than, say, tobacco and alcohol?[40] Should these messages come with the tacit assumption that the 'war on drugs,' which has entailed US overseas intervention in Panama, Columbia and Mexico—not to mention at least some instances of government drug-dealing—is somehow benevolent?[41]

Surely not.

The Disease Spreads

One of the major discoveries we have made has been the role of the Pentagon in network television. Even David Robb's expose only pointed to a handful of TV shows being affected by the military but the lists we've received through the FOIA have been astonishing. All told, the Pentagon has worked on 1133 TV titles, 977 of them between 2004 and 2016. These include: *American Idol*, *The X-Factor*, numerous Oprah Winfrey shows, *Ice Road Truckers*, *Battlefield Priests*, *America's Got Talent*, *Hawaii Five-O*, *War Dogs*—the list goes on (see Appendix B).

While much of DOD cooperation on most television shows in particular is likely just courtesy and the shows would never have had the potential to say something more critical of American power, it demonstrates the scale, reach, and intent of the Pentagon's activity. Nor should we be too sanguine about the lightweight nature of some of these programmes. For example, the Pentagon has worked on numerous cookery shows, including *Big Kitchens*, *Masterchef* and *Cupcake Wars*. In doing so, it at least does something to associate itself with the creation and provision of food, rather than the destruction of life. Or take an even weirder association: the DOD's substantial efforts in Hollywood from the 1950s onward to manipulate material that encouraged a belief in UFOs, for a range of opaque reasons, as recorded in exemplary detail by Robbie Graham in his book *Silver Screen Saucers* but otherwise ignored in scholarship and mainstream media.[42]

The Pentagon-friendly historian Lawrence Suid scoffed at David Robb's suggestion that Phil Strub is one of the most powerful men in Hollywood, calling it 'an absurd statement which has no basis in fact.'[43] Strub himself claims that his role as the Pentagon's man in Hollywood 'is like being a minor eunuch in the court of imperial China.'[44] The fact is that Robb's statement is even truer now than it was back then, and the evidence we have for it is much stronger. It is unusual and unhealthy for a field of primary research to be so heavily dominated by one scholar, Suid, and for access to significant documents to be almost entirely concentrated in that person's hands, apparently in line with the wishes of the DOD.

Over the past four decades, Suid has catalogued the material on DOD influence with great skill and precision but while he has revealed with one hand, so he has concealed with the other. Such an approach has saved the DOD from embarrassment. By now, just twelve years after Suid's last book was released, the Pentagon has worked on over a hundred more films and it is our understanding, based on IMDB searches and patchy DOD lists that he missed about a hundred from the pre-2004 period. Even by just sticking to the films he has directly discussed in published work, Suid has missed opportunities to mention the ethically dubious script changes for these products, including: *Clear and Present Danger*; *Tomorrow Never Dies*; *Rules of Engagement*; *Black Hawk Down*; *Goldeneye*; *Tears of the Sun*, and *Thirteen Days*. Instead, he either neglects to mention the changes or implicitly normalises the DOD's actions, such as when he dismissively says the original script for *Contact* contained a 'silly depiction of the military'.[45] Beyond that, although Suid does catalogue TV shows that depict the military, he does not systematically identify whether the DOD worked on them, let alone shaped their content. We counted 156 such products pre-2004 and 977 since Suid's last book.

In 1941, a Senate Investigation called the Hollywood movie studios 'gigantic engines of propaganda.' The Director of the Office of War Information, Elmer Davis, explained in 1942: 'The easiest way to inject a propaganda idea into most people's minds is to let it go through the medium of an entertainment picture when they do not realize that they are being propagandized.'

What had seemed like distant history is now contemporary reality. The engines are back in action—bigger, better, and at full throttle. But this time, no one knows it. This time, there is no Nazi threat. This time, the engines are turned on us.

THE CIA: IN FROM THE COLD, SHELTERED IN THE CINEMA

The CIA's influence on Hollywood has, by any measure, been much smaller than the DOD's, but it is larger than general coverage of the topic would have you believe. Although there have been many books published about the CIA since the 1960s, the Agency's role in the entertainment industry has become the subject of serious scrutiny only since it created an Entertainment Liaison Office in 1996.

Even in the contemporary period, with few bargaining chips aside from knowledge and access to official headquarters, the CIA has continued to present itself merely as an advisory entity in the entertainment industry. The Agency's website describes its ELO in banal terms, saying, 'Our goal is an accurate portrayal of the men and women of the CIA, and the skill, innovation, daring, and commitment to public service that defines them... We are in a position to give greater authenticity to scripts, stories, and other products in development. That can mean answering questions, debunking myths, or arranging visits to the CIA.'[46]

Documentation indicating anything to the contrary has long been sparse and scarce.

As such, any interpretations pushing a more conspiratorial line about CIA activity in Hollywood have been received cautiously within the scholarly community, and the notion that it has systematically interfered in entertainment has been explicitly shunned in the mainstream.[47] However, the CIA's first ELO, Chase Brandon, has given contradictory interviews about which products he helped to make, indicating that the Agency have sought to minimise the public's awareness of their influence.[48] As such, we should proceed with caution not to overestimate or underestimate the CIA's activities in the industry. By paying closer attention to the available facts and documentation, this chapter examines each era of CIA activity in Hollywood and shows that, at every point, the scholarly scepticism towards the existence of systematic CIA influence in Hollywood is wishful thinking at best.

1943—1965

Even by the early-2000s, there were indications that the CIA had a more significant influence over early Cold War Hollywood than anyone had previously known. Scholars had long been aware that the film adaptations of George Orwell's *Animal Farm* (1954) and *Nineteen Eighty-Four* (1956) were directly affected by the CIA.[49] In the case of *Animal Farm*, the changes to the ending of the film were designed to encourage revolutions against communist dictatorships, ironically just as, in the real world, the CIA was overthrowing the democratically elected governments in Iran and Guatemala and launching operations against Sukarno's independence government in Indonesia. E. Howard Hunt, one of the CIA agents behind the Agency's coup in Guatemala, was involved in negotiations with Orwell's widow for the rights to these film adaptations.[50]

In the late 1990s, Francis Stonor Saunders and David Eldridge found letters proving that the head of censorship at Paramount regularly wrote to an anonymous individual at the CIA to tell how he promoted narratives favourable to the Agency, especially to patch over the cracks in US race relations. Saunders and Eldridge published their findings in 1999 and 2000, respectively, with Saunders in particular characterising the discovery as part of a wider plan by the government to 'pay the piper' (the artistic industry) in the early Cold War, including its sponsorship of expressionist artwork for political ends.[51]

The Paramount man was Luigi Luraschi, who reported to his CIA colleague, known only as 'Owen,' that he had secured the agreement of several casting directors to plant 'well-dressed negroes' into films, including 'a dignified negro butler' who has lines 'indicating he is a free man' in *Sangaree* (1953) and in a golf club scene for the Dean Martin/Jerry Lewis feature *The Caddy* (1953). [52] Elsewhere, Luraschi claimed to have arranged the removal of key scenes from the film *Arrowhead* (1953), including a sequence where an Apache Indian tribe is forcibly tagged and relocated by the US Army. He also removed scenes from *Houdini* (1953), *Legend of the Incas (1954)* and other films where Americans were drinking heavily, and leaned on the writer of *Strategic Air Command* (1955) to ensure that America didn't appear as, 'a lot of trigger-happy warmongering people, just itching to drop atom bombs at the slightest provocation.' [53]

Although there is nothing to suggest that Luraschi was actually paid by the CIA, it is undisputed that his 'work' constituted a relationship with an anonymous individual at the CIA, whose own identity, activity, strategic aims and correspondence (even his replies to Luraschi) remain hidden to this day.

The discovery of Luraschi's letters raise questions about the spy links held by other major figures in Hollywood. Most directly, Luraschi noted how it was possible to 'kill a commie movie' by appealing to executives like Darryl Zanuck at 20th Century Fox who 'would not consciously do anything to help the Left.' [54] Zanuck had served in the Army Signal Corps during the Second World War and filmed the invasion of North Africa alongside John Ford's OSS film unit. After the war, Zanuck became a board member of the CIA-created National Committee for A Free Europe. He worked closely with both the Eisenhower and Nixon administrations. [55] C.D. Jackson, a former OSS psychological warfare specialist who worked for Eisenhower, described how Zanuck could be relied upon, 'to insert into scripts... the right ideas with the proper subtlety.' [56] The Luraschi documents were found among the papers of Jackson's secretary. Most recently,

Michael Ray FitzGerald wrote a commanding article drawing together the available evidence for a peer reviewed journal. FitzGerald emphasises that Zanuck was well above the level of a mere agent and was, in fact, one of the world's most powerful men at the time. In terms of propaganda on film, Fitzgerald pays particular attention to *The Longest Day* (1962), which totally erased the role of the Communists in defeating fascism in Europe.[57]

Luraschi's letters make it clear that the Production Code Administration (PCA) was 'a wonderful spot to keep a check on independents both from the standpoint of eliminating troublesome material as of injecting stuff.'[58] The PCA was controlled by the MPAA, which was run by another friend of the Agency, Eric Johnston, who served as MPAA president from 1946-1963. Johnston was also a high level political operative who worked for both Truman and Eisenhower, and maintained a friendship and correspondence with Allen Dulles. They discussed the film industry and Johnston reported back on his meetings with key Soviet officials, including when he played host to Anastas Mikoyan, Ambassador Stanislav Menshikov and Premier Nikita Kruschev when they visited the US. The letters between Johnston and Dulles are consistent with the idea that Johnston was providing the Agency with political intelligence.[59] Eldridge suggests that the reason Luraschi's correspondence with the CIA was short-lived was because, at the same time as his letters to 'Owen,' Johnston initiated an industry-wide program involving the State Department focused on achieving the same aims.[60]

As such, from the very earliest years after their creation, the CIA were recruiting assets within the highest levels of the film industry and using them to spy on Hollywood and to add and remove material from movie scripts. This is a far cry from the National Security Act's description of the CIA's mission being the, 'coordinating the intelligence activities of the several Government

26

departments and agencies in the interest of national security.'[61] Even the NSC's directive to allow for covert actions 'against hostile foreign states or groups or in support of friendly foreign states or groups' doesn't imply permission to alter film scripts to make Americans look less like drunken racists who enjoy nuking foreigners and abusing natives.[62]

On the screen adaptation of *The Quiet American* (1958), Jonathan Nashel argues that CIA operations officer Edward Lansdale helped producer Joseph Mankiewicz rewrite the script. In 1956, Mankiewicz sent his script to Lansdale so he could review it, along with a series of questions. Nashel cites a letter from Lansdale to Mankiewicz where he encourages the producer to make numerous changes to the version in Graham Green's original book, reversing Greene's political criticism of US involvement in Vietnam. The resulting film was profoundly different, ultimately presenting US intervention in a positive light. Of particular note, Greene's novel depicted the killing of a CIA protagonist because he is discovered manufacturing plastic explosives for an anti-Communist terror campaign in Indochina. For the film version, the plastic explosives became plastic toys—meant to be doled out to Vietnamese children, but the agent is brutally murdered by Communists anyway.[63]

A leading historian on the early Cold War relationship between the CIA and Hollywood, Simon Willmetts from the University of Hull criticises Nashel's analysis of Lansdale's involvement, arguing that the PCA, rather than Lansdale or the CIA, were the primary influence on these changes. In his book, *In Secrecy's Shadow: The CIA and Hollywood*, Wilmetts comments:

The principal alterations to Greene's story were made long before this correspondence [Mankiewicz-Lansdale] took place and were carried out in order to appease the industry censors in the Production Code Administration, not the

CIA. ... [Some people] appear to have lost sight of the fact that Lansdale is confirming changes to the novel that Mankiewicz had already made.[64]

It is true that Mankiewicz had already made numerous changes to the story told in the original novel by the time he wrote to Lansdale. Among them, the titular Quiet American secret agent Alden Pyle was re-characterised as a young man working for a benign NGO, in keeping with demands from the PCA not to depict government agents and agencies.

However, the PCA had nothing to do with the complete political reversal of the story, which turned Pyle from being naive and reckless into an all-American hero. They had no influence on the changes to the ending of the film, which blames a car bombing on communists, when, in the book, it is carried out by General Thế's CIA-supported militia. Lansdale's letter to Mankiewicz encouraged this reversal, saying 'go right ahead and let it be finally revealed that the Communists did it after all.'[65]

[Above] Fowler (Michael Redgrave, left) confronts Pyle (Audie Murphy, right) after the car bombing in Saigon.

Willmetts is right that Lansdale confirmed changes to *The Quiet American* that Mankiewicz had already made, but he overlooks the fact that the pair had met in Saigon two months earlier while Mankiewicz was scouting film locations. While we do not know what was said between Landsdale and Mankewitz, it is almost certain they discussed the script, otherwise why would Mankiewicz have subsequently sent it to Lansdale and asked for his opinions? As such, while in the letter Lansdale was encouraging changes that by that point had been made, he was involved in the production two months before sending that letter. Put another way, given the content of Lansdale's letter, why would we assume that he hadn't encouraged this reversal of the politics of the book when he met Mankiewicz two months earlier? Given that CIA director Allen Dulles subsequently intervened to help the production get permission to film in Vietnam, it is clear that the Agency approved of these changes.[66]

Similarly, on the production of *Animal Farm*, Willmetts says that Alford (along with historians Dan Leab and Tony Shaw) 'fail to point out the crucial distinction between the CIA's covert sponsorship of a *foreign* production company for the purposes of anti-Soviet propaganda, and the relationship which existed between the *American* film-industry and government departments such as the FBI and the Department of Defense for the purposes of public relations' [original emphasis]. This is technically true, but, in practice, *Animal Farm* was watched extensively by Western audiences, so the distinctions between domestic PR and overseas propaganda operations are irrelevant. Indeed, the CIA's practice of sending narratives into foreign markets, knowing full well that they would find their way back to the domestic population, was revealed during the Church Committee hearings as a tactic to evade laws on propagandising the public.

Willmetts himself discovered that *Men of the Fighting Lady* (1954) received CIA production assistance. According to an internal CIA memo in 1953, covert ops specialist Tracy Barnes went to Hollywood to 'show to certain MGM representatives an unclassified version of the film' about American pilots in the Korean War.'[67] While the memo therefore takes pains to establish that the CIA was not initiating a film project, it also makes clear that MGM couldn't use the footage without the CIA's permission. The production was thereby locked into the Agency's sphere of influence for when it decided to proceed.

Willmetts also traced the influence of American intelligence on Hollywood back to World War Two. He reveals that, during the war, the OSS ran a film unit comprising 300 Hollywood directors and technicians.[68] They produced training, surveillance, and propaganda movies including concentration camp films that were used during the Nuremberg trials.[69] Of course, this was all in the context of a much larger and well acknowledged cooperative relationship between the studios and the government as part of the war effort, which included numerous stars like John Wayne and Ronald Reagan helping to sell war bonds and work on propaganda projects—more justifiable, of course, during the struggle against Nazism than at other points in modern history.

Willmetts solidified the case that, immediately following the war, the OSS provided production support to three films glorifying their wartime activities—*O.S.S.*, *Cloak and Dagger* and *13 Rue Madelaine* (all 1946), though assistance was withdrawn from the latter after disagreements between wartime head of the OSS Bill Donovan and producer Louis De Rochemont over the accuracy of the movie.[70] *O.S.S.* features dialogue where a senior instructor tells a room of recruits that 'we need a central intelligence agency,' promoting this idea before the CIA even existed (and, though Willmetts did not mention this, before the phrase appeared in any government document). Willmetts acknowledges in a press release, though not explicitly in his book, that, 'Without Hollywood's help the CIA might not have been established in the National Security Act of 1947'—a fair claim but an astonishing one to underplay so gratuitously.

Despite documenting the OSS film unit in detail, Willmetts neglects to mention a 1943 OSS memo on The Motion Picture as a Weapon of Psychological Warfare. This document describes how to use not just individual movies but the entire industry as a weapon of national power and psychological warfare. In sum, it functions as a crude manual for what the CIA would later attempt to do. It says that motion pictures are 'one of the most powerful propaganda weapons at the disposal of the United States' and 'a potent force in attitude formation' that 'can be employed on most of the major psychological warfare fronts' including the domestic civilian and military population.[71]

Meanwhile, the CIA worked to ensure that Hollywood films did not depict them in any form in their early years. In one case, they managed to remove all references to themselves from the 1951 comedy, *My Favorite Spy*. A memo from that year records how a lawyer for Paramount approached the Agency seeking to ensure that three CIA character names bore no resemblance to those of real-life CIA agents. While Willmetts mentions this memo, he focuses on a handwritten note at the bottom that describes *My Favorite Spy* as 'a lousy picture' that 'makes no reference to CIA' and, in consequence, 'no further action' was to be taken.[72]

Actually, the memo makes clear that the original script explicitly referred to the Agency, and another handwritten note says that they told the lawyer to 'omit all references to CIA.' As such, the reason why the finished film (lousy or otherwise) 'makes no reference to CIA' is because the CIA leaned on the producers to change the script. This was successful and thus there was 'no further action' to be taken.[73] It is an explicit example of movie censorship by the Agency during this period.

The CIA did not just prevent the entertainment industry

from referring to them directly. They also protected the historical reputation of their predecessor, the Office of Strategic Services (OSS) (1942—1945). We discovered that, in 1956, through a network of informants and assets centred in CBS, the CIA learned that a small-time company, Flamingo Films, was developing a series of films about the exploits of the OSS in the Second World War. The Agency then engaged CBS to develop a rival product to muscle Flamingo Films out of the market, without ever intending to help CBS actually produce their series. This operation was successful and neither the Flamingo Films nor the CBS series were ever put into production.[74]

In 1961, the CIA suffered its first high profile failure when its attempt to invade Fidel Castro's Cuba was defeated at the Bay of Pigs, resulting in hundreds of deaths on both sides. In the aftermath, the CIA started using films to massage their public image, eight years earlier than Willmetts contends when he highlights 1973's *Scorpio*. While previous films had received production assistance from the Agency or mentioned the CIA, the first to do both was actually the James Bond movie, *Thunderball* (1965).

Although there is no evidence of the CIA directly manipulating the *Thunderball* screenplay, they did affect its source material. The book of the film was written at the height of the friendship between author Ian Fleming and CIA director Allen Dulles. Professor Christopher Moran, author of *Company Confessions: Memoir and the CIA*, gained access to correspondence between Fleming and Dulles and attributes the increasingly positive portrayal of the CIA in the later Bond novels to this blossoming friendship. He writes: 'Out of respect for his American friend, Fleming generously agreed to include in his later novels an increasing number of glowing references to the CIA. Nowhere was this more apparent than in *Thunderball*.'[75]

[Above] Bond and Domino rescued by a CIA front company.

We found that there was some direct CIA assistance on the film adaptation of *Thunderball* itself, too. At the climax, Bond and his lover, Domino, are rescued from the Caribbean Sea via a plane equipped with a skyhook. The plane and the skyhook apparatus were loaned to the production by Intermountain Aviation, a CIA front company. The provision of the skyhook was negotiated by Charles Russhon, a former Air Force officer who was hired by Bond producer Albert Broccoli as a technical advisor and liaison with the government. Russhon had invited the CIA to a special screening of *Goldfinger* at MPAA headquarters in 1964, while *Thunderball* was in development.[76] This might seem like a trivial detail of government production support but these rarely-seen technologies helped turn the Bond films into the world's premier spy brand. Adjusting for inflation, *Thunderball* was the first Bond film to gross over $1 billion, in part thanks to the added production value provided by the Agency. This not only helped the Bond franchise but also the Agency, as Bond was the first movie series to feature a CIA character—Felix Leiter—and he was portrayed very positively.

So, the CIA did have a tangible—and at the time secret—influence on Hollywood in the early Cold War, in terms of:

preventing undesirable projects from being made; altering the political content of entertainment, and using movies to promote themselves. Willmetts argues that they didn't exert much pressure on the industry because they didn't have to—the PCA and libel laws discouraged filmmakers from portraying government agencies. [77] However, the PCA could be sidestepped with permission from the relevant government agency, hence why the producers of the OSS-assisted film *O.S.S.* got away with having the name of a spy agency as the title of their movie. Similarly, libel laws only come into effect after a film is released, so, in order to maintain their total absence from cinema, the CIA had to be pro-active.

Newly released documents in the CIA's Crest archive show that, during the 1950s, the Agency refused or avoided all direct requests for production assistance as they 'deliberately cherish[ed] anonymity.'[78] The Agency managed to keep its name out of all films from its inception in 1947 until a very brief reference in Alfred Hitchcock's *North By Northwest* in 1959, and even then there was no focus on the Agency in any film until *Dr. No* (1962), followed by *Charade* (1963) and *Operation C.I.A.* (1965). This had real consequences for the CIA's ability to conduct covert operations without the public knowing, as Willmetts acknowledges when he calls the CIA in Hollywood an 'absent presence' that managed to curtail the representation of its 'controversial covert activities' by refusing to cooperate with filmmakers.[79]

[Above] The first allusion to the CIA ever in a Hollywood film, namely North by Northwest (1959), which even then only shows the CIA's name partially on screen.

One final example from this period illustrates the CIA's attitude to cinema. When Warner Bros. approached them in the early 1950s seeking technical advice on an unspecified film, they were told that the CIA 'would not only be unable to afford such guidance but that we would take every step to discourage the production of a picture which purported to represent current US espionage.'[80] Take every step? This mind-set shows that the CIA, at least, did not believe the libel laws and the PCA were enough to maintain their desired level of secrecy, despite Willmetts' protestations to the contrary.

All told, the CIA in the early Cold War could hardly be characterised as taking a neutral or hands-off approach to Hollywood, as has been argued in the leading scholarship to date. In fact, we rather suspect that most people coming new to this field, assuming they value transparent democracy, would be unhappily stunned by the CIA manipulation documented just in Willmett's generally excellent book, let alone the numerous additions we've made and the even more disturbing context that evolved in its aftermath.

1966—1986

Richard Helms took over as CIA chief in 1966 and appeared to adopt a more relaxed posture to active Hollywood cooperation. For the next two decades, the CIA had little involvement in cinema and, on the rare occasions that it did, it exercised weak and indecisive control over the productions. But was all as it seemed?

In April 1972, the producers of *Scorpio* (1973) visited CIA headquarters and shot footage at Langley. It was the first time in the Agency's history that such a visit had been permitted.[81] The resulting film was a paranoid thriller that depicted reckless and corrupt CIA officers assassinating their own agents. Ironically, a few years earlier, Helms had turned down a similar request from the producers of *Topaz* (1969), a Hitchcock-directed drama that, according to Willmetts, was, 'more palatable for CIA public affairs than *Scorpio.*'[82] It certainly appears possible, even likely, that the CIA made an error over *Scorpio* by helping facilitate the production of a movie that presented them in a grim light.

However, we now know that the CIA was aware that the film had changed its name from the mundane 'Danger Field' to the more menacing 'Scorpion' before the filming at Langley took place.[83] It is at least possible that what many interpret as a negative portrayal of the CIA actually conforms to the Agency's desired public image at the time. Some other circumstantial evidence gives weight to the idea. Helms also accepted an invitation to the set of the thriller *Three Days of the Condor* (1975), again a film that cast the CIA as murderous villains. He spoke for hours with the movie's star Robert Redford—although by this point Nixon had removed Helms from office. The CIA monitored the resultant news coverage of Redford meeting Helms and, some years later, the then CIA General Counsel, John Rizzo, hinted that the Agency themselves may have provided assistance to the film. Rizzo said:

It had the cadences of what real CIA people do, and what real CIA people are like... Even some of the scenes in the movie—a lot of the action is set in a CIA cover facility that several years later I found myself in a place that looked almost exactly like that movie. I don't know how they did it but they managed to replicate what a real CIA cover facility was like.[84]

(Above) Robert Redford's CIA analyst listens to a realist rationalisation for CIA activity.

If there really was a tacit CIA approval for the *Condor* script, it would suggest that the CIA was actually at ease with being represented in such threatening terms. The final scene of the film rationalises the CIA's criminal activity, as ultimately it is only the Agency that appear able to protect the flow of oil that is vital to the nation's survival. Similarly, on *Scorpio*, as director Michael Winner put it, 'We only show the CIA killing nasty agents.'[85] If the CIA really was, or is, happy to present such a cruel image of itself, this takes CIA manipulation of entertainment down ever darker alleyways. In the absence of better evidence, we can only err on the side of caution but keep an open mind.

Helms approached MPAA president Jack Valenti on multiple occasions in the late-1960s and early-1970s pushing for screen adaptations of E. Howard Hunt's spy novels because he thought the books 'gave a favourable impression of the Agency.' Valenti even interviewed Hunt at Helms' request. Meanwhile, an agent at the CIA's Domestic Contact Service provided copies to an executive at Paramount's parent company. In May 1972, Helms and other CIA officials, along with White House staffers, attended a special screening of *The Godfather* at MPAA headquarters in Washington D.C. Helms gave another set of Hunt's spy novels to Valenti, who in turn provided them to Charles Bludhorn, another Paramount executive. This led to some confusion within Paramount, who thought that the CIA had given up on the idea. Though it seems Helms was trying to revive it, he then ditched the plan entirely.[86]

In 1977, the Agency set up an Office of Public Affairs (OPA). CBS became the first news crew to be allowed to film at CIA headquarters, and the low-budget feature, *Telefon* (1977), was later granted the same permission.

The first half of the 1980s was a yet more barren period of CIA activity in Hollywood, though even the incoming director, Bill Casey, attended specials screenings of *On Golden Pond, I Love Liberty* and *War Games*, hosted by Jack Valenti and the MPAA.

Bill Casey, Reagan's CIA director, adopted a more secretive public posture in the 1980s. However, again there are some tantalising indicators that the CIA still had an interest in manipulating Hollywood. In 1985, *The Man with One Red Shoe* became the first movie to be produced with the help of former CIA agents. Others, including Frank Snepp—the first former officer to have a script vetted and cleared by the Agency—made similar efforts but their projects were never produced. *The Man With One*

Red Shoe employed Polly Dean and Penny Engle as technical advisors to help actress Lori Singer, 'better understand the actual work of being a female spy.' According to the transcript of an episode of *Morning Edition* provided to the CIA by a media monitoring company, Dean and Engle were, 'recruited by another ex-CIA case officer, Robert Cort, who has begun a second career as a producer at 20th Century Fox.'[87]

Investigative journalist Nick Schou substantiated a murky story first reported in the *New York Times* in 1987.[88] Shou explains:

[Marlon] Brando was trying to secure the rights to a story involving Iran-Contra and a cargo handler, who was shot down over Nicaragua. [former CIA officer] Frank Snepp tried to arrange a meeting at Brando's residence, where they were going to secure the rights to this movie. But they found that they were being outbid by a really shady production company nobody had ever heard of, which basically didn't even really exist. Frank Snepp was ultimately able to confirm that it was really [Iran-Contra operative] Oliver North, who was trying to orchestrate a bidding operation to try to prevent this movie from being made.[89]

In this context, can we really be sure that the CIA wasn't playing a role even greater than the one we outline above? More to the point, why isn't all of this much more freely available? Why can't we simply answer these questions immediately? What has gone wrong with the democratic system and the free flow of information that we are not permitted to see files about, of all things, *very old fictional movies.*

1986—present

In 1986, *Top Gun* was a great success as a Navy promotional film. In its wake, the CIA reconsidered its approach to Hollywood.[90]

After fostering a friendship with spy author Tom Clancy, the CIA gave permission for *Patriot Games* (1992) and then *Mission: Impossible* (1996) to become the first movies to film at Langley headquarters since the 1970s. A trickle of other celebrities began to visit Langley. They tried to develop a series akin to *The FBI*, this time based on CIA operations files, though this fell apart when the Agency insisted on editorial control.

[Above] Harrison Ford walking into CIA headquarters, 1992.

In 1996, these truncated media initiatives coalesced into an actioned strategy. Chase Brandon, a twenty-five-year veteran of operations and cousin of the Hollywood star Tommy Lee Jones, became the CIA's ELO. While Brandon's IMDB page and other sources include less than half a dozen credits, circa 2014 he temporarily maintained a website listing a much broader range of projects that he helped to produce.[91] In reality, it was revealed that, for ten years until his retirement in 2006, Brandon had provided script input and technical advice on *Enemy of the State* (1998), *Meet the Parents* (2000), *Spy Game* (2001), *The Bourne Identity*, *The Sum of All Fears* and *Bad Company* (2002), *The Recruit* (2003), *Meet the Fockers* (2004), *The Interpreter* (2005), *Mission*

Impossible III, *The Good Shepherd* (2006), and *Charlie Wilson's War* (2007). He also worked on major TV series including *JAG*, *24*, *The Agency* and *Alias*, and assisted with over a dozen other TV programs alongside books and several unmade productions. Brandon was also involved in the Tom Berenger TV movie, *In the Company of Spies* (2000), which filmed at Agency headquarters with real CIA operatives appearing as extras. [92] In addition, Brandon worked on documentaries and factual TV serials including *The Path to 9-11*, *Covert Action*, *Top Secret Missions of the CIA*, *Stories of the CIA*, and *Greatest Intelligence Agency*.

When interviewed by Jenkins, the CIA's 2007-08 ELO Paul Barry (Brandon's successor) said 'The added value we provide is at a story's inception. We can be a tremendous asset to writers developing characters and storylines.' [93] This certainly appears to have been the case in the Brandon era when, according to CIA chief of public affairs Bill Harlow, Brandon spent 'many hours' on the phone pitching ideas to writers. [94]

Jenkins also interviewed former CIA officer Tony Mendez, who advised on *The Agency* and helped produce *Argo*, who testified that Brandon was 'very adept at wielding his influence,' especially during a film's early stages. [95] The main writer for *The Agency*, Michael Frost Beckner, explained that he maintained contact with Brandon while producing the series and that the CIA's liaison frequently persuaded him to incorporate certain storylines and technologies into the script. One example was a hi-tech biometric scanner than could detect terrorists in airports. Brandon admitted to Beckner that this technology didn't exist but encouraged him to include it in the series as psychological warfare, since 'terrorists watch TV too'. [96] In light of these remarks, one wonders again whether more menacing films like *Three Days of the Condor* might indeed have fitted CIA requirements precisely.

Another idea that Beckner sourced from Brandon was that a Predator drone could be armed with a missile and used as a weapon of assassination. In the episode titled 'Peacemakers' this is used by the CIA to kill a rogue Pakistani general who is trying to start a war with India. Only weeks after this episode aired a real Predator drone armed with a Hellfire missile was used to kill a rogue Pakistani general. Beckner commented on these curiously predictive and accurate story points, saying, 'I'm not a big conspiracy theorist but there seems to have been a unique synergy there.'[97]

Brandon also had a central role in helping to create the CIA training thriller *The Recruit* (2003), starring Al Pacino and Colin Farrell. Publicly, the screenplay was written by Roger Towne, who also wrote *In The Company of Spies*. Brandon appears in the DVD special feature but captioned merely as a CIA case officer, not their Hollywood liaison or anyone creatively involved in the movie. However, Brandon is credited as a technical advisor on *The Recruit* both on IMDB and on his own website, where Brandon also listed Towne as his screenwriting partner and *The Recruit*'s Jeff Apple as his producing partner. Brandon's role in ghost-writing *The Recruit* was confirmed by Jenkins, who obtained private documents in 2013 proving that Brandon wrote the original treatment and early drafts of the script. Given that Brandon and Towne also worked on *In the Company of Spies* in the late-1990s and that the films contain moments of identical dialogue, it is likely that Brandon wrote, co-wrote, or had a lot of influence over that script as well, and that Towne was his pawn. Exactly why Towne allowed Brandon to use him as a front is not known, though it might be relevant that prior to *In the Company of Spies* Towne was not credited on a successful screenplay in 15 years. Similarly, Jeff Apple had not produced a major film since 1993's *In The Line of Fire*.

[Above] Al Pacino plugged into a lie detector, The Recruit.

The treatment and early drafts of *The Recruit* that Brandon created were clearly motivated by political concerns. In one scene that Brandon wrote, the head of the CIA's Clandestine Service says, 'We did slay the great dragon [the Soviet Union]. But in the new world order we are learning that there are a multitude of poisonous snakes.' The 'snakes' are then identified, with terrorism being the Agency's 'number one priority' but also 'North Korea, Libya, Iran, Iraq, Colombia and [most absurdly] Peru.'[98] In another scene, the recruit, James Clayton (Farrell), tells his recruiter, Walter Burke (Pacino), that the CIA are 'a bunch of old, fat, white guys who fell asleep at the wheel when we needed them most.' This criticism of the CIA's failure to predict 9/11 is countered by Burke who says that outsiders 'don't know shit.' Likewise the movie repeats an old Agency motto that 'Our failures are known, but our successes are not,' a line that also appears in the Brandon/Towne production in *The Company of Spies*.

In 2007, former associate general counsel to the CIA, Paul Kelbaugh, delivered a lecture on the CIA's relationship with Hollywood, at which a local journalist was present. The journalist (who now wishes to remain anonymous) wrote a review of the lecture which related Kelbaugh's discussion of *The Recruit* (2003). The review noted that, according to Kelbaugh, a CIA agent was on set for the duration of the shoot under the guise of a consultant, but that his real job was to misdirect the filmmakers: 'We didn't want Hollywood getting too close to the truth,' the journalist quoted Kelbaugh as saying. Peculiarly, in a strongly worded email to Alford, Kelbaugh emphatically denied having made the public statement and claimed that he remembered 'very specific discussions with senior [CIA] management that no one was ever to misrepresent to affect [film] content—EVER.'[99] The journalist considers Kelbaugh's denial 'weird,' and told our colleague, Robbie Graham, that 'after the story came out, he [Kelbaugh] emailed me and loved it... I think maybe it's just that because [the lecture] was "just in Lynchburg" he was okay with it – you know, like, no one in Lynchburg is really going to pay much attention to it.'[100]

Whether CIA officers exerted this kind of influence over scripts other than *The Recruit* is not known, and FOIA requests for relevant documents from this period have only turned up a few articles from the CIA's in house magazine *What's News at CIA?* Still, since Brandon left the post we know that his successors have worked on: *Race to Witch Mountain* (2009), *Salt* (2010), *Argo* and *Zero Dark Thirty* (2012), *Dying of the Light* (2014), *Mission: Impossible—Rogue Nation* (2015), and *13 Hours* (2016). The inclusion of the Agency logo, seal and/or footage of the CIA headquarters suggests that they were also involved in other films such as the remainder of the original *Bourne* trilogy, *The Interview* (2014), *Spy* and *American Ultra* (both 2015). Likewise, the Agency has continued to support major TV series (*Homeland*, *Covert Affairs*) and documentaries (*Extraordinary Fidelity*, *Air America: The CIA's Secret Airline*, *The Secret War on Terror* and *Game of Pawns*). While he was Agency director, Leon Panetta even appeared on an episode of *Top Chef*, which painted the CIA in the familiar hallowed terms and even showed the Director skipping dessert to attend to vital business.[101]

In keeping with the CIA's general approach, no documents have been released on any of these more recent productions. There is one exception—*Zero Dark Thirty*. In response to a FOIA lawsuit by Judicial Watch and subsequent requests by media outlets, hundreds of pages of emails, memos and other records are now in the public domain. While there has been substantial media criticism of the CIA over their role in *Zero Dark Thirty*, this has led very few to step back and look at the bigger picture. However, the model of cooperation revealed by these documents is instructive. Screenwriter Mark Boal and director Kathryn Bigelow were already developing an Osama Bin Laden-themed movie with the help of the CIA at the time of the Abbottabad raid in May 2011. They instantly switched focus to the new story and were granted unprecedented access to CIA officials and locations used to prepare for the raid.

Boal agreed to share his scripts with the Agency to ensure they were 'absolutely comfortable' with his portrait of them in *Zero Dark Thirty*.[102] One memo summarised a series of conference calls where Boal verbally shared his screenplay with CIA officers and they requested numerous changes, all of which Boal incorporated into his script.[103] According to the memo, these changes were not concerned with accuracy so much as 'to help promote an appropriate portrayal of the Agency and the Bin Laden operation.'[104] The CIA's changes included removing a scene where a drunk CIA officer fires an AK-47 into the air on a rooftop in Islamabad and the use of dogs in the lengthy torture scenes that make up the opening third of the film.[105] Perhaps most controversially, another change made the central character Maya less involved in the torture of prisoners, even though her real-life counterpart Alfreda Frances Bikowsky was so involved in the CIA's program that she has been labelled the 'Queen of Torture.'[106]

However, despite effectively having script approval, the CIA made no objection to the underlying storyline that torturing 'terror suspects' ultimately led them to find Bin Laden. When the film was released the CIA's acting director, Mike Morrell, took the unusual step of issuing a public statement distancing the Agency from the film and saying that while they participated in the production, 'we do not control the final product.' Morrell went on to say that 'the film creates the strong impression that the enhanced interrogation techniques that were part of our former detention and interrogation program were the key to finding Bin Laden. That impression is false.'[107] If that impression is false then why didn't the CIA exercise the power Boal conceded to them and remove it from the script?

There would have been complete academic silence on the post-Cold War period of CIA-Hollywood cooperation were it not for Tricia Jenkins' 2012 book. However, Brandon updated his website around the point that Jenkins finished her second edition and, consequently, she said nothing about his involvement in *Charlie Wilson's War*, *The Interpreter* and some other products. These products included the hugely successful Ben Stiller comedy *Meet the Parents* and *Meet the Fockers*, which wrapped a core of neo-conservative paranoia in a family-friendly message of tolerance, with Robert De Niro's character seeming to have been influenced by Brandon.

[Above] Ben Stiller sees intimidating images of his fiancé's father in Meet the Parents. Originally, the images were going to be CIA torture manuals.

[Above] Robert De Niro with President Bill Clinton in Meet the Parents.

In an excellent unpublished Ph.D. thesis, David McCarthy reveals that during a conference call with Universal Studios about *Meet The Parents* (2000), the production team asked him what the CIA's kidnapping and torture manuals might look like, because they wanted Ben Stiller's character to find them on DeNiro's desk.

Uncomfortable with the idea, Brandon proposed that they make the CIA connection by showing 'a panoply of photographs' of DeNiro's character with international figures. The Universal executives loved the suggestion, and wrote it into the screenplay.'[108]

While the long-term influence of these productions is perhaps impossible to measure because there are too many films, and too many other factors influencing public opinion, the short-term effects can be assessed. A recent study showed that *Argo* and *Zero Dark Thirty* didn't just encourage public support for the specific institutions portrayed in the films, but also stimulated support for the security state and the government as a whole. A team led by Michelle Pautz surveyed the opinions of audiences both before and after they watched one of these two CIA-supported films, and found that around a quarter changed their views, or had their views changed. Whether the question was about support for the CIA or other specific agencies, the general level of trust in the government, faith in the White House (who are not depicted in either film) or belief that 'the country is headed in the right direction', all improved after watching these movies. In some instances over 30% of the audience gave different responses to these questions after watching *Argo* or *Zero Dark Thirty*. Pautz's study produced no evidence of public opinion going in the other direction – towards being more sceptical of the CIA, the government or politics in general – confirming that, at least in the short-term, these films are highly effective instruments of propaganda.[109]

Is Hollywood 'Full of CIA Agents'?

How much deeper does CIA involvement go into the entertainment industry?

In 2014, former Deputy Counsel or Acting General Counsel of the CIA, John Rizzo, wrote, 'The CIA has long had a special relationship with the entertainment industry, devoting considerable attention to fostering relationships with Hollywood movers and shakers—studio executives, producers, directors, big-name actors.'[110] It is ironic that such a statement from one of the CIA's most notoriously tight-lipped officials asserts the existence of such a power network less ambiguously than the major scholarly histories to date.

[Above] Mike Myers and his girlfriend Kelly Tisdale at CIA headquarters.

How many more 'Luigi Luraschis' are there working for the Agency in Hollywood? We've already mentioned a long line of stars who have publicly visited Langley. Others include: Robert De Niro; Tom Cruise; Dean Cain; Dan Ackroyd; Will Smith; Piper Perabo; Patrick Stewart, Kevin and Michael Bacon, Claire Danes, Mike Myers, and Bryan Cranston. George Clooney and Angelina Jolie have worked on films with the CIA and are among the small number of Hollywood stars who have joined the Council on

Foreign Relations. Writers and producers who have been to CIA headquarters or worked repeatedly with the Agency include: Tony Scott, Philip Noyce, Mace Neufeld, brothers Roger and Robert Towne, JJ Abrams, Craig Piligian, Jay Roach, Alex Gansa, Howard Gordon, and Doug Liman.[111]

Jennifer Garner made an unpaid recruitment advert for the CIA, whilst starring in the hit series, *Alias*. Her ex-husband, Ben Affleck, himself is a political player, counting among his friends the Rwandan dictator Paul Kagame—they've hung out at baseball games together. Affleck starred in the CIA and DOD assisted *The Sum of All Fears*, where he met Garner. That film ends with his character, rather creepily, jovially acceding to CIA surveillance as though being spied on makes him the luckiest gosh-darn guy in America.

In behind-the-scenes footage for *Sum of All Fears*, Affleck can be seen learning martial arts with the CIA's ELO, Chase Brandon. In an interview to promote the anti-Iranian feature *Argo*, Affleck joked, 'I think Hollywood is probably full of CIA agents and we just don't know it and I wouldn't be surprised to find this was extremely common.' The interviewer asked: 'Are you CIA?' to which Affleck responded, with a strained smile: 'I am, yes.' Obligatory awkward laughter then follows from the interviewer as the star adds: 'And now you've blown my cover.' Is it really too much to suggest that Affleck has a closer political relationship with the Agency than he is willing to discuss?

In 2013, the producer of *Pretty Woman*, Arnon Milchan, publicly admitted that he had used his position in Hollywood to steal US nuclear weapons secrets and help Israel build its bomb. He had been recruited by the Israeli government's long-standing senior official, Shimon Peres. Milchan said other Hollywood bigwigs were involved, including the recently deceased producer Sydney Pollack (*Three Days of the Condor, The Interpreter,*

Michael Clayton). Milchan's status had taken three decades to emerge.[112]

Hollywood may be even more politicised by the CIA than indicated above. Following the media attention and scandal over the help they gave the filmmakers behind *Zero Dark Thirty*, the CIA's Office of the Inspector General (OIG) carried out several investigations. According to the OIG, former CIA employees are bound by their secrecy agreements and are supposed to 'comply with CIA security requirements in their interactions with the entertainment industry'.[113] All written or oral presentations, which would include consulting for entertainment producers, are supposed to be vetted by the Agency's Publication Review Board, and the OPA are responsible for advising them on contact with the media. However, the OIG's report also recommends the creation of formal guidance for these processes, showing that these did not exist prior to 2012, so whether this process was adhered to is not certain. The OIG examined eight CIA-assisted productions and noted that, 'For only one of the eight projects was OPA able to provide a complete list of the current and former CIA employees who had been in contact with entertainment industry representatives in the course of CIA support to the project.'[114]

The report indicates that the CIA monitor, vet and approve the assistance granted by former agents to the entertainment industry. It is certainly true that on some projects, such as *Homeland*, the producers employ former agents and receive assistance from the CIA as well. Likewise the filmmakers behind *Salt* contracted former CIA officer Melissa Boyle Mahle as a technical advisor, but we discovered that they also attained full co-operation from the CIA and that the main creative team, including Angelina Jolie, had a video conference with active CIA agents.[115] Furthermore, it has been widely reported that the screenwriter behind the TV series *The Americans*—former CIA agent Joe Weisberg—has to send all of his scripts to the CIA's OPA for vetting prior to them being produced.[116] Similarly, comic book artist Tom King also used to work for the Agency and, 'as a former CIA operative, anything Tom King writes that involves the CIA needs to be vetted by the organization, not for accuracy but just to make sure that they don't say anything they shouldn't.'[117]

The report begs the question: do all former agents of the CIA who write, produce, or provide script consultation or technical advice to the entertainment industry have their work monitored, vetted, and approved by the Agency? There does not appear to be a hard-and-fast rule, but, if so, then this would substantially increase the number of productions that the CIA has influenced. Former officers who have recently worked in the industry include: John Strauchs (*Sneakers*); Henry Crumpton (*State of Affairs*); Rodney Faraon (*Blackhat*); Bazzel Baz (*The Blacklist*); Robert Baer (*Red, Rendition, Car Bomb, Syriana, Cult of the Suicide Bomber, Berlin Station*); Carol Rollie Flynn and John MacGaffin (*Homeland*); Tony and Jonna Mendez (*Argo, The Agency*); Mike Baker (*Spooks*); Joe Weisberg (*The Americans, Falling Skies*); Melissa Boyle Mahle (*Salt, Hanna*); Valerie Plame (*Fair Game, Person of Interest*); Robert Grenier (*Covert Affairs*); Sandra Grimes and Jeanne Vertefeuille (*The Assets*); Michael Wilson (*Burn Notice*), and Lindsay Moran (*Cars 2: The Video Game*).

All of the products discussed in this chapter in some way promote spying and the CIA either by glorifying mass surveillance, excusing torture, or just by presenting an image of the world as being full of threats. In particular, *The Blacklist* and *Spooks* employ a 'villain of the week' format, portraying almost anyone and everyone as a possible terrorist or master criminal. Likewise, *The Assets* and *The Americans* are based on real life stories of Soviet or Russian spies within the US during the Cold War, whereas *Salt* and *Homeland* pre-empted a renewal of hostilities between NATO and Russia. Chase Brandon himself became a freelance consultant in Hollywood, with products still listed but not yet having come to fruition. Peculiarly, Brandon also wrote a book on UFOs, which he promoted by claiming to have seen incontrovertible evidence of alien landings at Roswell in 1947.[118]

How Bad Could It Get?

We hope that the pages above are a bracing set of illustrations and revelations about just how politicised Hollywood is by powerful forces working in their own interests, especially for the Pentagon and CIA.

But, finally, let us turn to history to attain a sense of how serious this situation could become. In this context, we could talk about the Blacklist from 1947—1960, which took place under the broader auspices of the Senator Joseph McCarthy's Red Scare and which saw thousands of left-wing Hollywood workers, dubbed Communists, hounded out of the industry—the most famous of which were called the Hollywood Ten. This dreadful era of a fear and paranoia served no security purpose and has been well covered by scholarship.[119]

Less well known is the role of the FBI under its tyrannical director, J. Edgar Hoover, which continued either side of the Blacklist and all the way up to his death in 1972. Let us consider this in more detail here.

The FBI still operates in Hollywood but it no longer appears to be a major player in terms of depth, breadth or politicisation.[120] Under Hoover, this was a very different tale. The FBI set up their ELO in the 1930s, the first of its kind, and wielded their influence on projects like *G-Men* (1935), *House on 92nd Street* (1945), *The Untouchables* (1959—1963), and *The FBI Story* (1959). In 1954, Congress passed Public Law 670, which, at Hoover's request, contained a clause outlawing the commercial exploitation, including screen depiction, of the FBI without Hoover's permission. This led to references to the Bureau being removed from several products including *Goldfinger* on the grounds that, 'Fleming's stories generally center around sex and bizarre situations and certainly are not the type with which we want to be associated.'[121]

The highly deferential ABC TV series *The FBI* (1965—1974) thanked Hoover for his cooperation on the credits of all 317 episodes. More than 5,000 pages of internal FBI memos released under the FOIA reveal that Hoover controlled every aspect of *The FBI*, approving the cast and crew, the writers, the directors and every word of the script. Anyone suspected of being a 'pervert' or remotely connected to the 'worldwide Communist conspiracy' was banned from the show. Hoover also sometimes threatened to can the show to pressurise ABC News to bend to his will. Hoover dictated there were to be no depictions of the Mafia, violence, civil rights issues, and none of the onscreen agents were to be shown doing anything wrong such as wiretapping or even, God forbid, having a girlfriend.[122]

The FBI recruited high profile celebrities as informants within the entertainment industry. These included Ronald Reagan and his first wife Jane Wyman, Cary Grant, and, perhaps most famously, Walt Disney. From 1940 until his death in 1966, Disney maintained a relationship with the Bureau via their Los Angeles field office, and, in 1955, was promoted to a Special Agent in Charge contact, meaning he could run his own informants in Hollywood. Disney reported on suspected Communists and other undesirables, and testified before HUAC.

Alongside numerous high-profile authors, including Ernest Hemingway, Graham Greene, and John Steinbeck (himself a CIA asset), other major movie stars were also spied upon by the Bureau for political reasons, including Orson Welles, Marilyn Monroe and Haskell Wexler. Their status as some of the biggest screen stars of the 20th century did little to protect them against government surveillance and harassment.

Charlie Chaplin's 2,000-page Bureau file shows that, as a result of his left-wing beliefs, the FBI conducted lengthy investigations into his politics and his sex life, including pursuing leads offered by anonymous sources, clairvoyants and gossip columnists. Destroying Chaplin's iconic status became an obsession for the Bureau, who reached out to MI5 for help trying to dig dirt, though the British found nothing indicating he was a Communist, let alone a Soviet spy. In September 1952, Chaplin and his family left the US to go on a European tour to promote his new film, and, after consulting with Hoover, the Attorney General revoked Chaplin's re-entry permit, banning him from the country. Even though the Bureau's files concede that they had no evidence that could be presented in court to justify barring him from re-entering the US, Chaplin decided not to contest the decision and lived the final 25 years of his life in Switzerland. He did not return to America until 20 years later when he visited New York to receive an honorary Oscar in 1972.[123] In short, the FBI quietly ended the career of the greatest comedian of all time on the false grounds that he was a Communist.

In 1970, as part of its Counter Intelligence Program (COINTELPRO), the FBI decided to 'neutralise' a married and pregnant upcoming star, Jean Seberg, because of her financial support for the Black Panthers. Declassified documents show that The Los Angeles Times printed a lie that had been leaked by the FBI, namely that the father of Seberg's unborn child was a prominent Black Panther. Shocked by the story, Seberg immediately collapsed and went into labour. Her daughter died three days later. Seberg then attempted to commit suicide on the anniversary of the child's death every year until 1979, when eventually she succeeded. Just over a year later, her husband, Gary, also killed himself.[124] Hoover had been directly involved in the operation to ruin Seberg's life.

The most famous case of FBI persecution is that of Jane Fonda, who campaigned against the Vietnam War. She was most reviled for being photographed behind Communist weaponry in 1972, a mistake that she regretted but which left her open to the charge that she opposed US troops. Fonda had in fact worked with Vietnam Veterans Against the War, an organisation that believed individual soldiers should not be made scapegoats for policies designed at the highest levels of government.[125] Also, rather less well known, the FBI used false pretences to arrest her and acquire her personal records.[126] Politicians variously said 'I think we should cut her tongue off' and called for her to be 'tried for treason and executed'[127] and the Nixon White House seriously compared their surveillance and overall treatment of 'Hanoi Jane' with that of Soviet Premiere Brezhnev.[128]

The FBI was also able to impact films themselves. In 1992, *Salt of the Earth* (1954) was preserved in the US Library of Congress at the National Film Registry because it is deemed "culturally significant." The film was an inspiring drama about working men and women striking at an American owned zinc mine in New Mexico—think *The Full Monty* without the laughs. The FBI investigated the film's financing; the American Legion called for a nation-wide boycott; film-processing labs were instructed not to touch it; and unionized projectionists were advised not to show it. During the course of production in New Mexico in 1953, the trade press denounced it as a subversive plot, anti-Communist vigilantes fired rifle shots at the set, the film's leading lady was deported to Mexico, and from time to time a small airplane buzzed noisily overhead. The plane's buzzing played havoc with the soundtrack, moving the producer, Paul Jarrico, to wisecrack: "We'll make this picture again sometime. And next time we'll say, 'You've seen this great picture. Now hear it.'"[129]

Upon its release, all but 12 theatres in the country refused to screen *Salt of the Earth*. The film, edited in secret, was stored for safekeeping in an unmarked wooden shack in Los Angeles and received vitriolic reviews.

The prospect of the present-day DOD and CIA behaving with such impunity may seem remote. But we should bear in mind nor was there any sense of Hoover's widespread malevolence in any literature until well after his death. In fact, taken holistically, officials from all major elements of the national security state have presided over the cover-up of an extraordinary interlinked propaganda operation, with just enough cracks in the system to deny outright censorship or covert action. Deftly done, indeed, but they should be treated with the scepticism they deserve and the facts uncovered.

The relationship between national security and Hollywood could become considerably more toxic given the enormous surveillance capabilities of the National Security Agency (NSA). So far very little information has emerged on the NSA in Hollywood, and we can only assume that it has yet to become seriously involved, but an otherwise uncited article in the Baltimore Sun illustrates that they might yet jump into the game. Jerry Bruckheimer told the paper that the NSA have 'realized that to turn away Hollywood makes you an even bigger bad guy.' The article goes on to explain that the original screenplay for *Enemy of the State* (1998) depicted the NSA as employing brutal tactics in hunting down Will Smith, but, after NSA cooperated on the production and offered up an ex-employee as a consultant, 'Bruckheimer agreed to pin the wrongdoings on a bad-apple NSA official, and not the agency.' Bruckheimer predicted, 'I think the NSA people will be pleased. They certainly won't come out as bad as they could have. NSA's not the villain.'[130] Straight from the CIA/ DOD play-book.

[Above] NSA Headquarters, Fort Meade from Enemy of the State.

Conclusions

The scale, scope, and range of the CIA's activities in Hollywood are difficult to assess, even for their own Inspector General, let alone outside researchers. Following widespread reporting on the Agency's involvement in *Zero Dark Thirty*, the OIG carried out multiple investigations and found that the OPA's records were woefully inadequate. The OIG reported that 'OPA has not maintained a comprehensive list of entertainment projects that the CIA has supported and those projects that CIA has declined to support.' From a partial list of 22 projects covering 2007—2012, the OIG focused on eight and found that 'OPA was unable to provide documentation concerning the nature and extent of CIA's support to three of the eight projects' and 'provided limited documentation concerning support to the other five projects.'[131]

It is unacceptable, in a democracy, not to mention indefensible in a digital age, for such material to be stored but unavailable.

The OIG also found that officers met with entertainment producers 'off campus'—outside of CIA facilities—and sometimes in disguise and under a cover identity. In some instances, this was done without the OPA being aware of the meetings, and without anyone from the OPA being present or providing any guidance on what to say and what not to say. An investigation into potential ethics violations found that multiple officers received gifts and gratuities in return for their help on *Zero Dark Thirty*, including jewellery and an expensive bottle of tequila. The ethics report also made clear that it was unnamed officers not working for the OPA who reviewed and changed the script for *Zero Dark Thirty*.[132] Thus, the CIA are, at times, side-lining or bypassing their own OPA in providing assistance to filmmakers, and reviewing and modifying their creations, leaving little in the way of a paper trail for internal or external investigators to examine. They are acting with little accountability, if any, and leaving few traces of their actions.

In one documented instance this was done quite deliberately. The CIA's support to *Homeland* is now relatively well reported, and showrunner Alex Gansa has described how, before each season, they hold private meetings in an old CIA club in Georgetown with 'a parade of former and current intelligence officers, State Department people, journalists and White House staffers.'[133] However, the CIA has been involved since the very beginning of the franchise, as Agency emails illustrate that its star, Claire Danes, was given a tour of Langley and met with the Deputy Director while the first season was still in pre-production. Danes got into Langley with the help of an active CIA officer who formed the basis for *Homeland*'s protagonist Carrie—most probably Carrie Rollie Flynn, who has since appeared in promotional events for the series. Referring to Danes' visit, an email by then CIA director of public affairs, George Little, says, 'We will do NO press on this since it's low profile [their emphasis].'[134] How many other visits to Langley by entertainment bigwigs have been 'low profile'? How many other 'off campus' meetings have there been between CIA agents and film and TV producers?

The lack of accountability regarding the relationship between Hollywood and the CIA and other government officials is starting to be subject to federal oversight. The 2017 Intelligence Authorization Act is the first to require that the Director of National Intelligence, 'issue, and release to the public, guidance regarding engagements by elements of the intelligence community with entertainment industry entities.' The Act also requires each part of the US intelligence community to submit an annual report summarising each engagement with the entertainment industry, the work required, the cost and the benefits to the US government.[135] At the time of writing, neither the guidance nor the annual reports are available.

Like the FBI once did, the US intelligence agencies lurk in the shadows of the cinema. At crucial times, they operate the figures on screen like puppeteers. It is astonishing that they are allowed to do so without someone turning on the lights to show the strings. Only then can we cut them.

CASE STUDIES

~

The bulk of this book comprises a series of contemporary, major, mainstream cinematic case studies. We think this is the best selection of cases for several reasons.

Firstly, in terms of genre, these films encompass most of Hollywood's diverse output, including action-adventure, war films, political dramas, comedies, and science fiction. While it may be tempting to assume that the national security state only affects war films, this simply isn't true, and it's worth making that clear.

Secondly, most of these movies were directly impacted by the government, and the documentation we have on them needs more in-depth treatment than we have space for in the opening chapters.

Thirdly, most of the films we choose ultimately hold the same fundamental ideological assumptions, namely that American military supremacy is fundamentally benevolent. This underlying aspect to the politics of Hollywood cinema is a vital element that ensures Hollywood chimes with the interests of the state, or, at least, does not oppose them. More to the point, we show how the narratives could have gone the other way, but pressure from the powerful has made them markedly less critical products. This really is a close-up and gruesome look inside the ideological sausage factory.

Finally, we include some instances of filmmakers resisting state ideological controls and how this played out in production. In particular, we focus on Oliver Stone and Tom Clancy's chequered attempts to refashion American history and Paul Verhoeven's idiosyncratic takes on US power.

Avatar

[Above] CGI-generated military planes in Avatar

Avatar seemed to do the unthinkable. It is, undeniably, a film that is opposed to war, imperialism and environmental destruction. Not only that but it was made right in the belly of the corporate Hollywood beast and, even more remarkably, the industry supported it at full throttle and the result was the highest grossing film of all time.

James Cameron's blockbuster, *Avatar*, turns the usual colonial paradigm on its head, even though it emerges from the Murdoch Empire. 'The snarling vipers of left-wing Hollywood have been let off the leash,' cried the *Sydney Morning Herald*;[136] the *Pacific Free Press* called it 'the biggest anti-War film of all time'[137] and it was widely dubbed as *'Dances with Wolves* in Space.' On the surface, *Avatar* does indeed suggest that armed resistance to America's might is understandable and even noble—a simplistic message, so one can see why commentators with right-wing sympathies were prickly about the film. [138] Still, a closer examination reveals a more complex picture where the leftist vision is emaciated. As a consequence, the first comments by Rupert Murdoch himself upon watching *Avatar* were not about the film's politics, but rather about how exciting it would be to use its 3-D technology when screening Premiership football.[139]

Set in 2154, the RDA Corporation is mining a distant moon, Pandora, using US Marines for protection while the corporation hunts for a vital raw material called 'unobtainium.' In an attempt to improve relations with the native Na'vi and learn about the biology of Pandora, scientists grow Na'vi bodies (avatars), that are controlled by genetically matched humans. A paraplegic former Marine, Jake Sully (Sam Worthington) becomes an avatar, meets a female Na'vi, Neytiri (Zoe Saldana), and becomes attached to her clan in Hometree. Although Jake is supposed to be working for Dr. Grace Augustine (Sigourney Weaver), Colonel Miles Quaritch (Stephen Lang) has enlisted him to gather intelligence for a military strike that will displace the Na'vi and reveal the unobtainium that lies beneath their 'Tree of Souls.' Jake eventually commits to the Na'vi and works with their leadership to assemble a resistance coalition, which defeats the advancing corporation when Pandoran wildlife unexpectedly joins their ranks. The military personnel are expelled from Pandora, while Jake and the surviving scientists are allowed to remain. The Na'vi use the Tree of Souls to transplant permanently Jake's consciousness into his Na'vi avatar.

In *Avatar*, the US government is certainly vilified. Phrases in the film like 'shock and awe,' 'daisy cutters,' 'pre-emptive war,' and 'fighting terror with terror' tie the American aggressors quite closely to the real-world Bush administration. The leading bad guy is Colonel Miles Quaritch (Stephen Lang), who wants to use a pre-emptive strike to defeat the Na'vi and acquire their resources, despite the fact that it will destroy Hometree. He is the muscle behind Parker Selfridge (Giovanni Ribisi), the RDA administrator.

The Na'vi are undoubtedly sympathetic victims and, in stark contrast to *Stargate*, for example, they are not just passive, backward figures. Rather, they have a coherent voice, proper leadership and take a full role in the defence of their land. Neytiri even kills Quaritch, thereby delivering the decisive blow as he is about to kill Jake's human form. Still, in a manner similar to the ostensibly anti-war David O. Russell movie *Three Kings* (1999), key characters amongst the US invasion force are the leading figures in saving the day for the sake of the Na'vi: the heroic Jake, who tames a ferocious dragon which only five Na'vi have done before, the Marine, Trudy Chacón (Michelle Rodriguez), who switches sides ('I didn't sign up for this shit'), and Dr. Augustine, who earns her place in the Tree of Souls. Likewise, even though we are invited to respect the Na'vi, we are not required to identify with them—our heroes remain the humans, and US Marines at that.

Compare *Avatar* to, say, the low-budget South African sci-fi feature, *District 9* (2009), which explores similar themes but interrogates the South African power system in a more rigorous manner, notably by depicting the apartheid-style system with cold and brutal realism through the eyes of one of its seemingly unrepentant minions. In contrast, *Avatar*'s central figure is Jake, 'a warrior who dreamed he could bring peace,' but who develops through the Na'vi his naturally 'strong heart' and attractiveness to the forest's 'pure spirits.'

'The film is definitely not anti-American', clarified Cameron to the *New York Times*.

Similarly, by pandering to the film's lucrative merchandising potential and by chasing the PG-13 rating, Cameron sanitised the movie in key ways, particularly by having the villainous Quaritch and his men kicked out of Pandora in a happy ending that contrasts starkly with countless examples of such real-world struggles.

'We know what it feels like to launch the missiles,' said Cameron. 'We don't know what it feels like for them to land on our home soil, not in America. I think there's a moral responsibility to understand that.' [140] Cameron may have understood his moral responsibility, but he seems less willing to act on it. Despite campaigners appealing directly to him through a full-page $20,000 advert in *Variety*, Cameron neglected to make even a single public utterance in support of the 'real-life Na'vi' Dongria Khond tribe in India, whose people and environment are being uprooted by Vedanta, a British mining corporation. [141] The campaign group, Survival International, told Alford that Cameron's disinterest was "unfortunate" and added that 'It is a classic example of where a simple quote could have had a massive impact on a campaign.'[142]

Avatar is a significant shift in emphasis politically towards open criticism of US brutality, but it is restrained, as discussed above, and relies more on exploiting a global feeling of cynicism about the superpower—reflected in the film's even more incredible overseas takings—than it does on a systematic critique of US action. As such, it even struck a deal with those well-known anti-corporate environmentalists, McDonald's. 'The Big Mac is all about the thrill of your senses,' said the burger chain's US Chief Marketing Officer, Neal Golden, in an allusion to Cameron's visual spectacular. 'There's so much going on with the Big Mac. We think it's a perfect match for the movie.'[143]

The most instructive barometer of *Avatar*'s politics could be found in a *Fox News* interview with James Cameron at the point of the film's release. Since their ultimate sponsors at NewsCorp were one and the same, Fox was unable to unleash its customary baleful hyperbole about 'left-wing' Hollywood. For his part, Cameron appeared unwilling to recant the film's message but was content to couch it in language that sat well with his interviewer, just as he had with the marketers.

Buried several minutes into the interview, the Fox anchor asks the question: 'There's a little controversy about the storyline, whether it has anti-Americanism ... did politics enter into your head at all when developing this storyline or are people just reading into it?'

Cameron: I think they're reading into it and some people are taking away the right message and some people are taking away the wrong message. I just wanna go on the record as saying that I'm very pro-America. I'm pro-military. I believe in a strong defence. My brother is a former Marine who fought in Desert Storm and we got a lot of friends who are Marines. So, I made my main character in this movie a former Marine and he embodies the spirit of the Marine Corps and all that and it's what makes him a warrior even though he's in a wheelchair. He's disabled, he's still a warrior and he takes on every challenge head on as a Marine would.

Fox anchor: Well, you're talking to the father of a Marine so I'm glad to hear you're with the Marine Corps on this.

Cameron: Yeah, exactly....

With Cameron's all-American credentials established, he goes on to say that the film does contain two 'cautionary message[s]:'

One is against what we're doing as human beings, *not as Americans* [our emphasis], but as human beings to the environment, to the natural world. And the other one is a cautionary message which I think science fiction does very well which is to pay attention to how we deal with each other as human beings and what are the steps to war and when are our leaders accountable and not accountable and I kinda go after the idea of big corporations in this movie and how they are responsible for a lot of the ills of the world. And I don't think this is anti-America. We have a big technological, corporate civilisation worldwide and we need to make some changes if we're going to survive on this planet.

In response, the Fox anchor nods respectfully, moves on to ask Cameron about sequels, concludes the segment, and then starts talking with his co-anchor about 3-D glasses.[144] An undeniably important, obvious viewpoint alluding to the dangers of the current global system is given its 45 seconds of airtime on Fox, everyone is happy and no one fumbles the two billion dollars.

The film makes clear that the Marines are villainous corporate mercenaries, rather than tools of some future US government. Indeed, Jake makes it clear that although the Marines on Pandora are just 'hired guns,' back on Earth 'they're fighting for freedom.' What is the reason for this subtle change? We'd bet the DOD was behind it. The Marine Corps ELO reports say that they only assistance they offered to *Avatar* was 'courtesy support for verbiage in the script dialogue,' but they provided script notes and met with Cameron multiple times, including on set.[145]

Officers from the ELO attended the premiere three days before the film went on public release, and their reports kept track of the movie for well over a year, from pre-production through to its enormous success at the box office and its DVD release. In early 2010 the actors and producers went on a 'Navy Entertainment Program visit to 11th MEU [Marine Expeditionary Unit] and other units' that are part of CENTCOM.[146] Representatives from the ELOs of all branches of the military participated in a Comic-Con panel in 2011 and *Avatar* was one of the films attributed to the Marine Corps' officer on the panel.[147] All this just for 'courtesy support for verbiage'?

The case of *Avatar* points to other issues about the politics of Hollywood. What kind of social change can a film actually achieve? If Avatar had been less cowardly in its approach, what would have happened to Cameron? What good might have been achieved?

Black Hawk Down

Black Hawk Down was based on a book by journalist Mark Bowden. It served as a warning about the perils of US military intervention by recreating the October 3rd, 1993 US raid on Mogadishu ('the Mog') in Somalia, which resulted in the deaths of 19 US troops and nearly a hundred injuries. The US' main enemy was General Aidid, a Somali warlord and, during the raid, a solider called Durant was captured by Aidid's forces. The ostensible aim of US forces was to lead the humanitarian relief effort following a policy of starvation by Aidid's militia.

During the film adaptation, *Black Hawk Down*'s narrative was twisted in favour of US national security interests. It's one of the classic cases of DOD influence.

Bowden's book sensitively reflects concerns about US foreign policy and troop behaviour in Somalia during the early 1990s. He describes Somali characters as having understandable motivations for their resistance and meaningful relationships with their friends and families.[148] Bowden explains that the Somalis had seen six raids prior to October 3rd where the US troops often killed people indiscriminately. [149] During the first raid, the US accidentally arrested nine UN employees. On September 14th, the US assault force stormed the home of a man who turned out to be a close ally of the UN and was being groomed to lead the projected Somali police force; this led to 38 erroneous arrests. [150] On 19

September, after a bulldozer crew of engineers from the 10th Mountain Division was attacked by a band of Somalis, US troops fired into the crowd that had come to see the shooting, killing nearly one hundred people.[151] Previously, on 12 July, the UN authorised what became known as the 'Abdi House raid,' in which the UN tried to take out Aidid's leadership, instead massacring at least fifty Somali leaders drawn from across the political spectrum.[152] Bowden chronicles events that do not tally with the film's portrayal of American squeamishness about killing[153] and otherwise intimidating women and children,[154] including an incident where 'massive Ranger volley literally tore apart [a Somali woman] ... It was appalling,' says Bowden, 'yet some of the Rangers laughed.'[155]

Furthermore, Bowden reveals that the US threatened Somalia with an enormous attack in the event that Durant not be released unharmed by his captors. He quotes Somali ambassador Robert Oakley as sending a message to Aidid saying that 'Once the fighting starts again, all this pent-up anger is going to be released. This whole part of the city will be destroyed, men, women, children, camels, cats, dogs, goats, donkeys, everything ... That really would be tragic for all of us, but that's what will happen.'[156]

The reliable but broader discourse about the war was even more critical. African Rights' co-director, Alex de Waal, for instance, who pointed out that when the US troops arrived in Somalia the fighting had ended in all but one province in the south, and that according to the Red Cross and American Friends Service Committee, 80-90 per cent of the aid was getting through.[157] This raises the possibility that the war had other or additional unmentionable motivations, such as to stimulate US arms sales,[158] distract public attention from America's inability and/or unwillingness to solve the Balkans crisis with a PR coup,[159] acquire oil resources,[160] or even because UN Secretary General Boutros Boutros-Ghali harboured a longer-term rivalry with

Aidid's Habr Gidr clan.[161] US Major General Anthony C. Zinni, who directed operations in Somalia, said that women and children constituted two-thirds of the 6,000-10,000 Somali casualties that resulted from clashes with UN peacekeepers or in fights between rival Somali factions during the four months of US intervention in the summer of 1993.[162]

However, *Black Hawk Down* emerged like a grotesque parody of these alternative narratives. Military action is largely seen through the eyes of Eversmann and Garrison, who reflect official thinking on the US campaign. Eversmann—the 'everyman'—explains his attitude toward the Somalis: 'I respect them. Look, these people have no jobs, no food, no education, no future. I just figure that, I mean, we have two things we can do. We can either help or we can sit back and watch the country destroy itself on CNN.' Although the other soldiers display much less awareness of the political implications of their mission, they instinctively hold benevolent, interventionist views comparable to Eversmann and Garrison. When Eversmann cries 'did you see that?' in response to the Aidid-sponsored massacre in the opening minutes of the film, Durant requests to intervene militarily but he is not permitted due to UN regulations.

When the Americans capture Aidid's right hand man, Atto, he indulges in incorrect stereotypes about Americans. Paradoxically then, it is the American general who, after a six-week posting, gives the more credible account of events in Somalia—alleging genocide—even though he happens to be a leading figure in the invading military force. The real-life Atto, in fact, complained to the BBC about the film's portrayal of his arrest, saying that his colleague Ahmed Ali was injured on both legs and that his single car—not an imposing motorcade as the film depicts—was shot at least fifty times by US forces. He also claimed that people died during the attack.[163] On the DVD commentary, Ridley Scott and Jerry Bruckheimer admit that shots were fired at the motorcade and that Atto and his entourage then fled into a building to which the US laid siege, an incident which was omitted from the film.

Although the US causes civilian casualties in the film, this is not its intention. We continually hear warnings about the UN rules of engagement ('You do not fire unless fired upon!') and the military does not ever abandon these rules—even to the point of absurdity. Furthermore, their own sense of decency prevents them from killing armed and dangerous women and children, at least not without the appropriate expressions of misery and heartache.

Black Hawk Down provides a depiction of American suffering and innocence that is extreme even by Hollywood standards, juxtaposed with an evil or otherwise worthless enemy population. Lawrence Suid argues that the film is 'by no stretch of the imagination ... an argument to get back into Somalia ... if anything, it's the exact opposite!'[164] Suid's point is right in a narrow sense, namely that the film shows some of the dangers of US intervention for Americans. Still, *Black Hawk Down* implies that the US military can literally do no wrong and that, where the US does choose to fight, it must win at all costs, or else risk giving succour to the enemies of civilisation. Suid's further comment, that the film shows 'for our efforts, we were slaughtered,'[165] again points to the inability of certain commentators to recognise what were, at best, serious moral ambiguities over US intervention. Closing captions inform us that the US withdrew from Somalia after the battle and, watching it in the immediate post-9/11 world, it is hard to avoid the reading that such a 'cut and run' approach led to blowback against America.[166]

Ridley Scott said that he could have made *Black Hawk Down* without the Pentagon but 'I'd have had to call it "Huey Down,"' in a reference to the much smaller brand of helicopter.[167] He was joking of course—the film was completely reliant on the Black Hawks because he was recreating the Battle of Mogadishu in

Somalia where these helicopters were famously shot down.

The producers also changed the name of one of the characters, Ranger Specialist John Stebbins, because in real life he had been sentenced to 30 years in jail for raping and sodomizing his six-year-old daughter. Similarly, at the Pentagon's direct request, the filmmakers toned down its depiction of the military hunting a wild boar by helicopter, though it had been filmed.[168]

Black Hawk Down implies the US mission in Somalia is a tactical mistake on the part of Washington, but there is little indication that the authorities' motivations emerge from or are even consistent with private interests. Written captions at the start of the film establish that the US government sent the military to Somalia to stop the indigenous peoples from killing each other—and from starting to kill international forces—leading the 'response' of the 'world.' We are told that 'behind a force of 20,000 US Marines, food is delivered and order is restored [in Somalia]' and that US policy is to oppose a 'warlord' who is using 'hunger' as a 'weapon' against his own people. The official narrative was further elucidated in the film's companion documentary, *Good Intentions, Deadly Results*, which explicitly states that 'the most ambitious humanitarian mission in modern history' unfortunately 'ended in bullets, missiles and death' and that the moral of the story is that 'no good deed goes unpunished.'

Although Restore Hope was in reality an all-American operation, the film's cast is varied in nationality—McGregor is Scottish; Bana is Australian; Isaacs is English—which subtly renders the struggle multilateral. By this reading, the film is not just a US military disaster but a tragedy for Western civilisation itself. By the end, the idealistic Eversmann has become influenced by Hoot's attitude that no one 'back home' understands the motivations of military men, which are based around camaraderie only and that political values are unimportant in battle. Eversmann's transformation, then, further elevates the military above both the enemy and even Western civilians. The soldiers' rather less edifying attributes, such as parading around naked, using blow-up plastic sex dolls and masturbating in a parachute—as depicted in the book[169]—are conveniently excised for the silver screen.[170]

The filmmakers, including Bowden, often emphasised how *Black Hawk Down* was not a political film.[171] The film was promoted as a faithful recreation of the battle, with director Ridley Scott even emphasising that he thinks 'every war movie is an anti-war movie.'[172] Yet at the film's Washington premiere were such luminaries as Oliver North, Donald Rumsfeld, Paul Wolfowitz and Dick Cheney.[173]

Charlie Wilson's War

Based on George Crile's book of the same name, this fast-paced comedy might seem like a critique of Operation Cyclone—the US and allied policy to arm the Afghan mujahideen to fight against the Soviet Union, who had invaded Afghanistan. But, behind the tight-fitting skirts, Bond-style excessive alcohol consumption and rapid, sardonic dialogue lies a serious story that is only partly true.

Comparing an early and substantially different draft of the script with a later draft, and with the final movie, suggests that the filmmakers originally had significantly more radical intentions. These were unacceptable to powerful forces, which ensured the film was sanitised for their own ends. These changes fall into three distinct categories: (1) Charlie Wilson and Joanne Herring, two of three main characters in the film, were originally portrayed more critically and controversially; (2) the fact that the CIA supported the extreme elements of the Afghan mujahideen who later became designated global terrorists was removed; and (3) the scale and directness of the CIA's involvement, and therefore their responsibility, was downplayed.

Maverick Congressman Charlie Wilson (Tom Hanks) is approached by his friend Joanne Herring (Julia Roberts), who persuades him to visit the Pakistani leadership and support the Afghans' struggle against the Soviet Union. After attending the showing of *Courage is Our Weapon*—a documentary about the plight of Afghanistan produced and hosted by Herring—Wilson gets involved. Wilson and Herring both served as consultants on the film and, as a result, were in a position to exert some influence over how they appear in the cinematic adaptation of their lives.

While Wilson is shown to be a hard-drinking womaniser, one of his more serious indiscretions was wiped from the script. Just before he first visited Pakistan in 1980, Wilson was drunk-driving home over the Key Bridge when he rammed his car into another vehicle. Wilson was so inebriated that, believing he had simply hit the barrier, he didn't stop to check on the occupants of the car and drove on home. A modified version of this event appears in the 2005 draft script, where Charlie does stop and check that everyone was OK, but this was removed from later drafts. Likewise, a 1982 Congressional Financial Disclosures document suggests Charlie Wilson had several hundred thousand dollars' worth of holdings in petroleum companies, wheras the film explicitly has him declare only a modest salary.[174]

Meanwhile, Joanne Herring hired legal legend, Houston attorney Dick DeGuerin, to rattle NBC Universal, successfully ensuring changes to her portrait in the film including her previously smutty dialogue.[175] Wilson goes to visit an Afghan refugee camp where he is deeply moved but frustrated by the CIA's low-key approach. Charlie then befriends maverick CIA operative Gust Avrakotos (Philip Seymour Hoffman) and his understaffed Afghanistan group, who develop the strategy of supplying the Afghan Mujahideen with weapons and money, especially anti-aircraft guns to counter the Soviet helicopter gunships. The CIA's anti-Communist budget eventually grows from \$5 million to over \$500 million, each dollar matched by Saudi Arabia, and the Soviets are repelled. The film is bookended with Wilson receiving a major commendation from the CIA, but we realise at the end that his pride is tempered by his fears for the future, as 'the crazies have started rolling in [to Afghanistan]' and Charlie has found little Congressional support for rebuilding the country.

One of the major facts that the film leaves out but the original book makes clear is the existence of extreme elements among the mujahideen being supported by the CIA. *Courage is Our Weapon*—the documentary produced by Herring and shown to Charlie—was partly about Gulbuddin Hekmatyar, one of the leaders of a major group of rebels and a close associate of Osama Bin Laden. Herring had met Hekmatyar and had been charmed by him, and, even though she'd been told he was a 'dangerous fundamentalist, busy killing moderate Afghans, a man no self-respecting nation should support,[176] support him she did, and so did the CIA. Despite Hekmatyar being a narco-terrorist who liked to skin people alive, it was his gang that got the largest share of the billions eventually allocated for Operation Cyclone.

After 9/11 Hekmatyar was targeted (unsuccessfully) in a CIA drone strike and, the following year, became a US 'specially designated global terrorist' allied with Bin Laden. Indeed, Ed McWilliams, the former US special envoy to Afghanistan, confirmed the widespread assumption that the US itself gave Hekmatyar the bulk of its aid, and that former Islamabad station chief Milt Bearden tried, with some success, to prevent warnings of the coming maelstrom from reaching Washington.[177] The 2005 draft of the script includes a scene of a CIA briefing where they explicitly refer to supporting both Hekmatyar and Al Qaeda, but this was removed from later versions and the eventual film.

Bearden served as a technical advisor on the production and it seems likely that when he said that the film would 'put aside the notion that because we did that [support and supply arms to the Afghan mujahideen] we had 9/11,' he was tacitly referring to such cuts.[178]

The original script also emphasised other complexities in US foreign policy. In one scene Charlie angrily chastises Israelis for their war on Lebanon in 1982:

Charlie: Sabra and Shatilla, I just saw it. I thought the press accounts had to be blowing it out of proportion so I went to see it myself. Oh, my God, Zvi … what the fuck happened?

Zvi: Exactly what you've been told happened. Lebanese Christians came in and began slaughtering the Palestinians.

Charlie: This was supposed to be a surgical strike against the PLO. There are mass graves back there, the place is still on fire. They just told me the body count's up to 900, it's three days and they're still pulling bodies out. 900 civilians.

After being stonewalled by the Israelis, Charlie points out 'Your sentries let the Lebanese soldiers in… Didn't they. They watched while it happened.' Zvi eventually tells him, 'I don't lose much sleep over dead Palestinians.'[179]

Avoiding these complexities entirely, the final film presents a tale of the US winning a key military victory against the Soviet Union, which prefigured its collapse. Wilson, Herring and Avrakotos are the pioneers that work around the existing softly-softly US strategy, characterised by having 'the Afghans … walking into machine gun fire 'til the Russians run out of bullets.' Wilson and Co. are all-American heroes without whom the world would be 'hugely and sadly different.' But when Charlie tries to maintain US commitment to Afghanistan, he is given the cold shoulder. 'No one gives a shit about a school in Pakistan,' a Congressman tells him and, when Charlie corrects him he receives the response 'Afghanistan? Is that still going on?'

Meanwhile, the Russians are portrayed as brutal imperialists, gunning down hopeless Afghans whilst discussing marital infidelity. The Mujahideen are pitiful victims of what the Russians call the 'killing season,' though, as they receive greater American support, they begin to resemble the gun-toting warriors familiar from contemporary news coverage of Islamist terrorists. While Charlie Wilson's sympathies were with them, the sympathies of the watching audience are with Good Time Charlie. The Afghans themselves are reduced to Reel Bad Arabs—good for shooting or getting shot at, but very little else.

Another major facet that was changed was the ending of the film. The final cut is summed up by the jokey end caption from Charlie, which declares 'These things happened. They were glorious and they changed the world… and then we fucked up the end game.' The banner at the CIA's award ceremony declares, 'Charlie did it.' The ending of the original script was more Strangelovian. Similar to Crile's book, it concludes with Wilson hearing a 'teeth-jarring explosion' at the Pentagon on 9/11—a chilling scene in which the link is firmly established between US policy and its consequences. The original script hints at this throughout, with Gust Avrokotos repeatedly warning of the potential outcome of providing weapons—particularly Stinger missiles—to the mujahideen.

In the earlier script, Gust also breaks down the idea that the Soviets were simply genocidal invaders:

Gust: This is a two-year-old report. It's from the Red Cross. They were gathering statements from Afghan refugees regarding Soviet atrocities in their village. This woman said the Russian soldiers came in, gathered them in a semi-circle and you know what they did?

Charlie: What.

Gust: The Russians forced them to learn how to read and write.[180]

In typically dry fashion, Gust says, 'I'm not worried, though, 'cause I know if Islamic fanaticism ever gets outta hand, [*sic*] Joanne Herring and her friends will rise up to meet it with Christian fanaticism and then we've got ourselves a ballgame. And I wouldn't be concerned except we've just sent enough weapons over there to kill everyone on both sides.' This scene, along with the crash at the Pentagon, did not appear in the finished movie. Director Mike Nichols intimated that the scenes discussed above had been filmed but that he had left to them to 'curl up on the floor and die.'[181] The DVD contained no deleted material.

No draft of the script acknowledged the US' part in arming the mujahideen prior to the invasion and thus encouraging it to happen. In a 1998 interview with French news magazine *Le Nouvel Observateur*, former National Security adviser Zbigniew Brzezinski revealed he had 'no regrets' about the US having provided 'secret aid to the opponents of the pro-Soviet regime in Kabul' to encourage Moscow's intervention through a 'secret operation' in an effort to give the Soviet Union its own 'Vietnam War' in an 'Afghan Trap.'[182] Brzezinski later refuted these comments and said he was misquoted and that supporting the mujahideen with arms only happened after the Soviet invasion, demanding 'show me some documents to the contrary.'

One such document is the minutes of a meeting of the Special Coordination Committee—a top-level interdepartmental committee within the US government. On December 17, 1979, before the Soviet invasion, this meeting of top officials including Brzezinski concluded that 'we will explore with the Pakistanis and British the possibility of improving the financing, arming and communications of the rebel forces to make it as expensive as possible for the Soviets to continue their efforts.' Regardless of what Brzezinski did or didn't say to *Le Nouvel Observateur* about US intentions prior to the invasion, clearly there was already an international effort underway to arm the 'rebel forces' that they were trying to expand before even one Soviet tank entered into Afghanistan. Ironically, the earlier draft of the script does include Charlie quoting directly from the interview in *Le Nouvel Observateur*, saying, 'What's more important to the history of the world? Some stirred up Muslims or the liberation of Central Europe and the end of the Cold War?' Gust responds, 'there's such a thing as unintended consequences, especially when you've been as reckless as we have.' Naturally, this was removed and this entire question and controversy does not enter into any part of the film.

Indeed, it is the portrait of the CIA that is the most egregious deception in *Charlie Wilson's War*. The operation largely boils down to three guys—Charlie, Gust and Michael Vickers, a weapons expert who worked for the Agency throughout this period. Aside from a tiny number of other insignificant characters, as far as the watching audience are concerned, this was the CIA's team on Afghanistan (along with John MacGaffin, who appears but is never named in the film and is now the primary consultant on *Homeland*). In reality, the operation was much larger and included the likes of Milt Bearden, who, despite being a consultant to the film, is not depicted in it in any way. Likewise, MI6 and the British government as a whole are completely ignored. While Crile's book makes it clear that Wilson was a formal CIA asset and that Gust was his handler, the film reduces this to nothing more significant than a buddy comedy friendship. This is the story of an all-American triumph where half a dozen brave CIA officers and one drunken congressman took on the Soviet Union and won. If that sounds ridiculous and untrue, that's because it is.

Along with minimising the scale of Operation Cyclone, at least in terms of the number of CIA officers involved, *Charlie Wilson's War* also downplays how directly they were involved and thus how responsible they were for the consequences. Alongside Bearden, the film also involved then CIA entertainment liaison Chase Brandon as a technical advisor. It was likely his influence that encouraged this minimising of the scale and directness of CIA involvement in the Afghan jihad. The earlier scripts contain pointed references to the CIA's provision of Stinger missiles to the mujahideen, including warnings from Gust where he says, 'It's what's called a "Fire and Forget" weapon, that means anybody with a shoulder can operate it, are we okay with that? This line, along with a scene where Charlie shows off the spent casing from the first Stinger used to down a Soviet Hind helicopter, were excised. The 2005 draft even has Gust going out to Afghanistan to directly train the mujahideen alongside two other CIA agents. The 2006 draft turns this into two Pakistani agents, but still includes Gust. This scene does not appear in the film either.[183]

As the film developed, it was systematically stripped of almost any politically controversial material, and ends up telling an extremely diluted version of what is in Crile's book, which itself is not the most critical text about Operation Cyclone. The response to the film shows that this rewriting (of both the script and the true history) was successful. Although the *Investors Business Daily* complained that the film was evidence of liberal bias in Hollywood because it did not specifically celebrate Republicans' efforts in Afghanistan, [184] most commentators who examined its politics recognised that *Charlie Wilson's War* was highly supportive of the Reaganite initiative. Michael Johns, the former Heritage Foundation foreign policy analyst and speech-writer for George W.

Bush, praised the film as 'the first mass-appeal effort to reflect the most important lesson of America's Cold War victory: that the Reagan-led effort to support freedom fighters resisting Soviet oppression led successfully to the first major defeat of the Soviet Union.' Paul Barry, the CIA's Hollywood liaison following Brandon, called it a 'genuinely ... positive portrayal of CIA accomplishment.'[185]

Contact

[Above] A plane approaches the wormhole machine in Contact (1997).

Contact (1997) is unusually cerebral for a big budget, special effects-driven movie. It is essentially a film about abandoning old divisions and borders, overcoming differences and embracing the possibility of new frontiers. However, the producers wanted support from the DOD, so this progressive, futuristic vision was compromised and potentially subversive material was removed from the film.

While *Contact* is an alien contact story it does not involve the extraterrestrials arriving on earth. Instead they send instructions from outer space on how to build a wormhole machine to carry one person across the galaxy to meet them. As such, the film avoids the standard notions of good aliens vs bad aliens (*ET* vs *Independence Day*) and so the obvious government role of maintaining security or chasing the protagonists was not an option for the writers. Instead, the story mostly revolves around the conflict between science and religion, an essentially non-governmental issue, and how this impacts on the relationship between the scientific protagonist, Ellie Arroway (Jodie Foster), and her religious love interest, Palmer Joss (*Matthew McConaughey*).

However, within this dynamic, there is still room for a series of NATO-friendly assumptions. Fundamentally, Western technology and American science are shown to be superior, and, given the casting, one could argue that white American supremacy is a root of the story. The authorities are shown to be in control of information and that this is right and proper, and the general public are reduced to a cheering or booing mob. Despite the global (or even galactic) implications of the possibility of extraterrestrial communication, *Contact* rarely ventures outside America's borders. In this respect, *Independence Day* at least showed brief glimpses of how the alien invasion affected other countries and continents, whereas *Contact*'s narrow focus undermines the core message of the film about the benefits of overcoming such limited perspectives.

This undermining was exacerbated by the DOD's influence on the film. When the producers approached the Pentagon to rent some vehicles and helicopters the script was quite different—the military had a bigger role in the film but they were not portrayed well. As the Pentagon's own database on films records, 'Originally a fair amount of silly military depiction. Negotiated civilianization of almost all military parts. Minimal military depiction, but positive (benign). Allowed use of vehicles and helicopters for National Guard sequence.'[186]

This 'civilianization' also had the effect of removing some of the most politically relevant and subversive material in the script. One scene that was altered, likely at the request of the DOD, is when Ellie begins to decode a series of images hidden within the alien signal. In a meeting at the White House Ellie explains that the decoded images are blueprints for building a machine and speculates that it could be an advanced communications technology or some kind of transport device. In the original script the National Security Advisor suggests, 'It could just as easily be some kind of Trojan Horse. We build it and out pours the entire Vegan army.' The Chairman of the Joint Chiefs of Staff responds, 'Why even bother to risk personnel? Why not send some kind of doomsday machine? Every time an emerging technological civilization announces itself by broadcasting radio waves into space they reply with a message. The civilization builds it and blows itself up. No expeditionary force needed.' Ellie responds by telling the President, '[T]his is communist paranoia right out of War of the Worlds.'[187]

In the finished film this scene appears in modified form and it is the National Security Advisor and not the military who says, 'Every time they detect a new civilization they fax construction plans from space. We poor saps build this thing and blow ourselves to kingdom come.' Ellie's response about Cold War paranoia was cut, removing one of the few lines in the movie that was critical of the military and their mindset. While in the original script it is the military in this scene who appear neurotic, this fearfulness was 'civilianised' in the final version and the criticism of this mentality was removed. Similarly, another scene was excised where the candidates to go through the wormhole are shown a weapon they will take along for self-defence. This deletion included Ellie's objections that, 'I question the thinking behind sending the first ambassador to another civilization in armed—basically announcing our intentions are hostile,' and that insisting on taking a weapon is, 'xenophobic paranoia.'[188]

Another sequence in the September 1995 draft that features the military was also taken out of the final cut. In the original version, the President gives a stirring speech at the UN about the building of this great new technology and this is intercut with a military convoy and Apache helicopters approaching the construction site. The script describes how 'Encircling the installation is a vast graveyard of discarded aircraft—the detritus of Twentieth Century war-making.' [189] This is rather obvious symbolism representing how technological efforts are moving from the violence of the 20th century military industry to peaceful 21st century space exploration. In the final version this sequence does not appear, and there is no indication of military involvement in the construction of the wormhole machine.

In exchange for a few trucks for one sequence, the Pentagon effectively wrote themselves out of the script and demilitarised the whole story. As such, in this film where big ideas and widespread beliefs (in science and religions and by implication in politics) are subject to question and scrutiny, the military is the only area portrayed that is free from criticism. While they play only a minor role, they are not being shown through quite the same framework as the rest of the movie. The Department of Defense, along with the Treasury, Secret Service and NASA were thanked in the credits.

This process undermined *Contact*'s claims to being a truly progressive or radical film, but the military tried quite a different tactic on *Independence Day*. On that film one of the DOD's objections was that 'all advances in stopping the aliens are the result of actions by civilians' in contrast the 'anaemic US military response.'[190] They also had serious objections to the appearance of Area 51, as producer Dean Devlin explained, 'In fact, the United States military was going to support this and supply us with a lot of costumes and airplanes and stuff. Their one demand was that we remove Area 51 from the film, and we didn't want to do that. So they withdrew their support.' [191] Even when the producers 'civilianized' Area 51 and the officials responsible for it, this still did not satisfy the Pentagon's requirements for support.[192] Director Roland Emmerich elaborated, 'This is probably one of one of the biggest twists of the movie. In the middle of the movie, all of a sudden, you come up with Area 51. There's this mythology about this place where they keep spaceships. For Dean and I, it was the most important part because it ties together this mythology that people believe in to the movie. So it feels more real.'[193] Ironically, the Pentagon did provide promotional support to the vastly inferior sequel, *Independence Day: Resurgence* (2016), and even used this as a crossover marketing opportunity inviting people to join the army so they could fight aliens.[194]

However, demilitarising elements of movies to remove potentially embarrassments remains a preferred DOD tactic when rewriting scripts. In the Tina Fey war comedy *Whiskey Tango Foxtrot* (2016), the military allowed several days filming at Kirtland Air Force Base in exchange for civilianizing one aspect of the script they didn't like. The version the DOD reviewed, 'portrayed a US Army transport brake failure, resulting in it hitting a group of Afghani shoppers in Kabul, killing and injuring them. This was changed to an NGO vehicle.'[195]

Hotel Rwanda

Hotel Rwanda is about the true story of hotelier Paul Rusesabagina (Don Cheadle) during the 1994 Rwandan genocide, who saves his family and more than a thousand other refugees by granting them shelter in the besieged Hôtel des Mille Collines. The film had no CIA or DOD involvement. In fact, it was widely received as a movie that is extremely critical of US interests.

The standard story about Rwanda, replicated in the film, is that the US turned a blind eye to the hundred-day frenzy of genocide pre-planned by the Hutu government against the Tutsi minority and some moderate Hutus. Supposedly, the US was concerned about putting its troops in harm's way, especially given the debacle in Somalia the previous year; thus it ignored what

Gourevitch called 'the Jews of Africa' (the Tutsis) and became 'bystanders to genocide,' as President Obama's Ambassador to the United Nations Samantha Power famously put it.[196]

Salon magazine—usually well-versed in challenging establishment narratives—compared *Hotel Rwanda* favourably to 'the muckraking films that Warner Bros. turned out in the early '30s ... that aimed to shake up audiences' sense of justice and moral outrage.'[197]

In fact, *Hotel Rwanda* followed Washington's line on Rwanda and was based on a government-funded book written by Philip Gourevitch,[198] who worked closely with his brother-in-law, Secretary of State James Rubin.[199] It may be nothing more than coincidence, but military contractor United Technologies has major commercial interests in the region and one of its board members, Alexander Haig, also sat on the board of United Artists' senior partner MGM.

The problem is that consensus over the Rwandan tragedy is far from established, as the official narrative has come under sustained attack. Phil Taylor, former investigator for the International Criminal Tribunal for Rwanda (ICTR) claimed that 'for anyone who followed closely the 1994 crisis in Rwanda the highly-touted film *Hotel Rwanda* is merely propaganda statements interrupted by bouts of acting.'[200]

Some critics like Keith Harmon Snow argue that not only did the US fail to intervene to prevent 'genocide,' it intervened both before and after the massacres to ensure its side—the RPF— won. So, for instance, according to a French judge, it was Paul Kagame and his Tutsi associates who shot down the Hutu president's plane, killing all on board including President Habyarimana himself and President Ntaryamira of Burundi— commonly accepted as the trigger for the genocide.[201] This act was part of the Kagame-Tutsi final assault to seize power after a four-year war, with the assistance of the US-sponsored Ugandan military. A third Hutu leader, Melchior Ndadaye, an earlier president of Burundi, had been assassinated by his Tutsi military in October 1993, which was followed by an anti-Hutu pogrom that killed tens-of-thousands and drove hundreds-of-thousands of Burundian-Hutu refugees into Rwanda.

The RPF gained power and their preferred status in the West cleared the ground for Kagame and Yoweri Museveni— Kagame's ally and fellow US client and dictator (of Uganda)— periodically to invade and occupy Eastern Congo without 'international community' opposition to clear out the *genocidaires*. This led to the killing of hundreds-of-thousands of civilian Hutu refugees in a series of mass slaughters, and also provided cover for a wider Kagame-Museveni assault in the Congo that has led to millions of deaths in what has been commonly described as 'Africa's World War.'[202] This was again compatible with narrow Western interests and policy, as it contributed to the replacement of Mobutu with the more amenable Kabila and opened up the Congo to a new surge of mineral exploitation by Western companies.[203]

The subject of the film, Paul Rusesabagina, wrote in his autobiography that 'Rwanda is today a nation governed by and for the benefit of a small group of elite Tutsis… Those few Hutus who have been elevated to high-ranking posts are usually empty suits without any real authority of their own. They are known locally as Hutus de service or Hutus for hire.'[204] In December 2006, he wrote to the Queen of England to say that Kagame was a 'war criminal.'[205]

Hotel Rwanda certainly condemned elements of US policy towards Rwanda during the 1994 genocide, but it did so within ideological boundaries which ensured the film reflected the interests of US state and private power. *Salon* concluded, 'We know how little attention the West paid to the Rwandan genocide as it was occurring. The question is, how much attention will be paid to this movie?' [206] *Hotel Rwanda* generated a huge amount of news coverage and made $34 million on its $17 million investment. People are paying attention. The real question: should they?

The Interview

[Above] Unlikely Agents? James Franco and Seth Rogen join the CIA

Despite being a relatively low-brow comedy, *The Interview* is one of the most politically controversial movies of recent years. It depicts the CIA recruiting two flaky television producers—Dave Skylark (James Franco) and Aaron Rapaport (Seth Rogen)—to assassinate North Korean leader Kim Jong-Un. Skylark presents a celebrity gossip talk show and it soon emerges than Kim is a big fan, and invites the pair to North Korea for a rare and exclusive interview. The CIA immediately approach Skylark and Rapaport and convince them to use this opportunity to kill Kim using ricin.

The film was developed in response to real-life events. In early 2013, retired basketballer Dennis Rodman visited North Korea at Kim's invitation, playing in a special basketball game and leading a crowd in singing him Happy Birthday. Since then, Rodman has returned to Korea several times after reportedly meeting with the FBI. Rodman said, 'I have been contacted by the FBI and I met with them. They wanted to know what went on and who's really in charge in North Korea.'[207] This bizarre event inspired two comedy scripts—Fox's *Diplomats*, which was green-lit in February 2014, but was then dropped due to competition from Sony's *The Interview*.[208]

The film is clearly offensive to North Korea, not just in terms of representing its leadership but also in terms of eliding the historical and contemporary contexts of the US' bloody involvement in the peninsula. That much is obvious. More interesting is the film's production and reception. Pyonyang called it 'psy-ops' and this was dismissed out of hand by the Americans, but, on closer examination, the allegation seems accurate. This is a case study about a film as a weapon.

Instead of an intelligent satire of US interference in the fate of the Koreas, *The Interview* is a slapstick, gross-out buddy comedy where much of the humour centres around Kim's insanity and his attempts to 'honeydick' Skylark, i.e. fool him into thinking he's not so bad after all. When Skylark fails to smuggle the ricin into North Korea in a pack of chewing gum, the CIA drop more poison via a drone, leading to Rapaport having to hide the dildo-shaped case containing the ricin inside his anus. Meanwhile, the North Korean people are portrayed as foolish slaves who believe everything their Supreme Leader tells them, including that he can talk to dolphins and doesn't urinate or defecate.

In the summer of 2014—following a teaser trailer put out months before the movie's release—the Kim government declared *The Interview* an 'act of war' and promised: 'If the US administration connives at and patronises the screening of the film, it invites strong and merciless countermeasures.'[209] This was followed by the hack of Sony Pictures by a group calling themselves Guardians of Peace, which was discovered in late-November 2014, though it may have been going on for a year by that point. Gigabytes of data, among them copies of several unreleased Sony films and many thousands of internal documents and emails, were leaked onto the internet. Statements were issued by the Guardians of Peace demanding that Sony pull *The Interview* and not release it, and even hinted at bombings at theatres that showed the film. Eventually, the US government, after ignoring the question for a couple of weeks, decided suddenly that it really mattered to them, and the FBI declared that the North Korean government were responsible. Sony initially announced that they would not be releasing *The Interview*, before reversing this decision and putting the film out via independent cinemas and online streaming platforms.

It has been suggested that the Sony hack was not a hack, but a leak, either by a disgruntled employee at Sony or even as some kind of marketing stunt for *The Interview*. No evidence has emerged showing who released the files, let alone why, and no one has ever been charged in connection with the crime.[210]

However, the files do provide further details on the decisions being made within Sony and on their liaisons with other organisations during the production and in the run-up to the film's release. Of particular concern was the ending, where a tank fires a shell at Kim's helicopter and we see, in slow motion, with Katy Perry's *Firework* on the soundtrack, the shell strike and detonate, making Kim's head set on fire and then explode. After top-level discussions at Sony Pictures, including with chairman of the Sony parent corporation Kazuo Hirai, this scene was softened and made less gory. Hirai was concerned that the film, and the ending especially, would enrage Japan's volatile neighbour.

[Above] Kim Jong Un is finally assassinated in The Interview.

Concerned about the political impact, producers Rogen and Evan Goldberg reached out to Rich Klein of McLarty Media who suggested that the film could cause the North Korean government to take revenge. Klein later recalled saying, 'A physical strike in the U.S. would be beyond North Korea's capabilities, but we firmly believed that the North Koreans could try to stop the movie through a cyber-attack.'[211] Months later, on the day before *The Interview* was released, Klein wrote an editorial in support of the film calling it a 'subversive and damn funny movie' and suggesting that 'if copies are pirated in to North Korea, it is a very real challenge to the ruling regime's legitimacy.'[212]

Naturally, this storyline about the CIA using entertainment producers as a means of carrying out a covert operation begs the question of whether the CIA were involved in making the movie. However, the Agency are not depicted very well, as their recruits Skylark and Rapaport prove to be unreliable and thoroughly incompetent with Skylark frequently high on drugs (an easy role for Franco to play). The assassination plot has to be reworked several times to make up for their failings and missed opportunities. As such, the primary purpose of the film does not appear to be to make the CIA or America look good, but to make Kim look bad. The Supreme Leader is referred to as a 'modern day Hitler,' capable of nuking the entire West coast of the US. When he is eventually killed by Skylark and Rapaport shooting down his helicopter with a tank this is undoubtedly meant to be a positive outcome. So, whatever the CIA's failings in *The Interview*, they achieve their aim and we are meant to see this as a good result.

There is strong evidence that the CIA were involved in the production. *The Interview* includes footage of Langley that was also provided to the producers of recent productions that are known to have benefited from CIA support, such as *Zero Dark Thirty* and *Homeland*. According to emails leaked following the Sony Pictures hack, during a press 'visit the set' event someone let slip that a 'former CIA agent and someone who used to work for Hilary Clinton looked at the script.' One email exchange between executives Marisa Liston and Keith Weaver highlights their concerns about this slip, but as Weaver put it, 'Depending on how this comes up, this can go in any number of directions in terms of how it's interpreted.'[213]

Writer/producer and star Seth Rogen has made several statements about government involvement in *The Interview*, saying that, 'We made relationships with certain people who work in the government as consultants, who I'm convinced are in the CIA.'[214] This is another instance where academic commentary can be almost agonisingly tentative, with a major recent paper by Tricia Jenkins and Tony Shaw about *The Interview* saying, 'We must be wary of attributing too much credence to these statements of Rogen's, which might have been intended merely to boost publicity for *The Interview*.'[215] The assessment is dubious because this explicit comment by Rogen was published by the *New York Times* in mid-December 2014, after already months of media coverage of the movie and the subsequent hack, and at a point where Sony said they weren't releasing the film. Other similar statements are only public knowledge due to the leaked emails, which elevates these 'claims' by Rogen to more than just marketing speak. Furthermore, Rogen qualified his opinion about those he was 'convinced are in the CIA' explaining that, when Kim disappeared for a week, he emailed one of the consultants who reassured him that Kim was having ankle surgery and 'would be back in a couple of weeks.'[216] Sure enough, Kim was back in the public eye two weeks later. Given the secrecy around the North Korean government Rogen's assumption that the consultant worked for an intelligence agency is reasonable.

A few months after the film was released, South Korean activists started sending huge numbers of balloons into North Korea carrying tens-of-thousands of USB sticks and DVDs containing copies of *The Interview*.[217] This was before the film was available on DVD in many countries (including the UK), but none of the media coverage of the event addressed the large-scale copyright infringement inherent in this 'activism.'

This is virtually identical to CIA operations during the Cold War when balloons were used to drop millions of leaflets, copies of books and even terrorism training manuals to populations in Soviet states or countries with Left wing governments. It appears that the CIA not only quietly helped to make *The Interview* but were also involved in using it as a weapon of psychological warfare against the North Korean government. Whether this was effective is unclear due to the near-total absence of reporting from inside North Korea. In any case, it is doubtful than many citizens of North Korea own computers with USB drives. While Jenkins and Shaw's paper acknowledges this event, it neglects to draw any parallels with the CIA's equivalent Cold War programs, or to mention the question of copyright.

Just as this leak was predicted by Rich Klein in his review of the film, it was foreseen by Bruce Bennett of the RAND corporation. Bennett consulted on *The Interview* and was in communication with Sony Pictures CEO Michael Lynton, who sits on RAND's board of trustees. In another Sony email, Bennett assured Lynton that there was nothing dangerous about releasing the film, writing, 'While toning down the ending may reduce the North Korean response, I believe that a story that talks about the removal of the Kim family regime and the creation of a new government by the North Korean people (well, at least the elites) will start some real thinking in South Korea and, I believe, in the North once the DVD leaks into the North (which it almost certainly will).' Lynton responded, 'Spoke to someone very senior in State (confidentially). He agreed with everything you have been saying. Everything. I will fill you in when we speak.'[218]

The end of the movie sees an instantaneous revolt in North Korea as news of Kim's death spreads across the country. A few months later, this magically results in peaceful democratic elections with no sign of power struggles. This romanticises real CIA coups, which have consistently produced less democratic governments than they overthrew. As with the changed ending of *Animal Farm* (1954), the happy conclusion to *The Interview* promotes revolutionary violence. To a Western audience, this also promotes CIA covert operations including coup d'etats, but what about the North Korean audience? As one reviewer commented, 'The subject of "*The Interview*" is the political impact on North Korea of a worldwide media event such as "*The Interview*" itself.'[219] Seth Rogen put it more simply, saying, 'We were told one of the reasons they're so against the movie is that they're afraid it'll actually get into North Korea. They do have bootlegs and stuff. Maybe the tapes will make their way to North Korea and cause a fucking revolution.'[220]

There were multiple motivations behind the making of *The Interview*. But it is clear that, in part, it was deliberate propaganda, unnoticed by almost everyone in the country that produced and subsequently weaponised the movie.

The Marvel Cinematic Universe

[Above] The Avengers assembled.

The Marvel Cinematic Universe (MCU) has rapidly become the most commercially successful movie franchise of all time, but few are aware of the important role the Pentagon played in making that happen. Three out of the six films that comprise the first phase of the MCU benefited from full DOD cooperation. Here, we take a closer look.

Hulk

Military support for Marvel comic book adaptations began before the MCU even existed. *Hulk* (2003) was not a Marvel or Marvel-licensed film but it was based on a Marvel character. In exchange for providing script research assistance, military vehicles and filming at the Naval Air Weapons Station, China Lake, the DOD made substantial changes to the script. The story begins in the 1960s with Bruce Banner's father working on the genetic enhancement of mammals in a desert laboratory. He tests his serums on himself and sees no results, but then finds out that he has passed on the genetic abnormalities to his infant son. Decades later Bruce is working on near-identical research and is exposed to a massive leak of gamma radiation, which awakens his superpowers and allows him to turn into the Hulk. He is captured by the US military but escapes, leading to an extended pursuit across the desert and into San Francisco, where he is captured again. Meanwhile, his father, trying to duplicate what happened to Bruce, exposes himself to radiation and becomes the Absorbing Man, who takes on the properties of any energy or matter that he touches. There is a final showdown between the two, leading to the military bombing the pair as they fight. The Absorbing Man is destroyed while the Hulk escapes to the jungles of Latin America.

In February 2002, the Marine Corps ELO sent a set of script notes to the *Hulk* producers saying, 'The primary purpose of these notes is civilianize the desert lab and the direct action against the Hulk, leaving only one actual deadly military strike, against the Absorbing Man at the end. All the other military operations would be non-lethal and other unconventional attempts to contain, distract, or subdue the Hulk, or to provide reconnaissance information regarding him.'[221] The notes then list dozens of suggested changes, most of which were incorporated into the screenplay.

Such a recommendation is reminiscent of the DOD's farcical request that the *Independence Day* (1996) filmmakers eliminate 'any government connection' to Roswell and Area 51 and instead have a 'grass roots civilian group... protecting the alien ship on an abandoned base.'[222]

[Above] Five-way split-screen showing off military hardware in Hulk.

Some of these affected not just the military depiction but the overall story, as it appears that the script reviewed by the DOD included a more prolonged military pursuit of the Hulk throughout the film, rather than one big chase towards the end. Other alterations included changing the lab where Banner's father does his research from a military to a civilian facility. The notes say, 'If the physical look of the place is military, it would be good to make it clear that it's no longer an active military installation.' This was reflected in the dialogue, which states that the lab is under the authority of the president's science advisor, not the DOD. Along similar lines, the story's antagonist, Major Glenn Talbot—who physically beats Banner during his captivity, trying to make him transform into the Hulk—was turned into an ex-military officer working for a private contractor, again at the DOD's request.

The notes also refer a scene where the older Banner is talking with Bruce's girlfriend, saying, 'We don't understand the reference to "all those boys, guinea pigs" dying from radiation, and then "the germ warfare." Sounds as if there were evil military experiments, or is this just Banner's raving?' These lines were removed from the movie. Likewise, the codename for the mission to track and capture the Hulk was changed from 'Operation Ranch Hand' to 'Operation Angry Man' because 'Ranch Hand is a Vietnam era operation.' Though the script notes do not mention this the real Operation Ranch Hand was a program that saw the US military drop an estimated 20 million gallons of herbicides and defoliants on Vietnam between 1962 and 1971.[223]

Throughout the military's pursuit of the Hulk, the eponymous superhero smashes up a lot of military hardware, but according to internal Pentagon emails this wasn't a problem. An email discussing ideas for a scene where the military would use 'some cool toys' to subdue the Hulk suggests, 'Hulk can, after 1st attack, maybe pick up a car, etc. and throw it at and/or hit some of the troops... makes public more sympathetic to the militaries cause and gives General justification in taking it to the next level.'[224] The same email discusses how to 'get the JOINT aspect into it' and, while their specific suggestion wasn't used, the helicopters pursuing the Hulk bear the name and logo of the Joint Tactical Force West, a real joint forces military unit.

The DOD are not credited anywhere for their work on *Hulk*—the credits at the end of the film do not mention them, none of the military's IMDB pages refer to *Hulk* and the movie is not mentioned in the DOD's database of their involvement with Hollywood. It appears that the Pentagon do not want to draw attention to their role in drastically rewriting *Hulk*, which went way beyond providing notes on technical accuracy. As the script notes say, 'In the past we've usually been able to offer suggestions within the context of existing plot and characters. These, however, are pretty radical. I hope they don't have the effect of aggravating everyone, because we certainly aren't trying to intrude on the creative process. It's just that I see no other practical, straightforward way of communicating our concerns.'

Iron Man

While Hulk was rebooted a few years later during the first phase of the MCU, the first proper Marvel Universe movie was *Iron Man*. In it, a billionaire military industrialist is demonstrating his new missile system when he is kidnapped by Afghan rebels. They torture him and try to force him to build hi-tech weapons for them, so he constructs a prototype super-suit which he uses to kill most of them and escape their mountain lair. Back in the US, he announces that his company is no longer in the weapons manufacturing business and refines the suit, turning himself into a superhero.

This Pentagon-supported movie uses a slightly more subtle means than many films to convince the audience that war is good. Our protagonist, Tony Stark (Robert Downey Jr.), is initially shown as a carefree playboy, enjoying the profits from Stark Industries, the arms manufacturing behemoth he inherited from his father. Stark's capture and imprisonment appear to change him dramatically, which makes him much more appealing to ambivalent or anti-war audience members.

When Stark escapes and returns to the US he immediately tries to shut down the weapons manufacturing division of Stark Industries, announcing that he saw 'young Americans killed by the very weapons I created to defend them' and had 'become part of a system that is comfortable with zero accountability.' Stark declares that he has 'more to offer the world than making things blow up,' before creating an extremely efficient means of blowing things up. He develops the Iron Man suit and embarks on a mission to kill terrorists in Afghanistan.

Several reviewers fell for this conceit: the film was variously described as having 'a sprinkle of anti-war and redemption themes,' being a 'pacifist statement,' 'militantly anti-war profiteer,' and one saw Iron Man himself as a 'pacifist superhero' who 'shuns arms manufacturing ... [to] save Mankind.'[225] What this ignores is that Iron Man continues to make weapons of increasing sophistication and uses them for the exact same purposes as the Pentagon—killing generic Muslim terrorists.

None of these reviews highlighted the extensive US Air Force involvement in the film, perhaps indicating that their authors were unaware of this. Air Force Captain Christian Hodge, the Defense Department's project officer for the production, commented that the 'Air Force is going to come off looking like rock stars.'[226] In exchange for this very positive portrayal they helped with almost every aspect of the film, from script research and technical advice to on-location filming, providing aircraft and airmen as extras.

An early draft script of *Iron Man* from 2004 shows that it was originally far more opposed to war and the weapons industry than the version that made it into cinemas. In the earlier version, Stark's father, Howard, is still alive, and it is he who runs a massive weapons manufacturing business, which Tony opposes while working on developing advanced technologies that are peaceful. When others suggest that Tony adapt his inventions into weapons he rejects this, repeatedly saying '*No* military contracts.'[227] When Tony discovers that Howard, along with fellow military industrialist Justin Hammer, have been stealing his designs, weaponising them and selling them under the table to North Korea and other 'rogue states,' he fights back. Tony creates the Iron Man suit as a means of countering and struggling against the military industrial complex, rather than as a supplement to it as in the finished film. In one scene, Tony Stark confronts Justin Hammer, calling him a 'technology-laden sociopath.' Stark believes that the plot is just about making money but Hammer corrects him, saying 'Your father will settle for nothing less than the restoration of order to the world.[228] The original script not only criticised the moral corruption of the arms industry but characterised it as seeking to rule the world.

Several years later, the producers of *Iron Man* did not have a finished screenplay when they actually started shooting the movie, which meant that director Jon Favreau and star Robert Downey Jr. had to improvise a lot of the dialogue while they were filming. This is because almost all of the 2004 script had been jettisoned or radically altered. Howard Stark and Justin Hammer were watered down from military industrial megalomaniacs into the Obadiah Stane character who is merely selling weapons to terrorists to increase profits. Tony Stark briefly flirts with pacifism instead of being committed to it throughout, and he creates the Iron Man suit to take revenge on his captors, not on the arms industry. His sidekick, James Rhodes, was changed from chief of security at Stark Industries to the US Air Force liaison with weapons manufacturers. At the end of the film when Stane dons a bigger, more powerful armoured suit to fight Tony this is one of very few scenes taken from the 2004 screenplay, but here again there was a crucial change. In the original version, the suit that Howard uses to fight Tony is called War Machine—a direct reference to the military industry. In the film this name was dropped, only to be picked up in the sequel as the moniker for Rhodes when he steals an armoured suit and hands it over to the Pentagon so they have their own in-house Iron Man. Put simply, in the original script the 'War Machine' is a bad guy, in the finished *Iron Man* films he is a good guy.

With such a fluid script situation, it is likely that some of these radical changes were made at the behest or influence of Phil Strub and Chris Hodge, the DOD officers who worked on the film. The tone of the story was changed from being critical of the military industrial complex as a whole, to being a pro-military blockbuster with very limited criticism of a few bad eggs in the arms industry. It wasn't all smooth sailing. Phil Strub recalled an argument over one line where a military character says to another that people would 'kill themselves for the opportunities he has.' Strub did not like this line and wanted it to be changed, but the director refused. The argument was still running months later when it came to filming the scene. Strub recalled, 'Now we're on the flight lines at Edwards Air Force Base (California), and there's 200 people, and [the director] and I are having an argument about this. He's getting redder and redder in the face and I'm getting just as annoyed. It was pretty awkward and then he said, angrily, "Well how about they'd walk over hot coals?" I said "fine." He was so surprised it was that easy.'[229]

That even tiny aspects of the film were altered in keeping with the Pentagon's wishes shows that there is nothing in *Iron Man* that runs contrary to their agenda. While the Iron Man weapon is not owned or controlled by the Pentagon, it is on the same side and pursuing the same targets, and, as such, is in keeping with the Pentagon's overall mission philosophy. In the film, Stark keeps his creation and self-appointed mission a secret. The logic, that 'I don't want this [the Iron Man suit] ending up in the wrong hands. Maybe in mine it can do some good' is the core message of the movie: There are always going to be weapons, so aren't you glad our weapons are better than the enemy's? Contrasting this, the original script has Tony telling Justin Hammer that, 'Better weaponry isn't going to restore order anywhere.'[230]

The principal antagonist in *Iron Man* is Jeff Bridges' Obadiah Stane, an executive at Stark Industries who is clandestinely selling weapons to terrorists, and betrays Tony when he finds out. This crucial criticism of the weapons industry—that it is sometimes willing to sell to both sides of a conflict to make even more money—was diluted and condensed down into a small element of the bad guy's character. As is so often the case, a large systemic and institutional problem in the real world is reduced to the behaviour of a few bad apples in Hollywood-land. The other antagonists are all nameless Muslim terrorists who do nothing but shout and fire AK-47s, in the proud Hollywood tradition of Reel Bad Arabs. For all the anti-war rhetoric about 1/3 of the way in, the rest of the film is largely about America using superior military technology to blow away its enemies with impunity.

Iron Man 2

In the sequel, Tony Stark faces a number of new challenges, from the Pentagon trying to take control of the super-suits to a rival military industrialist who teams up with a Russian with his own version of the Iron Man weapon. The solution in all cases is the further destruction of Stark's cliffside mansion. The film opens with Stark engaging in an enormous vanity project—he leaps out of a military cargo plane and descends like an armoured angel onto a stage full of dancing girls. This is the opening of the Stark Expo, a vast technological theme park reminiscent of the World's Fair and other huge exhibitions that were so popular in the WW2 and early Cold War periods. This, Stark explains, is partly homage to his own father (who we see at a WW2 expo in *Captain America* the following year) but is also about Stark's own legacy. The reality, as Pepper Potts points out, is that 'the expo is your ego gone crazy.'

Nonetheless, the expo serves as the setting for both the opening of the film and the climactic battle sequences at the end, and reminds the audience of a time when the lines of battle were clear and the public believed that they were fighting for good. This setting, combined with one of the primary antagonists—Ivan Vanko—being Russian, successfully delivers that same feeling to a modern-day audience. The fact that Vanko is seeking revenge for Stark's father supposedly stealing his idea and thus his glory is a rather crude but useful metaphor for an image of contemporary Russia as a diminished superpower that is jealous of America's

103

status. Pointed references to North Korea, Iran and other contemporary 'enemies' only serve to cement these feelings in the watching audience.

Stark's other enemy is Justin Hammer, who we are told is the Pentagon's primary weapons manufacturer, played with typical aplomb by Sam Rockwell. In keeping with the original film's superficial criticisms of the arms industry, Hammer is shown to be corrupt. He teams up with Vanko to try to destroy Stark's legacy, and, in the process, ends up being arrested after Vanko's drone robots start shooting up the Stark Expo.

However, what most obviously separates Hammer and Stark is not that Stark is a good guy and Hammer is a bad guy. It is that Stark's technology works and Hammer's doesn't. Hammer isn't bad because he's a military contractor, but because his missiles don't land where he says they're going to land. So, the film does not criticise weapons manufacturers per se—Tony Stark continues to build and develop the Iron Man weapon throughout the film. He is always forgiven because his technology works and so it helps maintain an image of technological superiority and thus of American exceptionalism being just. The fact that he is not formally part of the Pentagon is debated but also forgiven, because, as Stark himself puts it, 'I've successfully privatised world peace' (he says while doing a Nixon-style two handed V for Victory sign).

[Above] Robert Downey Jr. on set at Edwards Air Force Base for Iron Man 2.

Just as with the original, *Iron Man 2* received full co-operation from the Pentagon. Primarily, this came from the Air Force but the Marine Corps also reviewed the script, provided extras, and technical advisors were on set during filming and Edwards AFB was again used as a major filming location. The DOD even had input on the visual design of the War Machine armoured suit as their database records that, 'the Air Force assisted in designing the war machine markings.' [231] Officers from Pentagon were also present for shooting the drone scene—the final battle where all of these elements coincide in one happy mess with lots of broken glass. The film was screened at Camp Pendleton prior to its full release, which the Marine Corps saw as a big success, 'bringing 1600 personnel to a 1350 chaired theatre.'[232]

The Avengers

Military support for the MCU continued, but on *The Avengers* (2012) the relationship began to fray. As recorded in reports of the Army's ELO, the DOD provided access to White Sands missile range for filming and a 'company of soldiers for the climactic battle scene.'[233] In exchange for this support, the DOD leaned on the producers to make efforts towards 'connecting one of the film's superhero protagonists, Captain America, with his US Army roots.'[234] However, unlike most other productions, there is no reference in the ELO reports to the DOD previewing the film prior to release, or any updates on how it had been received. This is because there was an argument during the shooting of the film and their collaboration stalled. Within days of *The Avengers'* release, news articles began appearing, quoting Phil Strub denying that the DOD had supported the film. 'We couldn't reconcile the unreality of this international organization and our place in it,' Strub explained, 'to whom did S.H.I.E.L.D. answer? Did we work for S.H.I.E.L.D.? We hit that roadblock and decided we couldn't do anything. It just got to the point where it didn't make any sense.'[235]

Journalist Spencer Ackerman noted that both F-22 and F-35 aircraft appeared in The Avengers, but Strub insisted that these were 'digitally inserted' and not real military aircraft loaned to the production. This is splitting hairs, because the aircraft we see getting blown up in the *Transformers* films or dropping like flies into the ocean in *Godzilla* are not really getting blown up or falling out of the sky. The fact remains that by the time F-35s appeared in *The Avengers* they had not yet flown a single combat mission, and thus could only have appeared with Strub's and the DOD's permission.

It appears one major problem was the scene during the climactic battle where S.H.I.E.L.D. launches a nuclear missile at New York city to try to fend off an alien invasion, without consulting the Pentagon. Strub said, 'We were really excited about the movie, but the more we tried to reconcile the S.H.I.E.L.D. hierarchy—this all-powerful, international paramilitary organisation who can do anything in any sovereign nation—we couldn't fit the US military into it. It just wasn't meshing. So we had to say no.'[236] Despite *The Avengers* being a superhero fantasy story, the Pentagon still could not accept the depiction of an organisation 'with its all-powerful international capabilities and weaponry that far exceeded our own.'[237] Clearly, the DOD has the same political concerns when it comes to the fiction of the MCU as they do with stories based on real-life events.

While the producers of *The Avengers* have never spoken publicly about this falling out, they deserve some credit for resisting government pressure and maintaining their creative freedom. While half of the first phase of Marvel films benefited from Pentagon support, there has only been one further collaboration since this disagreement over *The Avengers*—on *Captain America: Winter Soldier*. The second phase of the Marvel Universe has seen the studio team up with NASA and the Science and Entertainment Exchange to gain some added production value via the government, but not from the military or security agencies.

The Kingdom

The Kingdom had considerable potential to present a critical narrative about US foreign policy, specifically regarding its relationship with Saudi Arabia. Director Peter Berg cast Ashraf Barhoum (Colonel Faris Al Ghazi) because he had loved him in *Paradise Now* (2005).[238] Barhoum himself felt *The Kingdom* bore a different attitude toward the Middle East than other American movies in its attempt to see and understand the region and the conflict: 'this is our reality... very violent—and so our judgement of it will be very violent. But it will also be very human,' he said.[239] 'Certainly in my lifetime, military attempts to solve these problems don't seem to be working. Violence is just not going to work,' affirmed Berg.[240] 'I wanted to make a film that responded to the times that we were living in, a film that in 15 years my son, who's seven, will be able to watch and have a unique and a fair representation and understanding of what life was like for all of us who were living in this time.'[241]

What makes *The Kingdom* so notable is the director's apparently sincere efforts to engage in the political context and quite how twisted and reactionary that vision became. Why?

For a start, the plot points towards standard jingoistic attitudes. The film depicts heroic FBI agents tracking down a particularly nasty group of terrorists in Riyadh. All the Saudis are shown to repress women and not give them a voice (Jennifer Garner's role was scarcely more than eye candy). The final shot of a little Arab boy being told 'we are going to kill them all' seems to be intended to warn us of the dangers of a cycle of violence but there's another obvious reading that these little brown kids all-too easily become terrorists.

[Above] The aftermath of a suicide bomb, The Kingdom

Jack Shaheen, an advisor on *Three Kings* (1999) and *Syriana* (2005) pointed out that Berg could have provided a more nuanced depiction of Saudi Arabia by taking inspiration from documentaries like *The Saudis* (CBS) and *Amarco Brats*. He suggested that the central characters could have discussed how terrorism adversely affects all people and that Americans and Arabs should work in unison to protect the innocent.[242] Shaheen's expertise was not requested. There were several Saudis on set who provided cultural advice, though one, Berg said, was distanced from the project after he developed a crush on Garner (without meaning to belittle the issue of Jennifer's safety, one might at least ask the question—who didn't have a crush on her?).[243]

Berg acknowledged: "If you look at the trailers and teasers, *The Kingdom* could be perceived as jingoistic, overtly pro-American. That's clearly not the message of the film. My goal was to try to present Muslim culture in a way that wasn't inflammatory, but that showed humans, families, people trying to live their lives. There has to be a moderate Arab population, or everyone over there would be dead…"[244]

The audience response suggests that Berg didn't strike his intended tone, as he admitted to attending preview screenings in Sacramento, California where:

The audience started clapping very intensely and very aggressively, and I sat there thinking I'd really fucked up and had made something that appealed to the most bloodthirsty, violent, militaristic component of our culture… Afterwards we had this focus group of 30 people and everyone sort of talking about the film in very emotional terms, and they were responding to the message at the end… They were finding the film provocative, at which point we were like, "Maybe we should think a bit more about how we release this film and put a little more thought into it.[245]

However, Berg claims that follow-up screenings, including

with European Muslims, allayed his original concerns. He recalls: 'If the specially invited Muslim traditionalist crowd of South London-istan [Wandsworth] could take it, the theory went, everywhere else would be a doddle... the cheering and laughing and clapping that was there in the American audience was all there, and then some, in London.' Afterwards, a focus group was asked to explain why they had rated the film 'excellent' on their scorecards. 'A Muslim woman put her hand up—full head covering, the robe. She leaned forward and said, "Kick-ass action."'

To be fair to Berg, his perspective seems earnest. He visited Saudi Arabia in 2006 for two weeks of research and commented:

You're in the middle of a Muslim city and there was a war between Israel and Lebanon going on at the time. It's disorienting; the culture is so different. It takes a while to look someone in the eye before they smile. But I made great friends with many Arabs while I was there, which reinforced my belief that the great majority of Muslims are not violent religious extremists.

And yet the central question that comes out of Berg's long justifications for *The Kingdom* is, did he really need to have the idea reinforced that most Muslims aren't 'violent religious extremists'? Maybe he'd been watching too many movies.

'I wanted to make a film that dealt with the Middle East and dealt with religious extremism, but I first and foremost wanted to make a film that people would be thrilled at,' Berg added. The danger, again, that a well-meaning film-maker ultimately knows that thrills—violent in this case—are more important than the political perspective. 'I'm aware that audiences are cheering when Jennifer Garner kills an Arab in one scene,' Berg admitted. 'That's not a reaction I entirely anticipated, but I do understand it. I don't think it's a jingoistic cheer for killing Arabs because I've seen

Arabs applaud at that moment too. I think, I hope, it's more a "good guy beating a bad guy" moment.' Maybe—but it is notable that Berg provides the self-serving interpretation at every turn.

'The American public is certainly not as educated as it could be about the realities of the Middle East,' says Berg. 'I've been surprised how very few Americans understand that Osama Bin Laden is a Saudi, that 15 of the 19 in the planes that knocked down the Trade towers and the Pentagon were Saudi.' This appears to be the main point of the opening montage which walks us through US-Saudi relations. And now that we are all 'educated' with the knowledge that Saudi Arabia is the focal point of modern terrorism, what then? It's hardly an advert for a US-Middle East student exchange programme.

In addition to the DOD and FBI support, *The Kingdom* received advice from Rich Klein of Kissinger McLarty Associates—the international strategic advisory firm (officially split since 2008) headed by the infamous proponent of realpolitik and war crimes Henry Kissinger. Rather like asking Ronnie Kray to proofread an encyclopedia of gangsters. 'It became an exercise in honesty,' Klein informed the *New York Times*, somewhat strangely, as though those 'honesty' muscles were not subject to a regular work out.[246]

The nature of Kissinger McLarty Associates' advice is not known.

There surely are action films to be made—in the vein of *Three Kings* and *Syriana*—that are set against the backdrop of the US' support for the most brutal regimes. *The Kingdom* is not one of those movies. Berg seems to have had higher, even laudable, ambitions, rather than simply informing us that Saudi Arabia is a hive of terrorism. 'What we are doing now is creating new generations of haters,' he asserted passionately, referring to the inflammatory consequences of US foreign policy.[247] His point is no doubt true but blame also lies closer to his door than he wants to believe.

Lone Survivor

As one of very few Pentagon-supported films set in the War on Terror that is based on a real-life story, *Lone Survivor* is important in shaping public perceptions of present-day foreign and national security policy. Amongst the regular cinematic diet of *Godzilla* and *Transformers, Lone Survivor* stands out as a gritty and apparently realistic story that is representative of wider events. The up-close-and-personal nature of the film belies the startling inaccuracies, exaggerations and stereotypes that underpin almost every scene and sequence.

The Pentagon knowingly altered the critical scene in *Lone Survivor*, even though it was based on the account of the only survivor of the real events, because it did not suit their PR agenda and desired public image. This fact alone puts the lie to the Pentagon's claims that their involvement in Hollywood is motivated by concern for authenticity and technical accuracy, as well as revealing some of the true reasons for that involvement.

[Above] Mark Wahlberg and the other SEALs in Lone Survivor.

The film and the book tell the same basic story. Four members of SEAL Team 10—Mike Murphy, Matthew Axelson, Danny Dietz and Marcus Luttrell—are sent on a reconnaissance mission to try to locate Taliban commander Ahmad Shah in Eastern Afghanistan. They are discovered on a mountainside by local goat-herders and debate whether to kill the goat-herders or release them, knowing that releasing them means being discovered by the Taliban. They let them go, leading to a massive firefight on the hillside. Three of the SEALs are killed, leaving one, Marcus Luttrell, the Lone Survivor.

However, there are stark differences between the original book, on which the original script was closely based, and the finished film. In the book, the four have an argument, with one SEAL (Axelson) in favour of killing the elderly man and two kids and one (Dietz) refusing to make the decision. Luttrell is initially in favour of executing them but then the unit leader, Murphy, points out that if they kill unarmed civilians then they will be attacked by the 'liberal media' back home. This sways Luttrell, who rants at great length in the book about his hatred for liberals. Axelson then suggests that they do it and then just lie about it, even when it comes out in the papers, basically saying that they should commit a war crime and then cover it up. Eventually the four have a vote: Axelson votes for killing them, Dietz abstains, Luttrell is against, so Murphy makes the decision and decides to let them go. In the book Luttrell writes, 'It was the stupidest, most southern-fried, lamebrained decision I ever made in my life. I must have been out of my mind. I had actually cast a vote which I knew could sign our death warrant. I'd turned into a fucking liberal, a half-assed, no-logic nitwit, all heart, no brain, and the judgment of a jackrabbit.'[248]

In the final film, this scene is profoundly different. There is no mention of liberals or the liberal media and no suggestion of killing the goat-herders and covering it up. Luttrell is shown always to be in favour of letting them go, and it is he, not the team leader, Murphy, who brings up the issue of media exposure. However, unlike in the book, Luttrell's argument is apolitical and is about them going to prison rather than being attacked by the press. In the film, there is no vote, the team leader simply decides they're going to let the goat-herders go. In short, in the book, the SEALs talk about being attacked by the liberal media, discuss committing a war crime and covering it up, and take a vote. In the film, they talk about the story coming out and them going to jail, and don't discuss covering up the murder of unarmed civilians, nor do they take a vote.

Based on Luttrell's book of the same name, *Lone Survivor* is one of a trio of recent movies to feature US Navy Special Warfare commandos on a real mission that would become very high-profile—the others are *Zero Dark Thirty* and *Captain Phillips*. All three of these productions were assisted by the Navy, leading to the sense that the 'quieter professionals' (Naval special forces) are beginning to build a public profile for themselves. Certainly, the real-life story of Operation Red Wings is compelling and violent so it is no surprise that both the book and film were commercial successes, the movie making back over $150 million on a $40 million budget. However, the film contains numerous inaccuracies including that, 'Luttrell didn't flatline, Shah probably wasn't a member of al Qaeda, and the final battle depicted in the film never happened.'[249]

One of the more significant inaccuracies was the size of the Taliban force that killed three of the four members of the SEAL team and shot down a Chinook helicopter carrying another sixteen members of the US Special Forces. Different accounts range enormously: journalist Ed Darack's book, *Victory Point*, citing military intelligence reports, puts the number at 8-10 fighters but the medal citation for the SEAL team leader says there were up to 50. Luttrell himself has been very contradictory on this issue, writing in his after-action report (according to Darack) that there were 20-30, but in the book of *Lone Survivor* he says there were as many as 200. The film's script describes at least 50 Taliban fighters that Luttrell manages to fend off before he escapes.

Lone Survivor was produced in close co-operation with the US military, particularly the US Navy Special Operations Command and Navy Special Warfare Groups. They provided training footage that was used in the introduction to the film, helicopters including Chinooks and Apaches, along with other vehicles, and Kirtland Air Force Base in Albuquerque was a major filming location. Former Navy SEAL Harry Humphries was hired as a producer and consultant who helped director Peter Berg and the crew negotiate with the Pentagon.[250] The production employed several former SEALs, including, Luttrell to act as on-set consultants and technical advisors during filming. Meanwhile the Navy also allowed two SEALs, Raymond Mendoza and Scott Fox, to go on leave so they could provide pre-production training and consultancy to the cast.

In exchange for this assistance, the Pentagon were granted script approval, which they used to completely rewrite the key scene in the film. Navy emails show that when the DOD were reviewing the script that the 'goatherder scene' was the major worry. In the original script, the depiction of the four SEALs debating whether to execute the goatherders to protect themselves from the Taliban was based closely on Luttrell's account, but Strub and the Navy were not happy with it. One email records how instead of rewriting the dialogue in the scene, Phil Strub explained their concerns to the filmmakers, because, 'I was hesitant to rewrite what Luttrell believes was said to the best of his memory.'[251]

However, the script notes provided by the Pentagon to Berg show that accuracy and realism were not Strub's or the Navy's primary concern in the goatherder scene. The notes say, 'While maximizing historical authenticity is our mandate we share responsibility for the reputations of the four SEALs and to their families' memories of them.'[252] Strub's explanation of the DOD's worries about this scene are redacted, but in a later email he confirms that the writers, 'used our notes as a kind of check-list, and addressed all of our concerns.'[253] Navy officers were on set during the filming of this scene to ensure that the agreed-upon changes were made.

Emphasising how realism and accuracy were less than primary concerns for the Pentagon and the producers of *Lone Survivor*, the US Army's ELO reports contain dozens of mentions of the film, but only one includes the line 'the Lone Survivor director, Pete Berg is committed to telling an accurate and compelling story.'[254] This sentence was omitted from all other entries about *Lone Survivor*, though the entries are otherwise largely identical with occasional updates. This omission, and the rest of their assessment, demonstrates that they were less concerned with accuracy than with the film's impact on the audience.

Most of the entries note, 'support of entertainment feature films like this reach far greater audiences than any single news media story about the actual events. Audiences going to see the film will voluntarily sit through a two-hour infomercial about the participation of Army Special Forces in one of our many joint missions.'[255] They even took time to note that at Spike TV's Guys Choice Awards in 2014, 'More than 50 soldiers were in attendance at this annual event. The Fort Irwin Garrison Commander, COL Braga, presented the "Troops Choice Award" to Mark Wahlberg for his portrayal of Marcus Luttrell in the US Army supported feature film, Lone Survivor.'[256]

Lone Survivor director and producer Peter Berg's career is littered with pro-military and otherwise pro-government productions, including the Navy recruitment/alien invasion movie *Battleship*, which is little more than *Transformers* on water. He developed a programme called *Superpower*, 'a television series featuring DoD weapon systems that have given the US a dominant edge,' though this was never produced.[257] Berg also produced episodes of *The Selection: Special Operations Experiment* and *The Warfighters*, as well as the TV documentary *Lone Survivor: Will of the Warrior*.

Berg's latest film saw him team up with Wahlberg again to depict the 2013 Boston Marathon bombing and the resulting manhunt. *Patriots Day* was made in close cooperation with the Boston police department and consulted with former Boston police Commissioner Ed Davis, former Marine Mike Dowling and agents from the FBI. Screenwriter Joshua Zetumer explained, 'I was also able to gain access to the FBI. I have a consultant friend of mine, Rich Klein, who works for a company McLarty Associates who in the past has put me in touch with people from the CIA. In this case, he had a contact within the FBI. I did many hours of interviews with FBI agents who worked on the case. That ended up being really helpful for shaping the narrative.'[258]

Rules of Engagement

Rules of Engagement was denounced by the American-Arab Anti-Discrimination Committee (ADC) as 'probably the most vicious anti-Arab racist film ever made by a major Hollywood studio;' the government of Yemen condemned the film as a 'barbaric and racist attack against Arabs and Yemenis,' urging all Arab states to boycott it and its studio.[259] CAIR wrote to Secretary of Defense William Cohen, saying that the film 'seems to justify the killing of Muslim men, women and even children … it also offers a very negative image of Muslims and Islamic beliefs.'[260] Naturally, with such glowing testimony, the film had received unequivocal support from the Pentagon, including the provision of the aircraft carrier USS *Tarawa*, as well as helicopters and personnel.[261]

(Above) The Marine Corps open fire on a crowd in Rules of Engagement.

The US embassy in Yemen is attacked during a protest so Colonel Terry Childers (Samuel L. Jackson) and his Marine unit are sent in to rescue Ambassador Mouraine (Ben Kingsley) and his family from the besieged embassy. During the rescue, Childers feels compelled to order his men to open fire on the crowd of protesters below, killing dozens of them. There is initially some ambiguity as to whether Childers and his Marines were taking fire from the crowd below or only from some snipers on rooftops opposite the embassy. Later, in court, prosecuting attorney Major Mark Biggs (Guy Pearce) argues that Childers murdered the crowd when he should have been shooting at the snipers instead. Childers' old Vietnam buddy-turned-lawyer Colonel Hayes Hodges (Tommy Lee Jones) proves that an Islamist terrorist network operates in Yemen, but not that the crowd was armed and hostile, or that National Security Adviser Bill Sokal (Bruce Greenwood) is withholding evidence to that effect (which he is). Biggs calls one of Childers' old Vietcong enemies, Le Cao, to testify, in an attempt to prove that Childers has a track record of war crimes. However, although Le Cao asserts that Childers executed his radio operator and illegally threatened to execute him, he also admits that he would have done the same thing had their roles been reversed. Ultimately, Childers is exonerated.

The film represents military authorities in especially glowing terms, embodied by the hero, Childers, who is rendered as a dignified and compassionate human being. Indeed, Childers and Hodges are such decent and magnanimous figures that they never refer to their enemies in racist terms—It is only when a drunken Hodges is at his lowest ebb that he fears Childers may have fallen prey to racial hatred. He confronts Childers and demands to know if he thought of the crowd as 'ragheads,' 'camel jockeys,' or 'fucking gooks.' Aside from this one drunken argument, the idea that a Marine may use racist language or have racist thoughts—even when outnumbered by heavily armed Islamist terrorists—Is unexplored, unthinkable. Indeed, the film revolves around the deep affection between two men of different races—Hodges and Childers—who emerge out of a racially harmonious army, and who never even raise it as an issue between themselves.

Although the civilian government in *Rules of Engagement* is vilified as selling out the military, it is fundamentally driven by diplomatic necessity rather than narrower interests. Sokal insists that the US must not lose its bases in Saudi Arabia, Jordan and Egypt because the US needs to stay friends with moderates in the region to avoid a bigger war. In reality, the US military has launched numerous lethal drone strikes in at least seven countries, including Yemen, and there are no demands from Middle Eastern governments to withdraw and close down bases in the region. In *Rules of Engagement*, we are invited to recognise the heroism of the military that enforces US policy, as though force is deployed for noble values, even while the politicians who give those orders adopt tactics that are detrimental to the Marines. Indeed, the government is presented as a restraining force, albeit an imperfect one, which holds to account any excesses by the military for the cause of world stability.

No such ambiguities exist over the American civilian anti-war protesters in *Rules of Engagement*, who are viewed as an ignorant and unruly mob, one of whom starts an unnecessary fight with Childers. The representation of protesters was similar in 2008's *Vantage Point*, in which the US President appears to be assassinated by Islamic terrorists just as he is announcing a celebrated new peace initiative between the Western and Muslim worlds. Strikingly, *Vantage Point* is told from no less than eight different perspectives—not one of them from the throngs of protesters depicted on screen, who carry pictures of the President defaced with banal messages, even whilst we the audience are encouraged to think the President is really a pretty good guy.

Still, in *Rules of Engagement*, as much as we are encouraged to sympathise with Childers' decision to 'waste the motherfuckers,' for the first half of the film the implication is that his order in the field could well have been morally and legally wrong. An intriguing premise, but this ambiguity is dramatically trounced by a remarkable and pivotal scene: Sokal decides to watch the CCTV tape from the embassy. We see footage of the incident, which shows very clearly that every member of the crowd was armed and aggressive. Childers' subsequent separate flashback shows the same thing and even includes a little amputee girl— initially a pitiful sight—angrily firing a pistol at the marines on the roof of the embassy. The tape confirms that the crowd were heavily armed and very hostile, and therefore that someone must have removed the weapons from the scene to make them appear the innocent victims of US military brutality. *Rules of Engagement* implicates every strata of Yemeni society in the terrorist atrocity—government, police, ordinary men, women and children.

The original scenes of the embassy confrontation clearly show unarmed Yemenis being gunned down by Childers and his troops, but the later footage directly, graphically and convincingly contradicts this by showing a hostile crowd on an objective record (the videotape), which the government is then compelled to destroy. The filmmakers' cack-handed botch-job was apparently the consequence of showing versions of the movie to test audiences. It fundamentally renders the film an unambiguous contest between US Marines, who make morally righteous judgements, and a world of civilians, who are prepared to lie and—in the case of the Yemenis—kill.

No doubt with a beady eye on this change was the Pentagon.

Other changes were more explicitly political, and helped develop the idea that the civilian parts of government aren't up to the noble standards of the military. The ELO encouraged the filmmakers to make Ambassador Morainn appear a 'real wet noodle.'[262] In the court room sequence, when Hodges tries to excuse Childers because of the difficulty of the task facing him, the ELO commented '"Dirty job" sounds as if the mission was already "bad." "Tough mission" would be more appropriate.' The dialogue was changed to reflect this.

At the end of the film, after Childers has been found not guilty, there is an exchange between Hodges and Biggs. Biggs says that he will be pursuing further charges against Childers in light of Colonel Cao's testimony, and asks Hodges to testify:

Hodges: I'll make you a deal. If you can tell me right now what the life expectancy was for a second lieutenant dropped into a hot

LZ in Vietnam in 1968, I'll tell you everything I remember about Ca Lu.

Biggs: One week.

Hodges: Negative. Sixteen minutes, Major. Sixteen fucking minutes. And that's all I remember.

This entire exchange was suggested by the Pentagon's ELO.[263]

Little context is provided for the weekly Yemeni protests which give any suggestion they are motivated by social grievances. Just two brief explanations are vocalised, both from Americans. In response to her child's question 'What's wrong, Mommy?,' as they cower beneath a desk in the besieged embassy, Mrs Mourain replies, 'The people are upset about some things... they're trying to get attention.' Sokal describes the protests in derogatory terms that are left unchallenged by the rest of the film—the protesters are motivated by 'the usual bullshit about American presence in the Gulf.' 'Presence', instead of 'political, economic, and military impact;' 'The Gulf,' instead of 'holy sites'—nothing that complicates the message that the Yemeni are fighting a 'bullshit' cause.

In his review of the film in *The Nation*, Stuart Klawans points out that the government blaming the military is hardly a standard response. For example, in July 1988, guided missile cruiser USS *Vincennes* attacked an Iranian civilian airliner, killing 290 people without provocation.[264] Middle East reporter Robert Fisk explained that the US government issued notes of regret for the loss of human life but never admitted wrongdoing, accepted responsibility, or apologised for the incident. Officially, the US continues to blame Iranian hostile actions for the incident and the men of the *Vincennes* were all awarded combat-action ribbons.[265]

Rules of Engagement was written by James Webb, Secretary of the Navy under President Reagan. It offers a militaristic right-wing viewpoint on US foreign policy: US enemies are contemptible; non-American victims are insignificant and, indeed, in this case, the victims are brutal maligned perpetrators. The film could have been, and perhaps was initially intended to be, a meditation on the moral ambiguities of state violence, but during production it became something quite different. At the climax of the film, the final show of solidarity between the two former enemy soldiers—Childers and Le Cao—further morally elevates military men above civilians and whitewashes the enmity between the US and Vietnam. This is presented as though indigenous victims of American military attack can and should forgive—even respect—US atrocities if only they can appreciate their benevolent intent.

Rules of Engagement's denouement might be compared to that of *Basic* (2003), in which we are led to believe a unit of Marines have killed each other but who have in fact faked their deaths so they can operate secretly in the war on drugs, an ending similarly prompted by test audiences. Hollywood's tendency to chase profit within an ideological system here had a profound effect on the ideology of a film and the original intent of its makers. Likewise, in *Swordfish* (2001), a CIA renegade robs billions of dollars, which is eventually revealed to be for financing a private army to kill a 'Bin Laden' figure.

Rules of Engagement was also reviewed by the Marine Corps ELO who provided multiple and extensive sets of script notes, much of which were incorporated. Many of these changes were concerned with the general portrayal of the military. For example, in a scene where the Marine Corps host a retirement party for Hodges, the original script had him flirting and dancing with a female superior. The ELO instructed, 'Majors in the Marine Corps do not conduct themselves as "Flirtatious and/or funny" when dealing with superiors. No colonel for that matter is going to be seen dancing cheek to cheek with a major. Suggestion: make Sarah Grant a civilian secretary or paralegal on Hodges' staff or, make her a lieutenant colonel who has been selected for colonel. If she remains military, though, the flirting should be toned way down.' These shots and indeed this entire character were removed from the film.

Similarly, there was evidently a scene where Childers undergoes a psychological evaluation before his court martial, leading the ELO to comment, 'Childers comes across as a bona fide nut case in the shrink's office... needs to be toned down.' This scene was also cut from the finished movie. In another scene, in Childers' house on the Marine Corps base, the Pentagon's notes say, 'Childers would NOT have a government issue pistol at his home. Lose the holster and put the pistol on the desk or in the drawer.' The scene was altered.

The Terminator franchise

Was there ever a film series that ever fell off a creative cliff quite as high as the Terminator? From indie success to mega blockbuster success and onto mediocrity, then, finally, formulaic drivel.

Unclear until now is the role played by the Pentagon in trashing this once celebrated franchise.

The *Terminator* franchise was originally described as 'anti-nuclear'[266] and 'anti-authoritarian.'[267] This was indeed the tone of the first two films, but by the third and especially the fourth in the series had been co-opted by the Department of Defense, with the result that it became a direct champion of the US military. Here, we focus on the 2003 and 2009 sequels, which tell us most about the franchise's approach to the US' role in the wider world.

Terminator 3: Rise of the Machines (2003) is set in the present day, just as the US military computer system, Skynet, has become self-aware and is spreading a global virus as part of its plan to launch a devastating nuclear attack against humanity. A team of human survivors send a reprogrammed T-101 Terminator (Arnold Schwarzenegger) back in time from the future to protect John Connor and Kathryn Brewster because they are destined to lead a successful war against the machines. Meanwhile, the machines send back a female T-X Terminator (Kristina Loken) to kill John and other potential members of the human resistance.

In *Rise of the Machines*, US deployment of nuclear force is portrayed as a major miscalculation caused by blind faith in technology and militaristic authority. At the heart of the military industrial complex is the feeble Robert Brewster—programme director of Cyber Research Systems' (CRS) autonomous weapons division, who is bullied by his Pentagon superiors into deploying Skynet.

Rise of the Machines provides little justification for the creation of such an extensive and sophisticated military-industrial complex. No designation, for instance, of the 'threats' from North Korea and Iran, pointedly referenced in *Transformers*. There is also the hint that the build-up has something to do with a culture of 'funding' in the Pentagon, which alludes to the importance of powerful economic self-interests like CRS. Indeed, Skynet itself is reminiscent of the space-based weapons systems famously championed by the US since the early 1980s, when President Reagan poured billions into 'Star Wars' technology. The *Terminator* franchise views with suspicion these technological developments and, in *Terminator 2: Judgment Day* (1991), our heroes even triumphantly demolish a major military-industrial facility.

The critique provided by *Rise of the Machines* is very limited. As always, our sympathies are with the Americans, from the vagrant Connor to the military commander Brewster. Additionally, in terms of the political philosophy espoused by the franchise, it rises little beyond Luddism and survivalism. Nor is there any indication that in the real world, at the time of the film's production and release, the US was engaged in controversial hostilities in Afghanistan and Iraq and was reconfiguring its nuclear weapons policy to permit their usage in the event of 'surprising military developments' and other circumstances.[268]

The nuclear war, when it finally comes in *Rise of the Machines*, has an air of inevitability which essentially provides closure. In the scene 'Mission Complete,' our heroes are safe, the T-X destroyed, other bunker dwellers are getting in touch on the airwaves as we see the missiles shoot into the air over golden cornfields and explode in beautiful mushroom plumes from outer space. The final words of the film—'The battle has just begun'— position the viewer to imagine the future of these characters and, indeed, the series did continue in *The Sarah Connor Chronicles* TV series (2008-09) and beyond.

Rise of the Machines did make a request for a day's filming at Edwards Air Force base in California with various non-flying Air Force aircraft as background. The DOD notes that the Brewer character is 'benign' but 'inadvertently responsible for playing a part in unwittingly creating conditions for the machines to take over and create nuclear holocaust.' The document notes that 'some minor changes were made to the script [not concerning the general per se] to accommodate minor concerns and approval was granted in writing on July 3. In new pages, director Jonathan Mostow rewrote the general's character as a negative character, so we withdrew support. Ironically the final version reverted to the "approved" script, with a benign general.'[269]

By the fourth movie, *Terminator: Salvation* (2009), the franchise had made a clear shift towards supporting establishment narratives, despite its earlier reservations. The DOD provided assistance and the film was shot at Kirtland Air Force Base.[270] A central theme is whether John Connor (Christian Bale) should prioritise striking a decisive military blow against the machines or rescue some captured humans, who are entombed—with shades of Auschwitz—by the Terminators. The classic 'humanitarian' war scenario.

For a world that is set just fifteen years after a global nuclear holocaust, the survivors are fancifully healthy, not to mention hairy. Indeed, people hang around the streets of Los Angeles, a US submarine patrols underwater and the Air Force still functions above ground. Radiation poisoning seems to be of little concern, even though two further nuclear explosions occur during the course of the film. The military actually conduct a heart transplant, in the midst of the war, in broad daylight, above ground. None of this is an issue for director Joseph 'McG' McGinty Nichol as he normalises the unthinkable. Instead, he concludes the film with words that were surely inspired by, or directly written by, the very forces that destroyed the planet in the first two films: 'Skynet's global network remains strong but we will not quit until all of it is destroyed.'

During periods of heightened popular concern about nuclear weapons, films like *Dr. Strangelove* (1963) and the British-made *Threads* (1985) engaged thoroughly with the serious consequences of conflict. Even the flash-forwards from the first three *Terminator* films hinted at a horrible futurescape of pain, deprivation and *ad hoc* guerrilla warfare. In contrast, producer Jeffrey Silver explained that the Department of Defense gave 'fantastic cooperation [to *Salvation*] because they recognized that in the future portrayed in this film, the military will still be the men and women who protect us, no matter what may come.' [271] *Salvation*'s sanitised depiction of nuclear war again indicates how filmmakers may omit politically disturbing material—even stretching narrative credibility beyond breaking point—for the benefit of their institutional backers.

Drained of its spirit, the *Terminator* franchise hobbled on to a fifth instalment, and a sixth is in the offing. In an effort to retain happy childhood memories for both authors and our audience, it's surely better to leave our analysis here.

Thirteen Days

Thirteen Days attempted to obtain DOD support but was ultimately turned down because it refused to kowtow to Pentagon demands. The result was surely a better piece of cinema and a useful living document of the Cuban Missile Crisis.

As impressive as this was, in this case study we will also show how *Thirteen Days* still manages to endorse the legitimacy and use of US power up to and including the right to use nuclear weapons. Not surprisingly, the credits reveal it did receive cooperation from the Kennedy family.

Thirteen Days is based on documented evidence from October 1962, during the Cuban Missile Crisis. The Pentagon gave a dismissive response to the film's script, complaining about the depiction of the downed U-2 reconnaissance plane and the characterisations of both General Curtis LeMay and General Maxwell Taylor (Chairmen of the Joint Chiefs) as 'unintelligent and bellicose.'[272]

Most of the action in *Thirteen Days* is seen through the eyes of Kenny O'Donnell (Kevin Costner), special adviser to the President. American U-2 surveillance photos reveal that the Soviet Union is in the process of placing nuclear weapons in Cuba. Once operational, these weapons would give the USSR first-strike capacity against US territory. The Joint Chiefs of Staff, under General Curtis LeMay (Kevin Conway), advise military strikes against Cuba, which could lead the way to another invasion of the island, but President John F. Kennedy (Bruce Greenwood) is reluctant to follow through because of the predictable retaliation from Moscow that could escalate to global nuclear war. Kennedy imposes 'quarantine' on Cuba, which eventually is effective in repelling most Soviet ships approaching Cuba, but he is ultimately forced to withdraw US nuclear weapons from Turkey and to guarantee not to invade Cuba in a secret deal that ends the stand-off.

The film portrays the Joint Chiefs as aggressive anti-Communists, who see warfare as a legitimate, effective and useful policy tool. O'Donnell says that they 'want a war' to 'make up for' the Bay of Pigs debacle and the film makes it clear that such a stance would likely have apocalyptic consequences. LeMay is depicted as a warmonger—excited by the idea of attacking the 'big red dog' that is 'digging' in the US's 'backyard'—and showing an arrogant carelessness about the consequences. At the same time though, we are invited to accept the theory, propagated by both military and civilian authorities, that 'appeasement only makes the aggressor more aggressive' and that, one way or another, the missiles must be removed from Cuba or else the world will be forced into war. Even Costner's character says the decision to apply immediate force could 'well be right.'

The American civilian authorities in the film are portrayed in glowing terms. The presentation of the civilian administration is consistent with the popular image of 'Camelot,' a description of Kennedy's thousand days in office which was initially propagated by Kennedy's speechwriters Arthur Schlesinger Jr[273] and Theodore Sorensen[274] and that still holds true in popular programming—including the TV series *R.F.K.* (1997), the made-for-TV movie *RFK* (2002), and the movie, *Bobby* (2006). Even the Soviet Ambassador Anotoly Dobrynin (Elya Baskin) in *Thirteen Days* says that John and Bobby are good men.

O'Donnell functions as the 'Everyman' character, who allows us, the audience, to get an insider's view of the Kennedy brothers' partnership. Rather than being a secretive association, then, the Kennedys are shown bringing us/O'Donnell into their lives and therefore enhancing the myth of open government in this period. They are prepared to put the world and their nation above narrower interests, Bobby exclaiming 'I don't care if this administration ends up in the freaking toilet!' When O'Donnell's wife tells him that he is smart, he responds wistfully—almost romantically—not like them,' as though there is something intangibly wonderful about the leadership of these two brothers. More broadly, the Kennedys represent something about America as a nation: the 'free world' that repeatedly emphasises a 'sneak attack' is counter to US values. As we shall see, this is in stark contrast to the historical record.

Americans, specifically the US authorities themselves, are the principal victims in the film. The rest of the American population is largely ignored, not to mention the Russians, the Cubans, and the rest of the world. Every member of the executive is shown to be under tremendous strain. The President is taking painkillers, is unable to sleep, and repeatedly expresses a lack of enjoyment in holding Presidential office at this time. Bobby feels pressurised to be brilliant and ruthless, which he claims almost tearfully does not come naturally to him. The film closes with a respectful President paying tribute to the fallen airman over-laden with respectful images of his coffin draped in the Stars and Stripes.

Meanwhile, the Soviets are duplicitous and conniving. O'Donnell equates the missiles with the ship that bombed Pearl Harbor, thereby associating the Soviet Union with imperial Japan and acting as though an attack was already under way. The Russian spy who makes an overture to the US turns out to have been a decoy. The Soviet Embassy is framed in ominous terms—shrouded in darkness, the iconic hammer and sickle fluttering in the breeze, smoke billowing from its chimney as it burns documents in preparation for war.

Some historical perspective from leading historians on the 13 days in question reveals just how deferential the film's narrative is to the Kennedy administration. The film misleadingly presents the Cuban Missile Crisis as being unprovoked by the US and solved exclusively by the Kennedys.

In truth, following Fidel Castro's overthrow of the Cuban dictator General Fulgencio Batista in January 1959, in the winter of 1959-60, Morris Morley says 'there was a significant increase in CIA-supervised bombing and incendiary raids piloted by exiled Cubans' based in the US. [275] Robert Kennedy led the top-level interagency group that oversaw Operation Mongoose, a programme of paramilitary operations, economic warfare and sabotage launched in late 1961 to topple Castro, [276] a programme which was 'the centerpiece of American policy toward Cuba from late 1961 until the onset of the 1962 missile crisis,' reports Mark White. [277] Robert Kennedy informed the CIA that the Cuban problem carries 'the top priority in the United States Government—all else is secondary—no time, no effort, or manpower is to be spared' in the effort to overthrow the Castro regime. [278] The chief of Operation Mongoose, Edward Lansdale, provided a timetable leading to 'open revolt and overthrow of the Communist regime' in October 1962. The 'final definition' of the programme recognised that 'success will require decisive US military intervention,' after terrorism and subversion had laid the basis. The implication is that US military intervention would take place in October 1962—when the missile crisis erupted. [279]

Raymond Garthoff is slightly more circumspect, arguing that there was 'no political decision or intention' to invade Cuba again before October 1962, but agrees that the Kennedy administration directed Mongoose and that it 'was not unreasonable for Castro and the Soviet government to be concerned over the possibility of intensified US hostile action against Cuba in 1962.' [280] Famously, Kennedy had aborted at the last minute an earlier CIA-sponsored invasion, leaving thousands of exiled Cubans to be killed by Castro's forces at the Bay of Pigs in April 1961. If the military had to 'make up for' the Bay of Pigs, as O'Donnell says, the civilian authorities were surely in the same boat.

US operations continued in Cuba during the tensest moments of the missile crisis. They were formally cancelled on 30 October, several days after the agreement between Kennedy and the Russian Premiere Khrushchev, but went on nonetheless. Garthoff writes that on 8 November, 'a Cuban covert action sabotage team dispatched from the United States successfully blew up a Cuban industrial facility,' and that 'the Soviets could only see' US actions as efforts 'to back-pedal on what was, for them, the key question remaining: American assurances not to attack Cuba.'[281] Even after the crisis ended, Kennedy renewed the terrorist campaign, and, ten days before his assassination, he approved a CIA plan for 'destruction operations' by US proxy forces 'against a large oil refinery and storage facilities, a large electric plant, sugar refineries, railroad bridges, harbour facilities, and underwater demolition of docks and ships.'[282]

The film ignores and denies overwhelming evidence for repeated US and US-sponsored 'sneak attacks' on Cuba, known about by Kennedy, and thereby provoking the 13 days of crisis. The film legitimises US civilian power in the Kennedy era and only criticises those military leaders still mired in the Second World War paradigm (the military behave honourably elsewhere). No wonder the Bush administration saw fit to screen *Thirteen Days* at the White House, even while the Air Force refused to show it.[283]

It is true that Kennedy handled the immediate 13 days of crisis with a cool head, in the sense that he did not follow the lunatic council of his Joint Chiefs. Still, who would ever know from Hollywood the part played by Vasili Arkhipov, the Russian submarine commander who prevailed on his fellow officers not to fire a nuclear torpedo, even though the first Soviet captain had given the order on 27 October? US destroyers under orders to enforce the Cuban blockade did not know that the Soviet submarines that Moscow had sent as protection for its ships were carrying nuclear weapons, so the Americans began firing depth charges to force them to the surface—a move the Soviets interpreted as the start of the Third World War. Arkhipov 'saved the world,' according to Thomas Blanton, director of the National Security Archive,[284] but his story is forgotten—replaced instead by a similar but fictionalised tale with a US-friendly makeover in *Crimson Tide*. In 2014, a documentary feature was released called *The Man who Saved the World*, about another Soviet officer, Stanislav Petrov, whose willingness to abandon protocol and not report an apparent American attack probably averted a nuclear war in 1983. The documentary, of course, was not American—it was Danish.

In fact, Kennedy's doctor had injected him with speed and steroids in the early days of the crisis, prompting speculation that his initial belligerence in contemplating an air strike on the Soviets may have been caused by this and he had to be talked into the blocade.[285] If JFK had had to make a decision at that point, he would have attacked.[286] Nor was Bobby actually the architect of the secret negotiations that ended the crisis.[287]

Thirteen Days emphasises the difficulties of applying US force in a complex world but, in effect, akin to *The Sum of All Fears*, it excuses the executive in what would have been world-wide genocide/suicide. It is the US elites themselves, not ordinary people or even American citizens, that are shown to endure the burden of power, and it is only they—the heroic leaders of the free world—who are ultimately able to stave off disaster and pave the way for peace and stability. The film side-lines the real-world Kennedy administration's preoccupation with launching secret attacks, including an attempted invasion against Cuba, which persisted into the crisis and beyond. Rather, it buys into and perpetuates a glorious vision of the Kennedy administration that elides key narratives based on a lesser-known documentary record.

United 93

Paul Greengrass's *United 93* was generally received as a neutral piece of work with emphasis placed on its avoidance of a sensationalist style, through the use of unknown actors, its decentralisation of the famous 'Let's roll' line, and its use of hand-held cameras.[288] It is a literal depiction of what happened to Flight 93 on 11 September 2001, namely the terrorist take-over, the passengers rebelling and then crash-landing the plane in rural Pennsylvania. In other words, it was not a jingoistic piece of Hollywood trash, but rather a sensitively made piece of work that dealt respectfully with the human beings who all lost their lives on that day.

Still, a closer look at the film suggests it is not as neutral as it appeared. 9/11 had occurred whilst Greengrass was making *Bloody Sunday* (2002), which recreated the 1972 massacre in Northern Ireland. Greengrass commented, '[9/11] made what I was doing seem a bit irrelevant. But then, as we carried on working, it became for me oddly relevant, because *Bloody Sunday* was really about how we overreacted, how we militarised the early stages of the conflict and made it much worse.'[289]

United 93 raised no such issues, so it is hard to see how Greengrass saw it as 'oddly relevant.' The film's 'Bible,' as Greengrass put it in his DVD commentary, was the Bush administration's official *9/11 Commission Report*, which simply presented the events as described on the day. Perhaps this is what Bush had in mind when he said 'See, in my line of work you got to keep repeating things over and over and over again for the truth to sink in, to kind of catapult the propaganda.'[290]

In our analysis, we are not making any solid claims about 9/11 itself but we are saying that, in stark contrast to the way it was marketed, this film is a political construction over a highly contentious set of events that is, yet again, favourable to the propaganda needs of the national security state.

This 2006 docudrama is an unusual movie for two key reasons: It was the first big budget Hollywood film based on the 9/11 attacks, and it had no formal script—the dialogue was largely improvised. As a result, when the producers, Michael Bronner and Lloyd Levin, approached the DOD to ask for production support, there was no script to review. Instead they provided Phil Strub with detailed treatments, and Levin, along with the director Paul Greengrass, had a conference call with the DOD in November 2005 where Greengrass 'expressed his intentions to accurately and realistically portray the US military.'[291] This persuaded the Pentagon to agree to providing assistance, including on-set advisors for the scenes depicting the military.

Passengers aboard the hijacked United Airlines flight 93, as depicted by United 93.

The film rotates between three stories: the passengers onboard United Airlines flight 93; the fourth plane on 9/11, which crashed in Shanksville; the response to the hijackings at Federal Aviation Administration (FAA), which centres in the North East US; and the North Eastern Air Defence Sector (NEADS) ops control room. This multi-pronged approach means that *United 93* provides a convincing, seemingly-accurate account of what happened that morning. This sense of authenticity is enhanced through the use of semi-improvised dialogue, shooting with handheld cameras, and some people playing themselves in the film, including FAA National Operations Manager, Ben Sliney.

This unusual method of production lent the film much more authority than Hollywood films usually receive, even ones based on real events. BBC film critic Mark Kermode has repeatedly cited *United 93* as proof that the 'conspiracy theories' about the 9/11 attacks are wrong. In one article, he wrote that he had seen internet documentaries about the attacks that advanced theories that 'sounded like baloney' to him but 'just to be sure, I contacted respected British film-maker Paul Greengrass.' Why Kermode would choose to ask a film-maker rather than, say, a historical or political expert of some kind is not apparent. By the time he wrote this article, several academics, including Nafeez Ahmed, Peter Dale Scott and David Ray Griffin had published multiple books casting doubt on the official story or arguing in favour of an alternative theory. Nonetheless, Greengrass told Kermode, '9/11 has replaced the Kennedy assassination as the epicentre of this great upsurge of conspiracy theories, and flight 93 is right at the heart of it. Do I believe those conspiracies? No. The stuff about the plane being shot down is simply not true. But you have to ask why a document as exhaustive and accountable as the 9/11 Commission report has failed to dispel these myths.'[292]

One reason that many did not find the 9/11 Commission report convincing is that it presented a third story of why the military failed to intercept (and/or shoot down) any of the four hijacked aircraft. The first version emerged in the days immediately after the attacks, saying that no jets were scrambled until after the Pentagon was struck at 9:38am. The second story came in the form of a timeline published by the military on September 18th which contradicted this by saying that two sets of jets were scrambled prior to the Pentagon being struck. This second story places the blame on the FAA by saying that, because the FAA didn't notify NEADS quickly enough, the jets could not get there in time. This is also the version told to the 9/11 Commission in 2003 by Major General Larry Arnold and his close colleague Colonel Alan Scott. Arnold was the commanding general of NORAD's Continental Region and was centrally involved in the military response as the attacks unfolded. Scott and Arnold testified that the military were tracking flight 93 before it crashed, and were in a position to shoot it down. However, by the time of the Commission's report in 2004, a new story had emerged that painted the military in an even better light. According to tapes of communications at NEADS, the FAA did not notify the military about the last three planes until after they had crashed, and so NEADS were completely off the hook for failing to intercept them.

Given the scepticism and criticism, along with testimony from FAA and NORAD officials that contradicted these mutually contradictory stories from the Pentagon, *United 93* played an important role in codifying the official account—that the military have nothing to hide and nothing to answer for. A report from the Air Force ELO details how this was discussed in a teleconference between Phil Strub and the DOD, NEADS, Otis Air National Guard base (who scrambled jets on 9/11) and other components involved. The report notes that:

No organization had any showstoppers to potential support. Discussed support "wish list" from producer Lloyd Levin. All organizations appear to agree on importance of accuracy of military depiction and ensuring the director shows military within some context. Concern that viewers might misinterpret actions by controllers as "mistakes" when training, normal procedures, and "fog of war" might explain their actions.[293]

Fortunately for the military, there were two technical advisors from NEADS on set throughout the filming of these scenes.

The narrative in *United 93* is largely based on the third version reported by the 9/11 Commission, though it does contradict it somewhat. While the Commission's report says that the FAA did not inform NEADS about flight 77—which hit the Pentagon—until it crashed, in the film we see the officials at NEADS learn about the plane nearly 15 minutes before the Pentagon is struck. However, *United 93* does repeat the Commission's story that the FAA did not tell the military about flight 175—which hit the second World Trade Center tower—or flight 93 until after they crashed.

The film adeptly avoids this controvers. The audience spends large portions of the screen time with the passengers on flight 93, watching them eating breakfast and chatting with each other. Even after the hijacking we are provided with numerous shots from on board the plane that add nothing to the story except to establish, repeatedly, that the passengers are scared. This has the effect of padding out the screen time without making it clear that for approximately 90 minutes the military are doing virtually nothing. Each time we cut back from the plane or the FAA offices to the NEADS centre, nothing has progressed, they are still having the same conversations as when we left them. This jumping between narratives helps create a sense of chaos and confusion but without explicitly portraying the military as incompetent or negligent in allowing the attacks to continue. Had the film focused not on the passengers on the plane but on the military going around in the same circles for over an hour while thousands of people were being murdered then it would have been an equally realistic, but far more critical, movie. Equally, if the film only told the story of the passengers then it would have done nothing to help the military avoid scepticism and criticism about their role in the 9/11 attacks.

The effect of this creative decision to focus on the passengers is particularly apparent in the final half hour of *United 93*. After the Pentagon is hit at 9:38am, we see the NEADS boss Kevin Nasypany urging his staff to keep working, and see FAA boss Ben Sliney issue a national ground-stop, ordering every plane in the country to land. After that we do not see the FAA or NEADS again, and the final 25 minutes of the film are devoted entirely to events on the plane. Even according to the film's narrative, by this time, the FAA had known about flight 93 for 20 minutes and had informed the military liaison at their headquarters, so what were the military doing while this last half hour of action was taking place? According to Scott and Arnold, they were tracking flight 93 and were prepared to shoot it down if it turned towards Washington DC. According to *United 93*, they weren't really doing anything because the FAA still hadn't told them about flight 93 being hijacked, even after three major buildings had been struck by planes.

However, this version of events is even contradicted by reports from the Air Force ELO, which mention that 'Bronner is scheduled to interview Maj Daniel "Nasty" Nash (pilot who flew F-15 looking for Flights 11 and 93)' [294] and that 'Conducted conference call between script writer and Lt Col Steve O'Brien, pilot in command of Minnesota ANG C-130 involved in searching for two of the hijacked aircraft, including Flt 93.'[295] If the military were never told about flight 93 until after it crashed then why were they looking for it? Similarly, why was there nothing in the film about these pilots looking for flight 93?

Other reports from the ELO make it clear that they were very happy with the movie, even providing access to NEADS officers for interviews for DVD bonus features. They viewed a rough cut of the film at Universal Studios concluding, 'Overall positive AF depiction, primarily of Northeast Air Defense Sector ops floor and Combat Air Patrol over Capitol building in moving closing of the movie.'[296] This final shot of jets flying over the Capitol, along with the caption 'America's war on terror had begun' were removed from the final version of the movie.[297] Instead a sombre series of captions explains how military commanders were not even notified that flight 93 had been hijacked until minutes after it had crashed, and that the nearest jet was still 100 miles way. These captions come before the dedication to the victims of the September 11th attacks, showing that impressing the (third) official account of events was foremost in the producers' minds.

The ELO reports note how, when trailers for the film first started to appear, some people objected that it was 'too soon' after the real events. When *United 93* was released, the Air Force breathed a sigh of relief, writing, 'the first major film on 9/11 had a good opening week, drawing $11.5 million over the weekend and is the #2 movie in the nation. More importantly, it is getting good critical reviews.'[298]

The Bush administration welcomed the release of *United 93* with open arms. Soon after the film's nationwide release date, 'tears flowed' at a 'very emotional night'[299] when the President 'invited relatives of some of the 40 passengers and crew members' for a private screening at the White House.[300] Attendance figures were not offered; the families had already had a private screening,[301] and the White House cinema only has 44 seats anyway, [302] so we might surmise that providing a cathartic experience for 'some of' those affected was rather less important to the incumbents than continuing to associate themselves with what they called the 'heroes' of flight 93, who had struck what Bush called 'the first counter-attack to World War III.'[303]

Reflecting on the *Bourne* films, Greengrass says, 'we have to search for our own answers,' rather than rely on untrustworthy power systems. This is not an approach he applies to *United 93*. Greengrass didn't seem to care about the calls for a fresh enquiry into 9/11, or the concerns raised by serious commentators that Flight 93 might have been shot down by the military.[304] He says more than once that 'this thing was literally unimagined and unimaginable', despite the widely known warnings of just such an event. Rather, Greengrass felt that it was important for him to 'create a believable truth' as a 'good place to start a discussion'[305]

He commented:

A lot of people believe that Flight 93 was shot down by the military. I'm not knocking people who believe in conspiracy theories. What I'm pointing out is that conspiracy theories are comforting ... the truth is much more disturbing if you look at it for real and say, 'on that morning a small group of people hijacked a religion, hijacked four airplanes and had an entire civilian and military system break down inside an hour and if those passengers had not got up out of their seats the plane without a doubt would have hit the Capitol and flattened it.'[306]

It's hard to see what could be more 'comforting' in the dire circumstances of 9/11 than focusing on the day's one small victory,

141

based on a government-approved history in which al-Qaeda terrorists are clubbed to death by Americans.

Discussing the decision to shut down US borders in the immediate aftermath of the Twin Towers attacks, Greengrass points out that 'in the aftermath of a terrorist attack civilian life begins to close down, military response becomes predominant, the delicate systems of a democracy become compromised.'

Greengrass evidently recognises the dangerous trends within the US system. He just doesn't seem to appreciate that here he supported them.

Wag the Dog

Wag the Dog was lauded as a clever, liberal, independent film satirising President Clinton's policy and domestic problems. While we agree that it's a terrific movie, we also show inconclusive evidence that it had CIA influence. As such, it is worth considering this film, in part at least, as a CIA propaganda product making light of assassination, rationalising the military industrial complex, and removing the most subversive aspects of the book and other source material.

Wag the Dog (1997) tells the story of a president embroiled in a sex scandal who calls in the 'spin doctor' Conrad Brean (Robert De Niro) to find a way to control the media. Brean then recruits Hollywood producer Stanley Motss, and the two of them fake a small US war in Albania to distract the news media for a few days until the election. Despite the unabashed corruption (both sexual and democratic) portrayed at the heart of the American state, Wag the Dog did not have any trouble being released. It was produced during an unplanned break in the making of *Sphere* (1998), a big budget sci-fi adventure also directed by Barry Levinson and starring Dustin Hoffman. *Sphere* was suspended due to budget problems so Levinson directed the much cheaper and simpler *Wag the Dog* while *Sphere*'s situation was being resolved.[307]

In *Wag the Dog*, the US President is accused of sexually assaulting an underage girl. Brean and Motss, along with White House advisor Winifred Ames (Anne Heche), carry out an elaborate deception, complete with staged news footage, made up war heroes, and a fake soldier's funeral that actually takes place on a set constructed in a military aircraft hanger. They even invent a way for the public to show their enthusiasm for this fictional war—throwing old shoes over telephone lines in support of the supposedly lost war hero Sgt. William 'old shoe' Schumann (Woody Harrelson). This is successful, and the potential child molestor is re-elected president. However, movie producer Motss is so driven by his desire to tell amazing stories that he demands the right to tell people what he has done, resulting in him being killed by unseen government agents. The film ends with a newscast suggesting that a real war might be breaking out in Albania.

[Above] A humanitarian war is artificially constructed on television in Wag the Dog.

The *Wag the Dog* script is quite critical of US foreign policies and the domestic and international propaganda that so often accompanies those policies. It was based on the 1993 conspiracy satire, *American Hero*, by Larry Beinhart, which suggests that the first Gulf War was scripted as a means of getting George HW Bush re-elected. In *Wag the Dog* this biting satire was watered down by screenwriters Hilary Henkin and David Mamet into a relatively light-hearted black comedy. It depicts a small group of people within the government conspiring to fake a war and deceive the US and even the global population, all to protect a probable child abuser. However, this is primarily portrayed as absurd, with the likes of Willie Nelson (thinly disguised as country singer Johnny Dean) drafted in to help write ludicrously patriotic songs and help come up with merchandising and spin-off products. Motss and Brean have a fast-paced and very witty back and forth, treating what they are doing as though it is merely a clever and elaborate prank rather than a massive, politically-motivated public deception campaign.

The cynicism of picking Albania as the target because 'no one's ever heard of Albania' is glossed over as just another gag. In reality, by the time this film was made, the US and NATO had been involved in the ongoing wars in the Balkans for several years, covertly and then overtly. The Kosovo Liberation Army which was active at this time were supposedly ethnic Albanians fighting for independence from Serbia but actually were international jihadists supported by the Pentagon and the CIA. They were added to and removed from the State Department's list of designated terrorist organisations several times throughout the last 1990s and early 2000s.[308] This violence spilled over into Albania and Macedonia in the years after *Wag the Dog*'s release, making the film prescient not in terms of sexual improprieties in the White House but also in terms of the geopolitics of the Balkans.

The film also plays on the popular conspiracy theory about the government and Hollywood that surrounds Stanley Kubrick. As the story goes, Kubrick helped fake the footage of the 1969 moon landing while he was producing *2001: A Space Odyssey*, in exchange for highly developed camera equipment. Some theories say that *The Shining* contains various clues to this that constitute a confession by Kubrick (it is certainly true that there are visual and other allusions to the Apollo program in the film). This supposedly led to Kubrick's early death shortly after finishing *Eyes Wide Shut*, which tells a story about ritual sex magic among the American ruling class. In *Wag the Dog*, Stanley Kubrick is reborn as Stanley Motss, a film producer who helps the government deceive the public but is murdered to keep him quiet about what he has done.

However, it is Motss' partner in crime, Conrad Brean, who is the most important character. Though he is repeatedly asked what his job is and for whom he works, Brean always avoids answering. As director Barry Levinson notes, Brean is more than a mere spin doctor, he 'works on a much, much more convoluted, far more thoughtful and sinister level, than the concept of the spinmeister.'[309] It is heavily implied that he works for the CIA—when the Agency catches up with Brean and Ames, it is Brean who instantly recognises them, and expertly deals with them (while Ames is left jibbering excuses about being on medication). Likewise, when the CIA cut a deal with the other candidate in the election and publicly announces the end of the war, it is again Brean who immediately sees what has happened.

In one sequence, Motss and Brean fake news footage of an attractive young Albanian woman fleeing from her home having been 'raped by terrorists.' The actress pretending to be the Albanian woman, Tracey Lime (Kirsten Dunst), asks Brean whether she can put this on her resume. He responds by telling her that she cannot ever tell anyone that she did this. Tracey asks what they could do to her if she did say anything to which Brean

145

confidently replies, 'take you home to your house and kill you.' Finally, it is Brean who tries to explain to Motss what will happen to him if he blows the whistle on the deception campaign, and it appears to be Brean who gives the covert signal to two goons who then dispose of Stanley off-screen.

While he is not credited in any way on *Wag the Dog*, there are strong reasons to suspect that the CIA's Hollywood liaison, Chase Brandon, was involved in the production, and was the inspiration for the Brean character. 'Chase Brandon' and 'Conrad Brean' are similar names, and this was changed during the scripting phase (the character was originally called Ronald Brean). In the film, De Niro looks and talks like Brandon—this is the first movie since The Deer Hunter where De Niro has a full beard, for example. They do essentially the same job – acting as some kind of covert liaison between the government and the entertainment industry for the purposes of mass perception management.

At the time *Wag the Dog* was being developed, Brandon has just started his new job as the CIA's first entertainment industry liaison. He would go on to work with Robert De Niro on three films (*Meet the Parents*, *Meet the Fockers* and *The Good Shepherd*) and to co-write a screenplay with Hilary Henkin. Furthermore, Brandon worked on several films and TV shows that also employed former Marine Public Affairs Officer Dale Dye, including *Mission: Impossible*, *JAG*, *Spy Game* and *Air America*. Dale Dye was the credited technical advisor on *Wag the Dog*.

As such, the watering down of American Hero into the screenplay for *Wag the Dog* likely involved input from Chase Brandon, to the extent that De Niro even moulded his character to be more like the CIA's man. Perhaps the best illustration of how *Wag the Dog* fools the audience into thinking it is challenging the US military-intelligence establishment when it is actually promoting it is when Brean comes face to face with another national security official, Charles Young (William H. Macy).

Young explains that 'the spy satellites show it, Mr Brean. They show no war.' Brean responds, 'then what good are they if they show no war? I mean, why we spend a quarter trillion dollars a year on the Defense Department? What good are they if they show nothing?' He extends this logic, 'If there's no threat then where are you? Let me go one better. If there's no threat, what good are you?'

Having apparently exposed the entire military-intelligence complex as a sham, Brean then masterfully turns round Young, the conversation and the audience:

The war of the future is nuclear terrorism. It'll be against a small group of dissidents who, unbeknownst perhaps to their own governments, have blah blah blah. To go to that war you have to be prepared, you gotta be alert, the public has gotta be alert. Because that is the war of the future and if you're not gearing up to fight that war then eventually the axe will fall and you'll be out in the street. So you can call this a drill, call this job security, call it anything you like, but I got one for you: You go to war to preserve your way of life? Well this, Chuck, this is your way of life. And if your spy satellites don't see nothing, if there ain't no war, then you can go home and prematurely take up golf my friend, because there ain't no war but ours.

This cornerstone piece of dialogue is the movie in a nutshell: it starts out as an exposure of how the perception of widespread imminent threats is essential to the US security state, but takes the opportunity through very likeable characters to raise the idea that these threats are real and imminent.

When the curtain is pulled back in the Emerald City, the Wizard of Oz abandons all pretence of virtue or strength. Not so, the Wizards in *Wag the Dog*.

Tom Clancy movies

Tom Clancy is the artist most closely associated with the US national security state, especially the CIA and Pentagon. We include here a series of his films as case studies because they each adapt his books but, in doing so, all lose their subversive elements.

In the case of *Clear and Present Danger* and *The Sum of All Fears*, the changes were demonstrably the result at least in part of government changes.

While we are not holding up Clancy as a particularly laudable figure politically, the treatment of his films is illustrative of the declawing power of the Hollywood-government nexus, which misleads people about real events and political dynamics while portraying the security state as the only answer to a dangerous and hostile world.

The Hunt for Red October

The Hunt for Red October (1990) was several years in the making and was based on the novel by Tom Clancy published in 1984 by the US Naval Institute. It tells a tale of a prototype near-silent Soviet Submarine, the Red October, which is taken out for a test run and a training exercise by Captain Marko Ramius (Sean Connery). Ramius plans to defect and uses the exercise as a cover, sparking off an underwater race to see if he can get the submarine and its crew into US waters before the Soviet navy catches up with and destroys them. The Pentagon tracks these movements and suspects that Ramius is a rogue officer planning a nuclear strike against the US, but CIA analyst Jack Ryan (Alec Baldwin) realises the truth and manages to avert a catastrophe. By the end of the film, both Ramius and the prototype sub are safely in US hands.

The Hunt for Red October is one of the definitive pieces of Cold War fiction but it languished in development hell because no one was persuaded that an epic novel set primarily underwater could be cinematically exciting enough to compete with Rambo and James Bond. However, the CIA loved the book, so much so that they invited Clancy to their headquarters on multiple occasions in the years following its publication. Clancy became good friends with CIA directors of public affairs William Baker and James Greenleaf, and got to know several real-life Soviet defectors, presumably with the assistance of the government. There is even a popular in-house parody of *Red October* written by an unknown CIA officer, satirising the CIA leadership through their version of how they would react to the circumstances portrayed in the book. One former CIA analyst described it as so commonly-referenced among Agency employees that it is 'a shared cultural and institutional memory among the initiated.'[310]

Producer Mace Neufeld, who went on to produce the entire Jack Ryan series, bought the rights to the novel and, over several years, found ways to convince financiers and studios that it could be a successful film. In time, he would be proven right—the movie took over $200 million worldwide on a $30 million budget. Part of the reason for the success of both the book and the film was the devotion to realism and technical details, in many cases provided by the US military.

It probably helped that three of the principal actors—Sean Connery, Scott Glenn and James Earl Jones—had military experience. During pre-production Neufeld approached the US Navy for help, which, in exchange for some changes to the script, loaned the crew several submarines to stand in for both the Red October and the USS *Dallas*. The *Houston* made over 40 emergency surface blows to create the dramatic ending to the film where the submarines have to dodge their own torpedoes. The Navy also allowed the filming of flight deck scenes on the USS

Reuben James. Captain Michael Sherman, then head of the Navy's ELO, said, 'The problem with submarines is that when the public sees them, they are tied to a pier. We do a good job at sea, but we can't take the public out there.'[311] *The Hunt for Red October* helped solve this problem.

Patriot Games

Patriot Games was the first major movie since *Scorpio* (1973) to be granted access to film at the CIA's headquarters. The producers and other major creative staff visited Langley in July 1991 and then again in October, including being invited to see the Agency's Counterterrorism Center. Producer Mace Neufeld described how, when they entered the Center, rotating flashing lights came on to alert the officers there that they had visitors, saying, 'They all turned their backs on us so we couldn't see their faces.'[312]

One CIA memo sent to director Robert Gates from Public Affairs Officer Joe DeTrani outlined the filming request and noted that, 'Clancy's novels have cast the Agency in a positive light, as did the movie *Hunt for Red October*, based on his first and best known novel. We have discussed the film with the Paramount Pictures production team including the chief producer, the director and Ford. The team seems set on following the novel closely and retaining Clancy's view of the Agency.'[313] In the event, the script for *Patriot Games*, while loosely telling the same story as the novel, contained numerous details that were changed from the original book. Clancy was publicly irate, saying that of the 200 scenes in the movie 'only one corresponds with my book.'[314]

The CIA is not credited at the end of the film, though thanks are given to the DOD, the US Navy and the US Naval Academy, which was also used as a filming location. Nonetheless *Patriot Games* definitely retains Clancy's political approach: 'Tom (Clancy) didn't want us to do a left-wing movie. He didn't want us to portray the CIA as evil. We all tend to have our own opinions. We have a more left-wing attitude than Tom does, but we agreed we didn't want to make a movie insulting to the CIA. We all believe the CIA is necessary.'[315]

This is thrust in our faces in the opening sequence of the movie when Jack Ryan and his family are in London so he can give a presentation at the Old Royal Naval College in Greenwich. As they walk through London doing some sightseeing, they witness a gang of terrorists attempt an assassination on Lord Holmes, the Minister for Northern Ireland. While the British authorities are absent or hopelessly outgunned, former CIA agent Jack Ryan manages to take down three armed terrorists single-handed.

The rest of the story revolves around an ultra-violent splinter group of the IRA led by Sean Miller (Sean Bean) who try to take revenge on Ryan and attempt various plots against him and his family. This leads Ryan to re-join the CIA so his family can be given the full hi-tech protection of the Agency. Both British and American security agencies feature prominently in the film, including SO13, the SAS, the Diplomatic Security Service, Maryland State Police and the FBI's Hostage Rescue Team (who received Clancy as a guest during a visit to Quantico in 1988). All of these agencies are either portrayed as brave protectors of our society who are brutally murdered by IRA terrorists, or highly competent counter-terrorism agents who take down the bad guys without mercy.

In the original book the IRA splinter gang are Maoists being sponsored by the Libyan government. In the film, the Communist element was removed completely (probably due to it being produced after the Cold War had just ended) and the question of Libyan sponsorship is reduced to hints and implications. Still, the idea of Irish Republican terrorism being a product of state-sponsorship remains in the movie, echoing the popular news coverage that often made this claim.

While it is true that Gaddafi's government did provide assistance to the IRA, what this narrative overlooks is the overt and covert sponsorship of terrorism in Ireland by Western societies and governments. NORAID, or the Irish Northern Aid Committee, is a US-based organisation that raised millions of pounds in support of the IRA from the late-1960s onwards. In Boston, perhaps the most important city for NORAID with its large Irish-American population, this fundraising for terrorists was 'smiled on by many local politicians, and overlooked for a time even by the FBI.'[316]

Likewise, the British security services infiltrated the IRA and co-opted their opponents, the Loyalist UDA. Much of the violence in Ireland was the direct or indirect result of the involvement of British military and intelligence agencies on both sides of the conflict through secret agents including Freddie Scapaticci, Brian Nelson and John Black. Even the IRA's own mole-catcher, the 'angel of death,' John Joe Magee, 'worked for security services on both sides of the border.'[317] The man whose role it was to root out the British spies within the IRA was himself a British spy. According to a dossier produced by British intelligence whistle-blower Ian Hurst, as many as half of all senior IRA men were secret agents.[318]

In *Patriot Games* this dynamic is reversed and it is the terrorists who have a mole deep within the government. Watkins (Hugh Fraser) is an assistant to Lord Holmes but is secretly working for Sean Miller's gang. He tips them off, provides them with information and even assists them in an assassination attempt against Ryan and Holmes. Thus, the reality of the situation is inverted, once again making the terrorists seem far more dangerous than they really are and showing the government to be fighting against the odds to stop them.

Clear and Present Danger

On *Clear and Present Danger*, the DOD objected to, and successfully changed, the negative depictions of the White House, the National Security Advisor, and the government of Colombia.[319]

Other films laid greater claim to being critical, though almost invariably this only ever consisted of unsubstantial points. *Clear and Present Danger*, made with full Pentagon cooperation, is based on the novel (1990) by Tom Clancy, a hard-right Washington insider. It was co-scripted by self-confessed 'zen-fascist' John Milius, who was also behind films like *Conan the Barbarian* (1982), *Red Dawn* (1984), *The Hunt for Red October* (1990) and *Flight of the Intruder* (1991).

In *Clear and Present Danger*, US President Bennett (Donald Moffat) orders National Security Adviser James Cutter (Harris Yulin) to establish the secret and illegal 'Operation Reciprocity,' implementing a hard-line policy against a Colombian drug cartel, Cali. Cutter employs the help of CIA Deputy Director of Operations Robert Ritter (Henry Czerny) and they use government money to bankroll a secret army. Together, they set up acting CIA Deputy Director Jack Ryan (Harrison Ford) as the fall guy for their actions, but Ryan battles to save the troops and the truth.

Clear and Present Danger depicts the US military in reflexively positive terms—reluctantly obeying their shady civilian masters and engaging in daredevil operations that neutralise nefarious drug dealers and destroy their infrastructures.

More interesting is the film's depiction of civilian authorities, for, although it undoubtedly deplores the undemocratic tactics of the villainous Bennett-Cutter-Ritter triumvirate, all three are genuinely trying to defeat the drug cartels, which are a 'clear and present danger' to US national security, and to reduce the flow of narcotics into the US. The culmination of their plan comes when

Cutter makes a treaty with the villainous Felix Cortez (Joaquim de Almeida), whereby the latter would run the cartels without US interference in exchange for a dramatic cut of supply to the US and regular arrests for US propaganda purposes. This is certainly a deal with the devil but is arguably well intentioned, reflecting the Bennett-Cutter-Ritter view of the moral world as being shades of 'grey' rather than the 'right and wrong' equation preferred by Ryan.

The original script framed US policy in less favourable terms but fell afoul of the Pentagon's marker pen. For instance, the President says of the Colombian drug lords, 'Those sons-of-bitches ... I swear, sometimes I would like to level that whole damn country – and Peru and Ecuador while we are at it.'[320] The offending line was removed, along with any presidential references to 'payback,' 'Bustin' some butt' and his calling the dealers 'monkeys and jabaloneys.'[321]

No version of the *Clear and Present Danger* script cared to mention anything about the real-world effects of the US relationship with Colombia, the most salient being that while Colombia receives more US arms and training than any other nation in the world (with the exception of Israel and Egypt), it also has the worst human rights record in the hemisphere. [322] Commenting on Colombia in 1994, the year the film was released, Amnesty International reported that at least a thousand people had been illegally executed with impunity 'by the armed forces or paramilitary groups operating with their support or acquiescence,' while 'disappearances' and 'torture' were increasingly widespread.[323]

In *Clear and Present Danger*, the prevalence of other powerful characters—principally Ryan and Admiral James Greer (James Earl Jones)—suggests that the American political system also produces honest men who can rein in the kinds of abuses of protocol by the Bennett-Cutter-Ritter trio. In fact, the majority of American characters who work within civilian power structures are remarkably amiable: FBI Director Jacobs (Tom Tammi) even gives his secretary Moira Wolfson (Ann Magnuson) two days off just because she is in love. On his deathbed, outgoing CIA Deputy Director Greer emphasises the importance of the oath of allegiance public officials take to the American people, which Ryan dramatically sees through by shouting down the President in the Oval Office.

Bennett, Cutter and Ritter are therefore the exceptions, not the rule; what is more, they know it. Although they talk tough, they are under constant threat from the benign system, embodied by Ryan and Greer and symbolised by Congress. At the climax, we see close-ups of Bennett, Ritter and Cutter, all with blood-drained faces, desperately calling after Ryan who, with patriotic musical strains playing, solemnly swears to tell the truth in front of a congressional hearing. While the outcome is left open, Bennett-Cutter-Ritter's panicky manipulation suggests that they know Ryan will emerge triumphant. Power is only abused by minority elements and these are forced to act in secret, perpetually fearful of the system's all-pervading decency.

The principal victims of the film are Americans, especially the military and the majority of the civilian government. Ryan is shown under constant stress, trying to do the right thing while dodging political intrigue. At another stage, he and his government companions are ambushed from above by machine-gun-wielding terrorists. The terminally ill Greer struggles heroically to maintain the good name of the CIA. In a key scene, director Phillip Noyce intercuts Greer's sombre state funeral with images of the military coming under heavy fire from drug barons in the jungle. As Bennett mouths formal platitudes, the enemy soldiers kill US troops to the tune of 'America The Beautiful,' traumatizing the sole survivor—the patriotic Latino-American Domingo Chavez—and thus resuscitating the 'stab-in-the-back' myth from the Vietnam War. It is a narrative straight out of Stallone's *Rambo*.

At one point in *Clear and Present Danger*, US bombs kill some children who are family members of the drug dealers. Even here, the film makes a point of showing that the US military has not noticed the children. At the last minute, Clark sees them and hesitates in shock, implying that he would not have authorised the attack had he known they were present, but the missile is already on its way. One of the unidentified boys' teddy bears shows up in the rubble on the television news later that day, prompting a visibly distressed Cutter to terminate the military mission. And so, ironically, this scene in which the US kills children actually serves to demonstrate compassion amongst even the worst of America's leadership.

The original script for *Clear and Present Danger* framed US policy in more critical terms than the resultant movie. For example, the US President says of the Columbian drug lords in the movie, "Those sons-of-bitches... I swear, sometimes I would like to level that whole damn country—and Peru and Ecuador while we are at it." The offending line was removed, along with any Presidential references to "payback," "bustin' some butt," and his calling the dealers "monkeys and jabaloneys," all at the insistence of the DOD.

The DOD also made clear its '...obvious objections to portraying the highest level of US government engaging in illegal, covert activities...' Two notable ideas suggested by the DOD were for the on-screen President to establish to the Joint Chiefs of Staff (JCS) "that young Americans are dying in the streets because of this illicit drug activity in South America. The audience will clearly understand...the drug runners will not be seen as 'innocent' or 'unarmed.'" Similarly, it wanted the on screen F15s to be shown to be under direct threat from the drug barons. Both ideas were implemented.

Following this, we might ask some reasonable questions. Where is this abundance of sensitivity from the US national security apparatus towards the people of Latin America in the real world? Did an operative's tears smudge the ink of the Pentagon's Special Forces counter-insurgency manual, which states that establishing 'death squads' in places like El Salvador and Nicaragua is particularly effective because it 'forces the insurgents to cross a critical threshold—that of attacking and killing the very class of people they are supposed to be liberating'? Did US leaders visibly crumple with the shame of sponsoring these death squads? As a priest in El Salvador described:

People are not just killed [by the death squads] … they are decapitated and then their heads are placed on pikes and used to dot the landscape … Men are not just disemboweled … their severed genitalia are stuffed into their mouths … women are not just raped … their wombs are cut from their bodies and used to cover their faces. It is not enough to kill children; they are dragged over barbed wire until the flesh falls from their bones, while parents are forced to watch.[324]

The answers are all too obvious, except to a Hollywood hooked on schmaltz, wilfully ignorant of reality and in thrall to power.

The Sum of All Fears

The first attempt at rebooting the Tom Clancy cinematic universe saw rising star Ben Affleck take over from Harrison Ford as the protagonist, Jack Ryan. Like Ford, Affleck was invited to CIA headquarters and spoke with real analysts while preparing for the role, and George Tenet gave the filmmakers a personal tour. Years later, Affleck visited Langley again on multiple occasions and was

157

even granted permission to film there for *Argo*, leading to him cracking jokes in an interview about guys with M-16s bursting out of the woods when they drove through the gates a bit too quickly.[325] For *The Sum of All Fears*, the CIA's movie liaison, Chase Brandon, also provided on-set technical advice and appeared in a DVD special feature.

In the original book (published literally days before the fall of the Soviet Union), Jack Ryan proposes that Jerusalem be converted into an independent entity like the Vatican, run by a council of Jewish, Christian and Muslim leaders. This is hugely successful at accelerating the Middle East peace process, leading a small group of PFLP terrorists to seek a radical solution. They locate a lost Israeli nuclear weapon and, with the help of an East German scientist, turn it into a bomb and blow up the Superbowl, killing not just tens of thousands of people but also many senior military and government officials. This causes the desired reaction of provoking extreme hostility between the US and the Soviet Union, taking them to the brink of nuclear war. Jack Ryan intervenes and convinces the Soviet Premier to back down, averting the disaster. The terrorists then try to blame Iran for their actions to see if they can re-ignite the conflict that way, but this too is thwarted by Ryan. The President, who tried to nuke Iran before Ryan stopped him, is removed from power and the Palestinian terrorists are beheaded in a ceremony in Riyadh. The sword used to execute them is given to Ryan as a gift.

The only elements of this narrative that made it into the film version are the lost Israeli nuclear device being used to blow up a football game, and Jack Ryan talking down the Russians and saving the day. The script was rewritten numerous times, with original Jack Ryan director Phillip Noyce and Harrison Ford dropping out due to the problems they were having adapting the book. Clancy himself even joked on the DVD commentary that he was the 'author of the book that the director ignored.'

Nonetheless, the book was referenced in a US congressional hearing by Assistant Secretary for Homeland Defense, Paul F. McHale Jr. He was asked about the remote sensing technology for detecting explosives and WMD and, while replying, he said, 'With regard to explosives, the challenge is significant. With regard to weapons of mass destruction, it's even greater. ... a few years ago, Tom Clancy wrote a novel that focused on the transport of an improvised nuclear device across the Atlantic Ocean into one of our unprotected ports. And that novel's plot went on to describe the consequences following the detonation of that improvised nuclear device.'[326]

For the film, the Middle Eastern element was removed from the story completely, with the terrorists changed to neo-Nazis trying to spark off a nuclear war between the US and Russia so they can exploit this to set up a fascist European superstate. This change may have been made in response to a two-year campaign by the Council on American-Islamic Relations against using 'Muslim villains.' Interestingly, though, director Phil Alden Robinson said in a DVD extra that this change was made for purely creative reasons, because they felt it wasn't plausible that Arab terrorists could do all of the things they needed to do for the sake of the plot.

Whatever the reason for this change of focus, the removal of the Middle Eastern context and the Arab villains could qualify *The Sum of All Fears* to be considered a much more liberal film than any of its three Clancy-adaptation predecessors. However, by removing this element from the story entirely, the filmmakers also left out the idea that the many conflicts in the Middle East can be peacefully resolved. As a result, they did nothing to challenge the Hollywood consensus that the Middle East is simply a massive quagmire of religious, ethnic, racial, economic and political problems to which there are no solutions.

The CIA was not the only government agency to support *The Sum of All Fears*. It was the first Hollywood film to be allowed inside the Kremlin. More importantly, the Pentagon also provided extensive production assistance. When Fowler is rescued from his overturned motorcade it is real Marines in real Marine Corps helicopters who we see coming to his aid. B-2 bombers, F-16s and an aircraft carrier were all made available to the producers for filming, in exchange for further changes to the script. In one sequence where the aircraft carrier is attacked and destroyed by the terrorists, 'Pentagon officials said that was unrealistic, and they did not like the impression that a carrier was so vulnerable. In the end, the filmmakers accepted the Pentagon's assertion that the carrier would not be blown up and showed only its flight operations being destroyed.'[327]

However, the notions of nuclear terrorism being a credible threat and of the CIA being a diplomatic anti-war intelligence agency capable of saving the world remain front and centre in the script. While almost everything else about the book was changed or dropped, these two key ideas were retained, presumably with the CIA's encouragement and enthusiasm. Thus, the world is still a scary and threatening place full of genocidal terrorists, though for once they aren't Arabs, and the CIA are still the heroes.

Along similar lines, while in the book President Fowler and Ryan are deeply at odds, in the film they are close friends. In one of his many outings as the President, Morgan Freeman is at the football game when he gets a warning from Ryan about the impending nuclear explosion. He is rushed out of the stadium but the motorcade is caught in the blast wave, injuring Fowler and leading to his death. Ryan arrives just in time for a tear-jerking final conversation with his long-term ally, completely contradicting what happens in the book. Thus, the American state is shown to be unified and working together instead of beset by internal conflict, again removing a potentially subversive element from the story.

Oliver Stone: Thirty Years on the Front Line

Oliver Stone is one of the greatest screenwriters of his generation. As a subversive political figure in Hollywood, he has few, if any, rivals.

In Stone's *JFK* (1991), based on real historical events, US authorities are shown operating in service of the military industrial complex. Jim Garrison—an attorney played by Kevin Costner—and his legal team face a cabal of fascists which hold powerful positions in, and characterise the culture of, the US civilian and military elites. Mr X, an anonymous government-insider played by Donald Sutherland, outlines in detail how these forces hated the Kennedys for their progressive politics and arranged for JFK's murder, cynically using Lee Harvey Oswald as a patsy. The conspiracy included President Lyndon Johnson himself and utilized the Mafia and anti-Castro Cubans. These power systems are portrayed in frightening terms—faces concealed, operating in the dark, and associated with weird sexual rituals. Stone's loose sequel, *Nixon* actually characterises the political system as 'the beast,' incarnated as Larry Hagman's oil tycoon and Bob Hoskins' predatory J. Edgar Hoover. In a pivotal scene set at the Lincoln Memorial, a young peace protester tells the President he is unable to stop the war 'even if [he] wanted to' because he is not truly in control, which a stunned Nixon recognises as a fundamental truth that had previously eluded him.

In some senses, it is important to note that Stone built his *JFK* and *Nixon* narratives on an already powerful constituency: the Democrat Party. The principal victims of US power depicted in his films are supporters of the Kennedy dynasty. There is little discussion of the consequences of the war economy to people

161

outside the United States under President Kennedy and other administrations who were killed, injured and displaced in their millions. *Nixon* perpetuates the idea that Kennedy was innocent and unaware of CIA efforts to assassinate Castro, when even Stone's own script footnotes admit that this was not the case.[328] Such an approach to history suggests all will be 'like the old days' when the 'good guys' were in office, if only we can root out the villains. Kennedy remains America's last best hope in *Nixon*—the man that people 'want to be.'

Nevertheless, Stone's films *are* amongst the most radical attacks on US power to have been produced in mainstream cinema in the post-Cold War world. *JFK* was the decisive factor behind Washington's decision to release millions of pages of previously secret files about the Kennedy assassination. The 1992 Assassination Materials Disclosure Act is commonly referred to as the 'Oliver Stone Act.'[329]

Furthermore, when we consider Stone's full gamut of work, we see a quite comprehensive interrogation of US exceptionalism. Of note, *Platoon* (1986) extensively depicted the horrific rape of a Vietnamese girl by US forces; *Heaven & Earth* (1993) was shot entirely from the perspective of Le Ly, a Vietnamese woman caught between the fighting factions in Vietnam and forced into prostitution and poverty after living an idyllic life in the countryside. Although Tommy Lee Jones's character—a Marine who tortured Vietcong for Special Operations—is also a pitiful figure, it is Le Ly (who eventually becomes the Marine's wife) who is the principal sympathetic victim.

Stone made powerful, challenging films at quite a pace for quite some time. However, *Nixon* was released in 1995 and it is interesting to examine the subsequent two decades of his career, where it appears that the stress of being a political punching bag had taken its toll.

Nowhere was this declawing of Oliver Stone more apparent than in his *World Trade Center*, which told a story of heroic firemen trapped in the World Trade Center on 9/11, in what syndicated columnist Cal Thomas called 'one of the greatest pro-American, pro-family, pro-faith, pro-male, flag-waving, god-bless America films you will ever see.'[330] L. Brent Bozell III, president of the conservative Media Research Center and founder of the Parents Television Council, called *World Trade Center* 'a masterpiece,' and emailed 400,000 people saying 'go see this film.'[331] Stone also added some all–American machismo to his script: US Marine Dave Karnes sees the television news footage in his suburban Connecticut office, declares 'This country's at war!' and later predicts that some good men will be needed to 'revenge this' (*sic*). Karnes visits his pastor, tells him the Lord is calling him, gets a regulation haircut, dons his Marine uniform and drives straight to Ground Zero where he enters the disaster site. As the credits roll, we learn that Karnes re–enlisted for two more tours of duty and fought in Iraq.[332] In *Sight and Sound*, B. Ruby Rich calls Stone's Karnes 'a biblical warrior out of the New Testament by way of Vietnam,' and asks 'Did ex–military man Stone, like Karnes, snap back into some wartime persona and forget all the political positions and conspiracy investigations of his career?'[333]

Strikingly, prior to *World Trade Center*, Stone had repeatedly denounced the film industry, hinted at believing the 'inside job' story of 9/11, and had expressed the desire to make a balanced film about terrorism. In a panel discussion in October 2001, he exclaimed, 'there's been conglomeration under six principal princes,' referring to Hollywood corporations. 'They are kings, they are barons!—and these six companies have control of the world. Michael Eisner decides, "I can't make a movie about Martin Luther King, Jr—there will be rioting at the gates of Disneyland!" That's bullshit! But that's what the new world order is.'[334]

Stone was referring to his thwarted attempts to make *Memphis*, a film about the murder of Martin Luther King. In 1997, Stone was reported to be considering scripts about the activist Randall Terry and the Israel-Palestinian conflict.[335] Stone also considered making *Mission Impossible II* with Tom Cruise, which he said would be 'a vehicle to say something about the state of corporate culture and technology and global politics in the 21st century.'[336] None of this happened. Stone similarly turned down the offer to make *The Peacemaker*[337] (surely he would have made a more challenging picture out of it), in favour of making the apolitical *U–Turn* (1997), which his co-producer Dan Halfstad explained was about making a movie 'that wasn't going to be reviewed on the op-ed pages.'[338]

At the 2001 panel discussion, Stone called for a new film along the lines of *The Battle of Algiers* (1966), which had sympathised with Algerian terrorists resisting French occupation, and then elaborated:

You show the Arab side and the American side in a chase film with a *French Connection* urgency, where you track people by satellite, like in *Enemy of the State*. My movie would have the CIA guys and the FBI guys, but they blow it. They are a bunch of drunks from World War II who haven't recovered from the disasters of the '60s—the Kennedy assassination and Vietnam. My movie would show the new heroes of security, people who really get the job done, who know where the secrets are.[339]

Similarly, in 2003, Stone said:

If I had the youthful energy I had when I did *JFK*, and I could take all the abuse I would take—which I was a little ignorant of then—to do [a movie] about terrorism would be

164

a great contribution. But I don't know if it could get made or distributed because of the controversy it would arouse.[340]

In 2016, Stone returned to the big screen with *Snowden*, his first major political movie for 21 years, unless we are to count his remarkably tepid treatment of George W. Bush in *W* (2008). He faced the same old difficulties on *Snowden*, commenting:

It's a very strange thing to do [a story about] an American man, and not be able to finance this movie in America. And that's very disturbing, if you think about its implications on any subject that is not overtly pro-American. They say we have freedom of expression; but thought is financed, and thought is controlled, and the media is controlled. This country is very tight on that, and there's no criticism allowed at a certain level. You can make movies about civil rights leaders who are dead, but it's not easy to make one about a current man.

US companies refused to become involved in the *Snowden* project[341] and no studio was ready to support it. Stone and his producer had to finance everything themselves.[342] Eventually, financing came through from France and Germany, and the film ended up being shot in Germany as a German production.[343] Since the budget was too tight, Stone had to miss the funeral of his mother, who had passed away in America while he was filming.[344] It was all rather reminiscent of Stone's *Salvador* (1986), where Stone had put up his own money, turned down a director's fee, acquired Mexican and British money, since Hollywood's response was 'highly negative.'[345]

Even on the lacklustre *W*, the $25.1m production budget had to be raised independently and several actors turned down roles because of low fees and subject matter, as when Christian

165

Bale withdrew from the lead role, for example. Star Josh Brolin and Stone accepted points—money on the back of the project—rather than their usual fee.[346]

Stone's career has been a tremendous success and he has popularised some highly challenging political narratives. It just hasn't been easy, even for a creative tour de force like him. In 2017, Stone gave a speech at the WGA Awards: 'I've fought these people who practice war for most of my life. It's a tiring game. And mostly you'll get your ass kicked.'[347] Oliver Stone returned from Vietnam as a great man and artist but he remained forever a soldier on hostile terrain.

Paul Verhoeven

Paul Verhoeven is an example of another rare species in Hollywood—a director of popular, ultra-violent sci-fi fantasy movies that were obviously political and often explicitly critical of the US establishment. In particular, his collaborations with screenwriter Ed Neumeier and producer Jon Davison—*Robocop* and *Starship Troopers*—are regarded as cult classics, spawning multiple sequels as well as books, TV spin-offs and video games. Likewise, *Total Recall* inspired a forgettable remake and tie-in games. Few filmmakers have done more than Verhoeven to criticise and satirise American corporate power and the dangers inherent in the lure of money, though his successes were not just down to his abilities as a talented auteur—there were unique circumstances that permitted the production of this high-budget, politically subversive trio of movies.

Robocop (1987)

The film that saw Verhoeven break into Hollywood, *Robocop*, tells the story of Alex Murphy (Peter Weller), a cop in a futuristic version of Detroit which is beset by crime and poverty. So, quite like modern-day Detroit. Murphy is killed by a gang of thieves and drug-dealers headed by Clarence Boddicker (Curtwood Smith) and is resurrected as Robocop—a part-man, part-machine cyborg policeman. As Murphy gradually remembers what happened to him he seeks revenge against Boddicker and his gang, and against Dick Jones (Ronny Cox)—an executive at the corporation that created Robocop, who is secretly in league with Boddicker. In order to survive and ultimately win out over these forces, Murphy has to rediscover his lost humanity, and then violently lays waste to his enemies.

Verhoeven, Neumeier, and Davison used Robocop to criticise several major economic and political trends of 1980s America, which have only become more prominent in the 30 years since. The most apparent is privatisation of public services, as in *Robocop* the police, along with much of the rest of the city of Detroit, are run by Omni Consumer Products or OCP, a huge corporate conglomerate. OCP's executives are trying to build 'Delta City'—a new Detroit full of gleaming skyscrapers—and, in the process, are destroying 'old Detroit' by running the police service into the ground so they can replace the human officers with heavily-armed robots. When Dick Jones' plan for a fully artificial robot—ED-209—results in the savage killing of a junior board member the rival Robocop project headed by Bob Morton (Miguel Ferrer) is given the green light. This leads to an internal corporate struggle between Jones and Morton, culminating in Jones contracting Boddicker to murder Morton and to try to destroy Robocop.

As such, *Robocop* is more than a sci-fi fantasy, it also has prominent elements of a corporate conspiracy thriller and aspects ripped from exploitation cinema. Rather than gleaming futurism, the film adopts a decayed, post-industrial aesthetic with much of the action—including Murphy's death and the final showdown with Boddicker and his gang—taking place in a rusty, disused steel factory. This highlights how post-industrial economies no longer allow for corporations to grow by simply making more products for consumers, and therefore big business has to seek out new territory to conquer in pursuit of growth and profits. Public services provided by local or national governments are the primary targets of this process, turning the people within them from public servants into mechanisms for profit.

[Above] Robocop confronts a pair of would-be rapists.

OCP are depicted as a truly enormous company involved in all aspects of American life. Jones' eventual plan for the ED-209 robot is that 'After a successful tour of duty in Old Detroit, we can expect 209 to become the hot military product for the next decade.' When Jones and Morton have a confrontation, Jones declares, 'I had a guaranteed military sale with ED-209. Renovation programme. Spare parts for 25 years. Who cares if it worked or not?' Indeed, the design for the ED-209 was based on a Bell Huey gunship and the scientist who developed it in the film is named McNamara, both evoking the Vietnam war. Emphasising how in this world there is very little that isn't supplied by private businesses, when Jones instructs Boddicker to destroy Robocop, Boddicker asks, 'We're gonna need some major fire power. You got access to military weaponry?' Jones responds, 'We practically are the military.' Verhoeven commented that 'this situation is very close to fascism.'[348]

Another aspect of Robocop's subversive satire of the future of the American economy is the dehumanising of the people involved. As Murphy is converted into a trans-human entity, OCP see him not as a person inside a machine, but as their own property. This is most obvious when Morton and his assistant, Johnson (Felton Perry), are deciding which parts of Murphy's corpse they want to retain for the cyborg they are constructing.

Morton: We should lose the arm. What do you think?

Johnson: He signed release forms when he joined the force. He's legally dead. We can do pretty much what we want to.

Morton: (to doctor) Lose the arm.

Similarly, when Murphy's former partner Anne Lewis (Nancy Allen) first tries to remind Robocop of who he really is, she is confronted by Morton, who tells her 'He doesn't have a name. He's got a program. He's product.'

It is not just Murphy who is dehumanised. The rest of the police force are treated poorly by OCP, to the extent that they eventually strike, leading to chaos for the entire city's population. These two themes of recessive, post-industrial capitalism and the dehumanising of both workers and the public come together when Jones outlines his vision for Delta City to Boddicker, saying, 'Delta City begins construction in two months. That's two million workers living in trailers. That means drugs, gambling, prostitution. Virgin territory for the man who knows how to open up new markets. One man could control it all, Clarence.' It is clear that Jones sees the people building the new Delta City just like the police—as mere labour to be exploited while they actually turn the dreams of the OCP executives into a reality.

On top of this, the film is viscerally violent as robots and futuristic weapons rip through the flimsy humans made of flesh and blood. However, the notion that superior technology is a means of providing a recovery from the post-industrial economy is repeatedly shown in ludicrous terms. The satirical 'Mediabreak' newscasts that proclaim, 'Give us three minutes and we'll give you the world,' feature numerous stories of technology failing in dramatic and often lethal fashion. The first Mediabreak tells us 'The president's first press conference from the Star Wars Peace Platform got off to a shaky start when power failed, causing a brief period of weightlessness' (a reference to Reagan's 'Star Wars' missile defense program). Later in the film, another Mediabreak announces that the satellite-mounted laser defence had misfired and killed over a hundred people including two former presidents. This depiction is absurd at times but by emphasising the violent consequences of this military-economic-technological society, *Robocop* keeps these satirical exaggerations grounded in reality. Though they are sometimes ridiculous extrapolations of real trends, they are still relatable to the world the audience actually inhabits.

Robocop met with some resistance from the Hollywood machine. The producers approached the Pentagon for very limited support in the form of stock footage, but the assessment was that, 'DOD found nothing in the film beneficial to the department' and so 'the request for stock footage was denied.'[349] Likewise, the MPAA took objection to the finished film, initially giving it an X rating and insisting on numerous cuts to bring it down to the studio's desired R rating. Almost all the cuts toned down the violence and gore—the aspect of the film that helps ground it in reality. The scene where ED-209 murders the young executive was shortened and the shot where Robocop stabs Boddicker in the neck was removed. However, when it came to the 'melting man' scene where one of Boddicker's gang is soaked in a chemical poison and his skin begins to dissolve, the filmmakers and the studio held out. The MPAA wanted to remove the shot where Boddicker runs over the melting man in his car, splattering the corpse all over the windscreen. However, in test screenings this proved to be the most popular moment of the entire film, so Orion Pictures stood their ground and eventually the MPAA backed down. Despite these restrictions, the released version of *Robocop* is, in Davison's words, 'Fascism for liberals.'[350] It tells a fascistic story from a strongly left-wing perspective.

Total Recall (1990)

Verhoeven's big commercial breakthrough came with another film that defies casual genre definitions. A thinking man's action movie, *Total Recall* combines action and sci-fi elements with a twisty political spy thriller and a subtext about the uncertain distinction between memories, dreams and reality. A century in the future, in a world where humans are colonising other planets, Doug Quaid (Arnold Schwarzenegger) is a construction worker who dreams of moving to Mars. His wife, Lori (Sharon Stone), disagrees, so he goes to Rekall, a firm offering the implanting of memories of exotic get-aways, and buys a holiday where he is a secret agent. Something goes wrong, and this starts off an action-packed adventure taking Quaid to Mars where he joins up with the local resistance movement against the oppressive government. It is revealed that Quaid used to be Hauser, an agent for the Mars colonial government, and he is being used by the dictator Cohagen (Ronny Cox) to infiltrate the rebellion. Quaid rebels and kills Cohagen and his henchmen before activating an underground machine built by ancient aliens that creates a breathable atmosphere on Mars, freeing the oppressed people. However, throughout Quaid's journey it is ambiguous whether the events are real or an elaborate dream or fake memory planted by Rekall.

[Above] Arnold Schwarzenegger removes a homing device from his nose, Total Recall.

It was after seeing *Robocop* that Arnold Schwarzenegger suggested to the producers of Total Recall that they hire Paul Verhoeven to direct. Though neither Neumeier nor Davison worked on *Total Recall*, Verhoeven brought in several of the crew from *Robocop* including cinematographer Jost Vacano, production designer William Sandell, editor Frank J. Urioste, and special effects designer Rob Bottin. As a result, *Total Recall* incorporates several major thematic, tonal and stylistic elements from *Robocop*. The retro-futuristic aesthetic replete with high technology alongside cheap, neon-lit nightlife disguises a subversive story of brutal government oppression mixed with high-brow science fiction.

While *Robocop* focused on the machinations of corporate power, *Total Recall* targeted the violence and dehumanisation perpetrated by governments. The elaborate colony on Mars is largely run by a single dictator, and is partly populated by mutant humans, the victims of poor-quality domes in the early days of the colony. At one stage, when Cohagen is trying to capture Quaid, he shuts off the air supply to a section of the colony where most of the mutants live. The brutality of using access to air as a means to control people is emphasised at the climax of the film when Cohagen is blasted outside onto the surface of Mars and suffocates in visceral, eye-popping fashion. As in *Robocop*, Verhoeven used ultra-violence to leave no doubt about the consequences of oppressive systems, and his opposition to them. As Verhoeven put it, the colonial system is a metaphor for the real actions of the European colonial powers, or indeed for 'any kind of imperialism.' However, the ambition remains the same as in *Robocop*— Verhoeven described Cohagen's 'abuse' of the citizens of Mars as being the acts of a 'dictator who wants to get as much money out of it' as possible.[351]

Expanding this, while Quaid's moral status is as ambiguous as his mental state, the guerilla rebellion on Mars are portrayed very sympathetically. Both the mutant and regular human rebels are viciously repressed by Cohagen's forces, but they remain loyal to the cause. While the cab driver Benny (Mel Johnson Jr.) is dismissive, saying they just want, 'More money, more freedom, more air,' he comes across as callous, and later betrays Quaid and murders the leader of the rebellion. Likewise, the hangout for the rebels is a brothel populated by a variety of amusing and original background characters including a prostitute with three breasts and an infectious laugh. While the prominent female rebel Melina (Rachel Ticotin) develops into Quaid's love interest, she is a powerful and empathetic character in her own right, especially set against the traitorous Lori. The casting of Ticotin—who is ethnically Puerto Rican/Russian – and her triumph alongside Quaid over the very white and blonde colonial system provides an element of revenge fantasy for some members of the audience.

This likely contributed to the enormous commercial success that *Total Recall* enjoyed, while also advancing a radical anti-colonialist worldview.

The original edit of the film did run into some trouble with the MPAA, and, just as with Robocop, they initially rated it X. Changes were made to ensure an R rating, with Schwarzenegger commenting that he thought Verhoeven, 'Gave them that cut so they would have something to complain about, and then he would cut it down.' [352] Perhaps Verhoeven had learned from his experience with the MPAA over *Robocop* and approached the violence in *Total Recall* more strategically.

At a budget of around $60 million, *Total Recall* was one of the most expensive films ever made at the time of its production. While it is unusual that a studio would take a large financial risk on such a bizarre and politically controversial story, there were special circumstances that allowed Verhoeven greater than usual creative freedom. Adapted from a short story by Phillip K. Dick, the script underwent nearly a decade of rewrites comprising over 40 versions, with several stars and directors slated at different times. In 1987 producer Dino De Laurentis, whose company had started pre-production on the film, ran into financial difficulties. Schwarzenegger was enthusiastic about the script so when he learned De Laurentis was having to sell the project he called up Mario Kassar of Carolco Pictures and told him, 'That is the script you have to buy for me.' [353] Schwarzenegger, on whom Carolco depended to help bring in audiences, negotiated a deal where he not only got $10 million and 15% of the profits but also got to choose the screenwriter and director for the film. [354] He even intervened to keep certain expensive visual effects in the film despite objections from the studio, ensuring maximum creative freedom for the crew—a rare instance of star power being used to help make a more imaginative and politically subversive film.

Starship Troopers (1997)

One of the few subsequent sci-fi films to have achieved this is *Starship Troopers*, the only film Verhoeven has made with one of the big six studios. Set in a utopian future society, Earth is under attack by giant insects from the other side of the galaxy. A group of young friends sign up to the space-based military and fight back with technologically advanced weapons.

Starship Troopers reunited Verhoeven with the visual and special effects team from *Total Recall* and with Neumeier and Davison from *Robocop*. The consistencies in subject and style are such that viewers can imagine the world of *Starship Troopers* growing out of the world of *Robocop*, as giant corporations gave way to a totalitarian fascist state. Indeed while the characters in *Starship Troopers* are deliberately superficial and stereotyped, the world they inhabit is subtly constructed. In an early scene in a classroom the war veteran Jean Rasczak (Michael Ironside) indoctrinates his students, telling them that 'violence is the supreme authority from which all other authority is derived.' We subsequently learn that in order to vote, or go into politics, or even have children, the civilians of this world have to serve in the military and fight the giant bugs. Regular news updates show how the justice system is swift and brutal, executing people for minor crimes, and that most people are brainwashed with war hysteria and believe in the vital importance of fighting the insect threat.

As with most of Verhoeven's output, we immediately see the consequences of this violent, dehmanising society. The older people to whom we are introduced in the first act are military veterans who have suffered terrible injuries. Rasczak is missing a lower arm, a science teacher has been blinded by having acid splashed in her face, and the man on the desk at the local recruitment centre has lost both legs and an arm. When the protagonist Jonny Rico (Casper Van Dien) says that he's going to

175

join the Mobile Infantry (the space Marines) the recruiter (the triple amputee) congratulates him, saying 'Mobile Infantry made me the man I am today.' This sets up the rest of the film, as Rico sees his friends, his mentor Rasczak and his lover ripped limb-from-limb by giant arachnids.

[Above] A military recruiter bears the scars of the War on Bugs, Starship Troopers

While the recruiter's line is intended ironically, it contrasts sharply with two characters in recent DOD-sponsored films. In the Navy-supported *Battleship*, the wounded warrior character, played by a real life Army Colonel, 'was expanded significantly from the original cameo appearance to a major character instrumental to defeating the invading aliens and saving the planet—all while wearing an "ARMY" t-shirt.'[355] Meanwhile, in *Whiskey Tango Foxtrot*, the DOD were persuaded to support the film, in part, because near the end Tina Fey's character, 'visits the home of a young Marine who had suffered the loss of both legs in combat. His character is the complete opposite of the stereotypical "wounded warrior," as he and young family are doing quite well, and sets the reporter in pursuit of a new, positive life style.'[356]

While the team behind *Starship Troopers* were using black humour to criticise the use of wounded veterans to promote militarism, the DOD continues to do this, and not just in Hollywood movies.

Starship Troopers was based on Robert Heinlein's novel of the same name, but while Heinlein glorified the fascistic, militaristic future he portrayed, the trio behind the film satirised it. Verhoeven said they thought of themselves as 'fighting with the book' and described how the film is an attempt to tell two stories, one of, 'young boys and young girls fighting giant bugs, and then there is a counter-narrative of "by the way, these people are fascists."'[357] When *Starship Troopers* was released, the satirical dimension to the film escaped many critics, who saw it solely as a pro-fascist special effects extravaganza. Roger Ebert criticised the movie but credited Verhoeven with, 'faithfully represent[ing] Heinlein's militarism, his Big Brother state, and a value system in which the highest good is to kill a friend before the Bugs can eat him.'[358] Other reviewers described it as, 'Moronic dialogue and fascist bug slaughter,' and said '[it] lacks the courage of the book's fascist conclusions.'[359]

Over time, *Starship Troopers* has become a cult classic and in more recent polls and reviews it has fared better.[360] Former editor of AV Club Scott Tobias was especially positive, calling it 'the most subversive major studio film in recent (or distant) memory.'[361] But how did a film that was, in its director's words, 'politically incorrect' receive a $100 million budget from a studio like Sony? Verhoeven explained that it was because the upper management at Sony Pictures was in turmoil at the time, saying, 'the regime at Sony changed every three or four months... No one ever looked at the rushes because they had no time because they were fired every three or four months... We got away with it because nobody saw it.' However, when they turned in the finished film, 'They were stunned, flabbergasted that this movie was made... They didn't know how to handle it.'[362] As a result,

Starship Troopers was pushed back from a summer release to early November, and, unlike *Robocop* and *Total Recall*, did little more than break even at the box office. While Verhoeven did go on to make one more major Hollywood production, the *Invisible Man* remake, *Hollow Man* (2000), he described it as having, 'No signature at all anymore,'[363] causing him to return to making lower-budget features in Europe.

Though he only produced six films during his time in Hollywood, Verhoeven is best remembered for the dark subversive humour, deep politics and ultra-violence that characterise *Robocop*, *Total Recall* and *Starship Troopers*. No director has made clearer the brutal consequences of both corporate and government oppression in such vivid and gory style. However, he was the beneficiary of unusual situations at Carolco and Sony that allowed him to combine big stars, costly and innovative visual effects with radical narratives that challenge the status quo.

BREAK THIS MATRIX

~

Despite the under-estimated influence of the national security state, we are not claiming that it is the most important factor in shaping the politics of Hollywood. Corporate owners, producers, and directors still typically have considerable leeway to operate outside ideological state controls. They just rarely choose to do so.[364]

In *First Blood: Part II* (1985), Sylvester Stallone's Rambo fights his way through Vietnam—ten years into peacetime—to rescue American prisoners of war which, the film falsely implies, actually existed in the real world. Two years later, *Rambo III* (1987) had Stallone fighting the Soviet Union in Afghanistan, ironically in support of the forerunners to al Qaeda—official US government policy at the time. In *Rocky IV* (1988), Stallone's other iconic eponymous character gloriously humiliates the duplicitous Communists when he fights a Russian boxer closely associated with the Nazi Ayran ideal.

None of the Rambo or Rocky films received so much as government advice.

In 2013, *American Sniper* heroised US Navy Seal veteran Chris Kyle who, in the real world, boasted of killing two hundred Iraqis, including women and children. The film had no government support but still became one of the most virulently reactionary war films ever made. Warner Brothers had simply bought the rights to Kyle's autobiography and then the project passed through several hands before ending up with Clint Eastwood as director. No deliberate   propaganda.

[Above] Director Steven Spielberg accepting an award from Defense Secretary, William Cohen.

Munich (2005) dramatized Israel's response to the Palestinian terror attacks at the 1972 Olympics. Although the media emphasised the film's even-handedness, the filmmaker Steven Spielberg said explicitly that he agreed with Israel's lethal retaliation.[365] Spielberg's sympathies do indeed come across in the film—the most celebrated 'anti-war'[366] scene is actually a two-and-a-half minute exchange between an Arab and an Israeli which, close textual analysis reveals, merely points out that the whole Palestinian struggle is both futile and immoral. The film had no government support and, ironically, it was the filmmaker, Spielberg who—although unreported in the usual Western news outlets—provided a million dollars' worth of aid to Israel during its 2006 invasion of Lebanon.[367]

There are comedies, too. Adam Sandler's *You Don't Mess with the Zohan* (2007) was made without government interference but nonetheless trivialised the Palestinian struggle in line with the US government's professed desire for peace in the Middle East whilst still siding emphatically with Tel Aviv.

(Above, left) A frame from the slapstick comedy, You Don't Mess with the Zohan. The goof-ball face of Adam Sandler's Israeli special forces hero briefly drops and he expresses hostility in an intriguing frame as he pushes a Palestinian off a roof to his death.

The Peacemaker (1997) was not the recipient of any government script changes, either. Indeed, it starred a notable anti-war activist (George Clooney), was the first film by liberal studio DreamWorks SKG, and was based on the book *One Point Safe*, by journalists Andrew and Leslie Cockburn. Between them, the Cockburns had authored books that were critical of the US-Israeli relationship, the US secret war in Nicaragua, and Bush-era Secretary of Defense Donald Rumsfeld.[368] Nevertheless, *The Peacemaker* went out of its way to emphasise how the US values the sanctity of civilian life—even when George Clooney's character insists that a marksman shoot a terrorist to prevent a nuclear explosion in New York, he still does not do so because a child is nearby.[369] Director Mimi Leder commented that 'we are a vulnerable world and we need to protect ourselves. That is a message I hope gets across with the film.' On such terms, *The Peacemaker* succeeds—it does indeed indicate that we need to 'protect ourselves' from the entire Middle East, particularly Iraq (which Clooney prevents acquiring chemical weapons) and Iran. The solution implicitly advocated is targeted state-sanctioned violence, including the violation of Russian airspace. It becomes clear that Leder really means that the US is 'the peacemaker' in her title and there is precious little indication that she is being ironic.

How can we explain the prevalence of such national security narratives, beyond the role of direct government interference?

The most obvious reason, and one we won't explore in any detail here, is that entertainment products rip their stories from news headlines, which, in turn, broadly reflect the views of political power systems.

However, there are also two other more interesting facets of the system that help shape the establishment-friendly politics of screen entertainment: ownership and advertising.

The 'big six' studios that own and distribute the vast majority of film and television content are: Universal (owned by Comcast), Warner Brothers (Time Warner), Disney (The Walt Disney Company), 20th Century Fox (News Corporation), Paramount (Viacom), and Sony Pictures (Sony). This concentration of ownership has obvious effects in terms of pushing shows towards safe narratives that don't offend the powerful. This much is obvious, but let's look at two specific cases where this power was clearly exercised: NewsCorp's reaction to a short spate of unconventional films made by its subsidiary, and CBC's reaction to a documentary it had been obliged to screen.

In 1999, *Fight Club* reached number one at the box office. The film raised the issues of consumerism, credit-culture, and the dangers of fascism. Rupert Murdoch, ultimate head of Fox, declared to his aides 'You have to be sick to make a movie like that.' In a brief, uncited article, *The New York Times* reported that Murdoch's personal dislike of the 'dark tone' of films like *Fight Club* and the Leonardo di Caprio movie *The Beach* had led to the unexpected resignation of studio head, Bill Mechanic.[370] Around the same time, Warren Beatty had made *Bulworth* 'in complete stealth,' without revealing any political content to the studio, and skilfully negotiated complete creative control owing to Fox having backed out of making *Dick Tracy*.[371] In the critically well received film, Beatty's down-on-his-luck Senator utters the great taboo word: socialism. In response, Fox released *Bulworth* to compete with the blockbusting *Godzilla* and it vanished into obscurity.

In 1997, Elaine Briere's *Bitter Paradise: The Sell-Out of East Timor* won the Hot Docs award for best political documentary, which usually results in screenings on CBC. However, Briere commented to us:

I offered first window to CBC but it was tossed around like a hot potato between three of their current documentary programs. It was lawyered, something that rarely happens with the CBC. They wanted several important changes including deleting the part about Pierre Trudeau [the current Prime Minister Justin's father], our then Prime Minister, meeting with [Indonesian dictator] Suharto several months before the Indonesian invasion of East Timor, taking out the part about Canadian oil and mining companies investing in Indonesia, and at one point even replacing me as a narrator, saying I was too subjective and not journalistic enough. *Bitter Paradise* never at any point claimed to be journalistic, but was a point-of-view documentary, an accepted genre of the day.[372]

Eventually, Briere saw no alternative but to work with a different distributor TV Ontario—but she told us about the film's ongoing problems:

Bitter Paradise was screened only once [on TV Ontario] in a strand called A View from Here when I got a call from the then head of TVO [who] said that INCO, Canada giant multinational nickel mining company based in Sudbury, Ontario, with large mining operations in Sulawesi, Indonesia, wanted the film off the air or they would sue TVO. (There was a short section on INCO's operations in Indonesia in the film.) INCO, at the time, was TVO's second largest corporate donor. They [TVO] told me not to go to the media and that they would handle it. I heard nothing back from TVO and the film never aired again. Normally it would have had four screenings on A View from Here.[373]

We are not disputing the right of business owners to control their own products but if this control is exercised in order to further political, self-interested, and controversial ideological ends, then we have every right to call them out. Studios present themselves as being responsive to their audiences and, typically, their parent companies like to give the impression that they operate a 'hands off' approach to their subsidiaries. In fact, we know this is simply not the case when there are important political narratives at stake.

Let's take a closer look at these advertisers. Product placement and merchandising deals for toys, clothing, novelizations, and soundtracks are attractive to movie-makers because, even if the movie fails, the manufacturer incurs the loss. Product placement in motion pictures is a billion dollar industry, involving the vast majority of the Fortune 500 companies[374] and, since the average movie costs $30m just to market, such deals can be vital.[375] *Die Another Day* (2002) made $70m from associated brands from twenty placements[376] and the Superman reboot, *Man of Steel* (2013) made $170m from over a hundred placements.[377]

The Bond films, *The World is Not Enough* (1999) and *Quantum of Solace* (2008), each earned over $100 million for similar in-film promotions, with beer manufacturer Heineken reportedly paying $45 million for a scene in *Skyfall* where Bond turns down his signature martini and instead takes a swig of the Dutch lager. *Smurfs 2* managed to cover more than its entire $105 million production budget with $150 million in placements.

Sometimes the product placements themselves raise further ethical and security issues. For example, guns are prevalent and often presented in unnervingly positive ways. In *From Paris with Love* (2010) James Reese is a low-level CIA operative, who has never killed anyone before. He is assigned to a grizzled special agent, Charlie Wax, played by John Travolta. Reese's first task is to help Wax smuggle a gun through French customs. Wax shoots several terrorists who work at a seemingly innocent madras restaurant, and then blasts holes in the ceiling to reveal a load of drugs. Reese learns that his fiancé is a 'sleeper' agent assigned to live with him and, although he does everything he possibly can to talk her down, she can ultimately only be stopped by Reese blowing a hole in her head. In the closing scene, Reese shows off his big new weapon and Wax nods approvingly, as though the whole movie was building to some kind of weird advert for handguns and spousal murder—which it basically is.[378]

(Above) John Travolta, head shaved, with a large product placed gun in From Paris With Love.

Other times, the investors in movies are not large corporations but other large governments. Beijing has become a force to be reckoned with, as it has hundreds of millions of dollars invested in the main Hollywood companies, meaning that challenging films like *Seven Years in Tibet* and *Kundun* are no longer possible. While writing and casting *Doctor Strange* (2016), Marvel changed the character of The Ancient One from a Tibetan man to a Celtic woman, and cast British actress Tilda Swinton in the part, in an effort to avoid politicising the Tibetan issue.[379] During the remake of *Red Dawn* (2012), Beijing received a leaked script and complained. The script had China as the principle villain, invading the United States just as the Soviet Union had in the original 1984 film. The producers consequently spent a million dollars re-editing the movie to make the invaders North Korea. The effect? An already reactionary premise became ever more hysterical.

The most obvious and broader impact of product placement on Hollywood is that the value placed on artistic quality is further diminished. Peter Bart, editor in chief of industry magazine *Variety* recalls his experiences of making the decision to move a film project to the pre-production phase ('green-lighting'):

The green-light meeting, when I first started at Paramount, would consist of maybe three or four of us in a room. Perhaps two or three of us would have read the script under discussion. And people said stupid things like, 'I kind of like this movie.' Or, 'I look forward to seeing this movie.' Inane things like that. The green-light decision process today consists of maybe 30 or 40 people. There's one group there to discuss the marketing tie-ins. How much will McDonald's or Burger King put up? There's somebody else there to discuss merchandising toy companies and so forth. Someone else is there to discuss what the foreign co-financiers might be willing to put up. So, everyone is discussing the business aspects of this film. And it's sometimes unusual for someone actually to circle back and talk about the script, the cast, the package— whether the whole damn thing makes any sense to begin with.[380]

Bart goes on to explain that the movies now being made are those which 'appeal to the marketing and distribution team most of all. [They] have the heavy votes.' In some cases, large chunks of script are generated with the primary aim of selling products. Just as insidious, though, explains David Lancaster, 'a fog of fudge and compromise hangs over almost everything'[381] and the order of the day is happy endings, light entertainment and an absence of disturbing political narratives.

A relatively new type of product placement has arrived in Hollywood in the form of foreign governments subsidising production costs in exchange for large-scale promotions of their countries. The Abu Dhabi Film Commission offers a 30% rebate on all costs incurred by productions seeking to film in the emirate, a deal that some of the biggest movies including *Fast and Furious 7* and *Star Wars: The Force Awakens* have benefited from. The neighbouring emirate of Dubai tailors its rebates and incentives to each production, which drew the producers of *Star Trek Beyond* to spend a reported $32 million filming there. They benefited not only from a rebate but also what Jamal Al Sharif of the Dubai Film Commission called 'soft incentives,' including 'hotels, equipment, studios, location fees, police, civil defence, ambulance.' As well as priority customs waivers, 'Dubai customs had to search 11 tonnes of goods in 24 hours [and] scan them. You can't find this in any other country. 10,000 square feet of warehouses were filled up with boxes of props.'[382]

The most striking example of this sort of national product placement came in *Spectre*, when the government of Mexico struck a special $20 million deal with the producers outside of the usual rebates and recompense schemes. According to documents hacked from Sony Pictures, in return for their investment, the Mexican government requested several major changes to the opening sequence of the movie. These included that the first Bond girl in the movie be a 'known Mexican actress,' the initial villain 'cannot be Mexican,' the local governor be changed to an international figure, that the sequence last at least four minutes and showcase both 'modern Mexico City buildings' and the Mexican Special Police Force. While both the government and the studio denied that this was part of the deal, the resulting film incorporated all of these elements.

The economic penalties for not buying into this system can be serious. In 1997, Reebok sued Tristar Pictures, claiming it had reneged on its promise to feature its placement prominently in the "happy ending" scene of *Jerry Maguire*.[383] The parties settled out of court, purportedly for millions, and the Reebok advert was reinstated for the DVD.[384] In a similar case in 1990, Black & Decker settled a $150,000 lawsuit out of court over a promotion it had developed for a drill that Bruce Willis ended up not using in *Die Hard 2*.[385]

There was also the case of the cartoon movie, *Iron Giant* (1999), an unusually sensitive Cold War allegory, which was a box-office flop despite receiving a spectacular 97 per cent rating on rottentomatoes.com (a website which processes all available movie reviews from established critics). The main reason was that the film had been poorly marketed by Warner Bros.[386] Writer Tim McCanlies explained:

We had toy people and all of that kind of material ready to go, but all of that takes a year! Burger King and the like wanted to be involved. In April we showed them [Warner Bros] the movie, and we were on time. They said, 'You'll never be ready on time.' No, we were ready on time. We showed it to them in April and they said, 'We'll put it out in a couple of months.' That's a major studio, they have 30 movies a year, and they just throw them off the dock and see if they either sink or swim, because they've got the next one in right behind it. After they saw the reviews they [Warner Bros] were a little shamefaced.[387]

Others took away a more reductive lesson from *Iron Giant*. 'People always say to me, "why don't you make smarter movies?"' said Lorenzo di Bonaventura, Warner Bros' president of production at the time. 'The lesson is: every time you do, you get slaughtered.'[388]

It appears that the film industry has not learned the mistakes of the recent past. *Transformers: Age of Extinction* (2014) was the fourth in a franchise that has broken records for the amount of product placement it includes in its movies. However, it ended up being sued for $27.7 million by the state-backed Chinese tourism company Wulong Karst Tourism. The film was co-produced with the China Movie Channel and the second half was almost entirely filmed in China. Wulong's logo was supposed to be digitally inserted into this section of the movie but this never happened. Michael Bay filmed a commercial for the company and left behind the sets and props for them to use for promotional purposes but this did not placate them so they sued Paramount in a case deemed very important given the expectations that the Chinese box office will surpass the US market very soon.

A glimpse of a possible future has been offered by Jay May, president of a Los Angeles-based product placement agency, who sees the logical outcome of Hollywood's commercialisation emerging on DVDs, where 'All of a sudden, a bar code is going to pop up letting you know something in that scene is for sale, and you'll be able to buy it right off the screen.'[389] Perhaps such a sales device could include the cigarette brands smoked onscreen by the likes of Sylvester Stallone and Timothy '007' Dalton—for which they each pocketed hundreds of thousands of dollars.[390] Maybe Desert Eagle guns used extensively by Arnold Schwarzenegger in pictures like *Commando* (1985), *Last Action Hero* (1993) and *Eraser* (1996) will be available at the press of a button.[391] Or could it be that we will soon simply be able to touch our screens and buy a stake in the Boeing weapons systems credited in the *Iron Man* franchise?

This is not as absurd as it might sound. The Austrian gun manufacturer, Glock, includes in its annual glossy brochure a round-up of the films and TV shows featuring their weapons. The 2011 edition praised Angelina Jolie for her use of Glock handguns in *Mr and Mrs Smith,* and claimed, 'Any GLOCK aficionado worth their salt knows that when Angelina shares the scene with the Austrian super gun it's hard to know where to look!'[392] A year after the release of *Lone Survivor,* a story hit the press about how Beretta had paid $250,000 to have their gun in the hands of the eponymous hero. Brand-In Entertainment, a product placement specialist, boasted on their website of their role in making this happen while Brian Graves, owner of a gun supplier in Colorado, said, 'Movies sell guns. When a TV show is aired or a movie comes out, everyone wants to say, 'Well, punk, do you feel lucky?' Remember that Clint Eastwood did Westerns, and those firearms sell big time today. Each and every time a new movie comes out and the 'hero' uses his trusty firearm, it gets looked at and talked about.[393]

How powerful are advertisers in determining output? In 1994, Michael Moore pitched *TV Nation* (1994-95) to NBC as 'a cross between 60 Minutes and Fidel Castro on laughing gas.'[394] Moore's show planned satirised hot topics like gun ownership, war, and trade agreements. How would the mainstream media handle a show that was opposed to the national security state and broader establishment whilst simultaneously appealing to a wide audience?

Remarkably, NBC provided Moore with one million dollars to make a pilot show for TVN. On seeing the pilot, one executive asked another, 'Can we sell any advertising on this thing?' They decided to test the show with a focus group and then with an entire town, which was an unusually thorough move but successful: TVN was commissioned.[395]

However, in December 1995, after 17 episodes, the Fox network decided not to pick up its option for more episodes of the show. According to Moore, this was despite receiving more supportive letters from the public than they ever had for any show and protests outside several Fox affiliates.[396] By January 1997, the BBC had raised all of the necessary money for an eight-episode long third season of TVN, receiving funds from TV networks in five different countries (Canada, Australia, New Zealand, South Africa and France) but it never came to fruition.[397] *TVN* has never been released on DVD or online and it has not been re-run since the mid-1990s, though a short-lived sequel series, *The Awful Truth*, was picked up and funded by Channel 4 in the UK for a 1999-2000 run and shown on Bravo. [398]

Moore's experience in the film world is comparable to that of Oliver Stone and Paul Verhoeven. Disney made the release of his *Fahrenheit 911* (2004) difficult by telling its subsidiary, Miramax, not to distribute the film because it feared the political fallout. Disney denied claims that it ditched the film because Moore was challenging the interests of its parent company, which had links with the Bush and Saudi Royal families.[399] Subsequently, CBS, NBC and ABC all refused to advertise the DVD in between their news programming, which stunned the distributor Sony, according to an investigation by the *LA Weekly*.[400] Moore was booed off stage and called an 'asshole' after winning an Oscar, followed by a series of telephone death threats and a massive dump of manure on his home, escalating to gun and knife attacks on him and his family—prevented by his personal security.[401]

Occasionally, subversive films secure a presence on the American market but cannot rightly be characterised as Hollywood productions because much or all of the money comes from overseas, as with *V for Vendetta* (dystopian thriller), *The Ghost Writer* (Roman Polanski's skewering of a Tony Blair-like ex-Prime Minister), and *The Constant Gardener* (British neo-colonial activity in Africa). In the case of the latter two, they were given grants by the German government which did not need to be paid back. Steven Soderberg's sympathetic biography of Cuban Communist Che Guevara, *Che*, was a successful two-feature production but which was substantially funded and produced by French and Spanish companies, and then foreign pre-sales covered $54 million of the $58 million budget.[402]

As we have seen, some inescapably challenging narratives retain a subversive veneer but are watered down so they don't have enough potency to contribute to a more substantive media debate. Sometimes these products are compromised by the national security state itself (*Black Hawk Down, Charlie Wilson's War*) and other times they are compromised by the producers (*Munich*).

Some films are ideologically subversive but hide it behind generic conventions, particularly science fiction (*Starship Troopers, Total Recall, Robocop, Hunger Games*), even to the point where it has no political capital at all (*Avatar*).

Some dissenting films really have some studio backing, including the work of Oliver Stone, Michael Moore, and modest successes like *Thirteen Days*. Still, we've seen the backlash to these initiatives and the additional challenges they've faced.

A handful of American films have arguably made it through the system, attracting mainstream investors and box office returns, without suffering significant flak or amendments. These include *The East* (a sympathetic albeit critical portrayal of environmental activists), *The Insider* (a direct attack on tobacco companies), and *Lord of War* (a critical perspective on the arms trade). Following the Iraq War, there was also space for a short spate of films—*Fair Game, Green Zone, Syriana*—made in the context of the invasion, which had split real world elite opinion.

Overall, then, Hollywood is a broad church when it comes to politics. But it is still a church. Its architecture is longstanding and has deep foundations. Dissent exists but typically it is tepid, almost invariably ignored, and may be punished. The bishops are the heads of the media monopolies flanked by their national security clergymen. It is fitting that the word 'propaganda' stems from eighteenth century Catholicism, where the Cardinals 'propagated the faith.' Modern audiences are the new congregation, supplied with a constant diet of miracles and moonshine.

But our recommendation is not that Hollywood should be making more critical films. Some of our own favourite films are as far removed from politics as anyone can imagine. No—our concern is simply that there should be much less national security cinema.

How can this be best achieved? We don't believe in censorship, nor do we believe in bans. In a free but more accountable society, there are two reasonable reforms that should suit anyone who has nothing to hide: the government should be required by law to make their files on Hollywood cooperation open to the public and studios should explicitly declare any cooperation in the opening credits of their films, television shows, and videogames. We suspect that this would spell the end for national security entertainment, as viewers turn off material that they will recognise as propaganda much more readily. Until that day, with Hollywood as America's dream factory, we will continue to live and die in a military industrial nightmare.

Appendix A
DOD Supported Films 1911-2017 – 814 items (117 post-2004 items marked by #)

We compiled the following list using Lawrence Suid's books, documents obtained through FOIA requests, and searches on IMDB for movies filmed at military locations or that credited the DOD. A small number that do not appear in these sources are also included based on media reporting.

2 Guns (2013)#
20,000 Leagues Under the Sea (1954)
36 Hours (1964)
55 Men at Peking (1963)
A Bell For Adano (1945)
A Bridge Too Far (1977)
A Few Good Men (1992)
A Gathering Of Eagles (1963)
A Girl in Every Port (1928)
A Girl in Every Port (1951)
A Girl, a Guy, and a Gob (1941)
A Guy Named Joe (1943)
A Private's Affair (1959)
A Sailor-Made Man (1921)
A Soldiers' Gift (2015)#
A Soldier's Story (1984)
A Thousand Acres (1997)
A Ticklish Affair (1963)
A Time To Kill (1996)
A Yank in Korea (1951)
A.W.O.L. (2016)#
Above And Beyond (1952)
Above The Clouds (1933)
Ace Of Aces (1982)
Act Of Valor (2012)#
Action In The North Adventures in Iraq (1943)
Aerial Gunner (1943)
Afghan Knights (2007)#
Air Cadet (1951)
Air Devils (1938)
Air Force (1943)
Air Force One (1997)
Air Strike (1955)

Airport '75 (1974)
Airport '77 (1977)
All Hands On Deck (1961)
All The Young Men (1960)
Aloha (2015)#
Ambush Bay (1966)
America (1924)
American Guerrilla In The Philippines (1950)
An American Consul (1917)
An American Girl (2008)#
An Annapolis Story (1995)
An Officer and a Gentleman (1982)
Anchors Away (1945)
Angel's Flight (1965)
Annapolis (1928)
Annapolis (2006)#
Annapolis Farewell (1935)
Annapolis Salute (1937)
Antwone Fisher (2002)
Anzio (1968)
Apollo 13 (1995)
Armageddon (1998)
Armored Command (1961)
Army Surgeon (1942)
At War With the Army (1950)
Atlantic (1943)
Atlantic Convoy (1942)
Attack of the Jungle Women (1959)
Avatar (2009)#
Away All Boats (1956)
Baby Blue Marine (1976)
Back To Bataan (1945)
Bailout At 43,000 Feet (1957)
Bamboo Blonde (1946)

Bamboo Prison (1954)
Bamboo Saucer (1968)
Basic (2003)
Bat#21 (1988)
Bataan (1943)
Batman And Robin (1997)
Batman Vs Superman: Dawn Of
Justice (2016)#
Battle At Bloody Beach (1961)
Battle Beneath The Earth (1967)
Battle Circus (1953)
Battle Cry (1955)
Battle Cry of Peace (1915)
Battle Frame (1959)
Battle Ground (1949)
Battle Hymn (1956)
Battle Los Angeles (2011)#
Battle of Los Angeles (2011)#
Battle of The Coral Sea (1959)
Battle Stations (1956)
Battle Taxi (1955)
Battle Zone (1952)
Battleground (1949)
Battleship (2012)#
Beach Red (1967)
Beachhead (1954)
Beast of Budapest (1958)
Beginning of the End (1957)
Beginning or the End (1947)
Behind Enemy Lines (2001)
Behind the Front (1926)
Beneath The Flesh (2009)#
Best Years Of Our Lives (1946)
Between Heaven And Hell (1956)
Beyond Glory (1948)
Big Jim McLain (1952)
Big Miracle (2012)#
Biloxi Blues (1988)
Birdy (1984)
Birth Of A Nation (1915)
Black Hawk Down (2001)
Blockade (1929)
Blue Eagle (1926)
Bolshevism on Trial (1919)
Bombardier (1943)

Bombers B-52 (1957)
Breakthrough (1950)
Bridge Of Spies (2015)#
Bridge to the Sun (1961)
Bridge Too Far (1977)
Bridges at Toko-Ri (1954)
Brink of Hell (1956)
Broken Arrow (1996)
Brother Rat (1938)
Bruno (2008)#
Buck Privates (1941)
Buck Privates Come Home (1947)
Buffalo Soldiers (2001)
Bullets, Fangs and Dinner at 8
(2015)#
Bye Bye Birdie (1963)
Cadet Girl (1941)
Call Me Mister (1941)
Call out the Marines (1942)
Camp Nowhere (1994)
Captain America: The First
Avenger (2011)#
Captain America: The Winter
Soldier (2014)#
Captain Eddie (1945)
Captain Newman, M.D. (1963)
Captain Phillips (2013)#
Captured (1933)
Cat Run 2 (2014)#
Caught in the Draft (1941)
Cease Fire! (1953)
Chain Lightning (1950)
Change Of Heart (1934)
Classmates (1914)
Classmates (1924)
Clear And Present Danger (1994)
Clipped Wings (1937)
Clipped Wings (1953)
Closing The Ring (2007)#
Cock-Eyed World (1929)
Combat Squad (1953)
Come on Marines (1934)
Command Decision (1948)
Contact (1997)
Contagion (2008)#

Convoy (1927)
Corregidor (1943)
Counter Measures aka Crash Dive 2 (1998)
Courage of Lassie (1946)
Courage Under Fire (1996)
Court Martial Of Billy Mitchell (1955)
Crash Dive (1997)
Cry For Happy (1961)
Cry Havoc (1943)
Cutaway (2000)
D-Day The Sixth Of June (1956)
Darby's Rangers (1958)
Dave (1993)
Day After Tomorrow (2004)#
Day Of The Dead (1985)
Dear John (2010)#
Decision Before Dawn (1951)
Deep Impact (1998)
Deep Six (1958)
Deja Vu (2006)#
Destination Gobi (1953)
Destination Tokyo (1943)
Destiny (1944)
Destroyer (1943)
Devil Dogs Of The Air (1935)
Devil's Brigade (1968)
Devil's Playground (2010)#
Die Another Day (2002)
Dinosaur (2000)
Dirigible (1931)
Dirty Bomb (2012)#
Dive Bomber (1941)
Don't Cry. It's Only Thunder (1982)
Don't Give Up The Ship (1959)
Don't Go Near The Water (1957)
Dondi (1961)
Down Periscope (1996)
Draft 258 (1918)
Dragonfly Squadron (1954)
Dress Parade (1927)
Eagle Eye (2008)#
Easy Come, Easy Go (1967)
Electric Dreams (1984)

Elizabethtown (2005)#
Empire Of The Sun (1987)
End Of Watch (2012)#
Enemy Below (1957)
Ernest Saves Christmas (1988)
Escape from New York (1981)
Eternal Sea (1955)
Everybody Loves Whales (2012)#
Executive Decision (1996)
Expendable Assets (2016)#
Extraordinary Seaman (1969)
Face Of War (1968)
Fantastic Four 2 (2007)#
Father Goose (1964)
Ferris Bueller (1990)
Fighter Attack (1953)
Fighter Pilot: Op Red Flag (2004)#
Fighter Squadron (1948)
Fighting Coast Guard (1951)
Fighting Devil Dogs (1938)
Fighting Seabees (1944)
Final Analysis (1992)
Fire Birds (1990)
Firefox (1982)
First To Fight (1967)
First Yank into Tokyo (1945)
Fixed Bayonets (1951)
Flag Of My Father (2011)#
Flags Of Our Fathers (2007)#
Flat Top (1952)
Flight (2012)#
Flight Command (1940)
Flight Deck (1988)
Flight for Freedom (1943)
Flight From Ashiya (1964)
Flight Lieutenant (1942)
Flight Nurse (1953)
Flight Of The Intruder (1991)
Flight To Nowhere (1946)
Flirtation Walk (1934)
Fly Away Home (1981)
Flying Fleet (1929)
Flying Leathernecks (1951)
Flying Missile (1950)
Flying Tigers (1942)

Follow The Fleet (1936)
Force Of Arms (1951)
Forever Young (1992)
Fort Bliss (2014)#
Fort McCoy (2011)#
Four in a Jeep (1951)
Francis (1950)
Francis Goes To West Point (1952)
Francis in the Navy (1955)
Francis Joins The WACS (1954)
Fraulein (1958)
Freddy (1978)
Freezer Burn (2007)#
Frogmen (1951)
From Here To Eternity (1953)
Frost/Nixon (2008)#
Fury (2014)#
G.I. Joe: Rise Of Cobra (2009)#
Gallant Bess (1946)
Gallant Hours (1960)
Gardens Of Stone (1987)
Gathering Of Eagles (1963)
Geronimo (1939)
GI Blues (1960)
Giant (1956)
Girls Of Pleasure Island (1953)
Go For Broke (1951)
God Is My Co-Pilot (1945)
Godzilla (1998)
Godzilla (2014)#
Goldeneye (1995)
Goldfinger (1964)
Good Guys Wear Black (1978)
Good Kill (2014)#
Gray Lady Down (1978)
Guadalcanal Diary (1943)
Guarding Tess (1994)
Gung Ho (1986)
Hair (1979)
Halls Of Montezuma (1950)
Hamburger Hill (1987)
Hanoi Hilton (1987)
Heartbreak Ridge (1986)
Hearts And Minds (1974)
Hearts In Atlantis (2001)

Heaven Knows Mr Allison (1957)
Hell Below (1933)
Hell Divers (1931)
Hell Is For Heroes (1962)
Hell To Eternity (1960)
Hellcats Of The Navy (1957)
Hello Dolly (1969)
Hello Mr. Annapolis (1942)
Hell's Horizon (1955)
Her Man o' War (1926)
Here Come the Jets (1959)
Here Come the Marines (1952)
Here Come the Waves (1944)
Here Comes the Navy (1931)
Here Comes the Navy (1934)
Hero Of Submarine D-2 (1916)
Heroes (1977)
Heroes (2006)#
Hidden Figures (2016)#
High Barbaree (1947)
Hit the Deck (1930)
Hold 'Em Navy (1937)
Hold Back The Night (1956)
Hollywood Canteen (1944)
Home Alone 3 (1997)
Homecoming (1948)
Homer And Eddie (1989)
Honor Bound (1988)
House of Bamboo (1955)
How I Saved The President (1996)
I Aim At The Stars (1960)
I Am Legend (2007)#
I Wanted Wings (1941)
I Was a Male War Bride (1949)
I Was in an American Spy (1951)
Ice Station Zebra (1968)
In Country (1989)
In Enemy Country (1968)
In Harm's Way (1965)
In Love And War (1958)
In The Army Now (1994)
In The Line Of Fire (1993)
In the Meantime, Darling (1944)
In the Navy (1941)

In The Pursuit Of Happiness
(2010)#
Inchon (1981)
Independence Day: Resurgence
(2016)#
Indiana Jones And The Last
Crusade (1989)
Invaders from Mars (1953)
Invaders From Mars (1986)
Invasion USA (1985)
Iron Man (2008)#
Iron Man 2 (2010)#
Iron Triangle (1989)
Is Paris Burning? (1966)
Island in the Sky (1953)
It Came from Beneath the Sea
(1955)
It Started with a Kiss (1959)
Jackknife (1989)
Jet Attack (1958)
Jet Pilot (1957)
Joe Butterfly (1957)
Johanna Enlists (1918)
John Paul Jones (1959)
Johnny Handsome (1989)
Join the Marines (1937)
Judgment At Nuremberg (1961)
Judgment In Berlin (1988)
Jumping Jacks (1952)
Jungle Patrol (1948)
Jurassic Park III (2001)
Karate Kid II (1986)
Keep 'em Flying (1941)
Keep Your Powder Dry (1945)
Keep 'Em Rolling (1934)
Killing Fields (1984)
King Kong (1933)
King Kong (1976)
Kings Go Forth (1958)
Ladies Courageous (1944)
Larger Than Life (1996)
Last Action Hero (1993)
Leatherrnecking (1930)
Legends Of Flight (2010)#
Let it Rain (1927)

License To Kill (1989)
Lieutenant Danny, USA (1916)
Life Flight (2013)#
Little Mister Jim (1946)
Lone Star (1996)
Lone Survivor (2013)#
Love and Sacrifice (1924)
Lt. Robin Crusoe U.S.N. (1966)
Mac And Me (1988)
Macarthur (1977)
Madame Spy (1918)
Major Movie Star (2008)#
Man Of Steel (2013)#
Manchurian Candidate (1962)
March or Die (1977)
Marching On (1943)
Marine Raiders (1944)
Marines Come Through (1943)
Marines Fly High (1940)
Marines, Let's Go (1961)
Marines, Let's Go (1961)
Master and Commander (2003)
Matinee (1993)
Max (2015)#
McHale's Navy (1964)
McHale's Navy Joins the Air Force
(1965)
Megaforce (1982)
Megan Leavey (2017)#
Memorial Day (2012)#
Men Of Honour (2000)
Men Of The Fighting Lady (1954)
Men Without Women (1930)
Merrill's Marauders (1962)
Midshipman (1925)
Midshipman Jack (1933)
Midway (1976)
Mike (1926)
Military Air Scout (1911)
Minesweeper (1943)
Miss Sadie Thompson (1953)
Mission over Korea (1953)
Mission: Impossible (1996)
Mission: Impossible 2 (2000)
Mister Roberts (1955)

Moneyball (2011)#
Moon Pilot (1962)
Moran of the Marines (1928)
Mr. Winkle Goes to War (1944)
Murder in the Fleet (1935)
Mystery Submarine (1950)
Mystic Nights & Pirate Fights (1998)
Naked And The Dead (1958)
Navy Blue And Gold (1937)
Navy Blues (1937)
Navy Blues (1941)
Navy Born (1936)
Navy Bound (1951)
Navy SEALs (1990)
Navy Secrets (1939)
Navy Spy (1937)
Navy Wife (1936)
No Man Is An Island (1962)
No Man's Land (1918)
Nobody's Perfect (1968)
None But The Brave (1965)
Northfork (2003)
Not with My Wife, You Don't (1966)
Nowhere Safe (2005)#
Objective, Burma! (1945)
Off Limits (1953)
Okinawa (1952)
Old Ironsides (1926)
On the Beach (1959)
On the Double (1961)
On The Threshold of Space (1956)
On the Town (1949)
One Man's War (1991)
One Minute To Zero (1952)
Onionhead (1949)
Operation Haylift (1950)
Operation Mad Bull (1957)
Operation Pacific (1951)
Operation Petticoat (1959)
Over the Top (1918)
Over There (2018)#
Pacific Rim (2013)#
Panama Hattie (1942)

Parachute Battalion (1941)
Parachute Nurse (1942)
Parrish (1961)
Patent Leather Kid (1927)
Patriot Games (1992)
Patton (1970)
Pearl Harbor (2001)
Pet Sematary (1989)
Pilot No. 5 (1943)
Pirates Of The Caribbean: On Stranger Tides (2011)#
Pork Chop Hill (1959)
Presidio (1988)
Pride of the Marines (1936)
Pride Of The Marines (1945)
Pride of the Navy (1939)
Prince of Tides (1991)
Prisoner Of War (1954)
PT-109 (1963)
Purple Heart Diary (1957)
Purple Hearts (1984)
Quicksands (1923)
Race To Space (2001)
Rain (1932)
Raise The Titanic (1980)
Random Hearts (1999)
Red Ball Express (1952)
Red Bull Express (1952)
Red Dawn (1984)
Reel Steel (2011)#
Remember Pearl Harbor (1942)
Renaissance Man (1994)
Retreat! Hell (1952)
Retreat, Hell! (1952)
Ride With The Devil (1999)
Robot Jox (1989)
Rockets Red Glare' (2000)
Rookies (1927)
Rules Of Engagement (2000)
Run Silent, Run Deep (1958)
Running Brave (1983)
Russkies (1987)
Sabotage (2014)#
Sabre Jet (1953)
Safe House (2012)#

Sahara (1943)
Sailor Beware (1951)
Sailors on Leave (1941)
Sailor's Lady (1940)
Sailor's Luck (1933)
Salute (1929)
Salute to the Marines (1943)
San Andreas (2015)#
San Francisco (1936)
Sands Of Iwo Jima (1949)
Saved from the Harem (1915)
Saving Private Ryan (1998)
Sayonara (1957)
Screaming Eagles (1956)
See Here, Private Hargrove (1944)
Serbian Scars (2009)#
Sergeant Mike (1945)
Sergeant Murphy (1937)
Sergeant York (1941)
Seven Days in May (1964)
Seven Sinners (1940)
Sharkfighters (1956)
Shining Through (1992)
Shipmates (1931)
Shipmates Forever (1935)
Show Of Force (1990)
Skirts Ahoy! (1952)
Sky Commando (1953)
Sky Devils (1932)
Slattery's Hurricane (1949)
Sleepless In Seattle (1993)
So Proudly We Hail (1943)
Soldiers in the Rain (1963)
Somebody Up There Likes Me (1956)
Son of a Sailor (1933)
Sound Off (1952)
South Pacific (1958)
Southern Comfort (1981)
Space Command (2016)#
Spare Parts (2015)#
Sphere (1998)
Stage Door Canteen (1943)
Stalug 17 (1953)
Stand By for Action (1942)

Star Spangled Banner (1917)
Star Spangled Banner (2013)#
Star Trek IV (1986)
Star Trek: First Contact (1996)
Star Trek: Insurrection (1998)
Starlift (1951)
Stars and Stripes Forever (1952)
Stealth (2005)#
Steel Helmet (1951)
Story Of G.I. Joe (1945)
Strategic Air Command (1955)
Stripes (1981)
Subconscious (2015)#
Submarine (1928)
Submarine Command (1951)
Submarine D-I (1937)
Submarine Patrol (1938)
Submarine Pirate (1915)
Submarine Raider (1942)
Suicide Fleet (1931)
Suicide Squad (2016)#
Sully (2016)#
Sum Of All Fears (2002)
Sunday Dinner for a Soldier (1944)
Surrender – Hell! (1959)
Swing Shift (1984)
Take The High Ground (1953)
Taken By Force (2010)#
Tank (1984)
Tank Commandos (1959)
Tanks a Million (1941)
Taps (1981)
Tarawa Beachhead (1958)
Target Earth (1954)
Target Unknown (1951)
Target Zero (1955)
Task Force (1949)
Tears Of The Sun (2003)
Tell it to the Marines (1926)
Telling the World (1928)
Teresa (1951)
Terminator 3: Rise Of The Machines (2003)
Terminator: Genisys (2015)#
Terminator: Salvation (2009)#

Test Pilot (1938)
Thank You For Your Service (2015)#
The A-Team (2010)#
The American President (1995)
The Andromeda Strain (1971)
The Angry Red Planet (1959)
The Avengers (2012)#
The Battle of the River Plate (1956)
The Bear (2010)#
The Big Lift (1950)
The Big Parade (1925)
The Bob Mathias Story (1948)
The Bridges At Toko Ri (1954)
The Bugle Sounds (1941)
The Caine Mutiny (1954)
The Cantebury Tale (1944)
The Client (1994)
The Core (2003)
The D.I (1957)
The D.I. (1957)
The Day The Earth Stood Still (1951)
The Day The Earth Stood Still (2008)#
The Deadly Mantis (1957)
The Dry Land (2010)#
The Fighting Roosevelts (1919)
The Fighting Seabees (1944)
The Fighting Sullivans (1944)
The Final Countdown (1980)
The Finest Hour (1991)
The Finest Hours (2016)#
The Five Year Engagement (2012)#
The Fleet's In (1942)
The Fleet's In (1928)
The Flight (1929)
The Flying Fleet (1929)
The Flying Marine (1929)
The Flying Missile (1950)
The Force Beyond (1977)
The Gentlemen from West Point (1942)
The Girl He Left Behind (1956)

The Glenn Miller Story (1954)
The Glory Brigade (1953)
The Great Escape (1963)
The Great Impostor (1961)
The Great Mail Robbery (1927)
The Great Raid (2005)#
The Great Santini (1979)
The Green Berets (1968)
The Green Dragon (2001)
The Guardian (2006)#
The Happiest Millionaire (1967)
The Haunting Of Sarah Hardy (1989)
The Hindenburg (1975)
The Hulk (2003)
The Hunt For Red October (1990)
The Hunters (1958)
The Incredible Mr. Limpet (1964)
The Innocent (1993)
The Invisible War (2013)#
The Jackal (1997)
The Last Full Measure (forthcoming)#
The Last Plane Out (1983)
The Last Time I Saw Archie (1961)
The Leathernecks Have Landed (1936)
The Lieutenant Wore Skirts (1956)
The Long Gray Line (1955)
The Longest Day (1962)
The Lost Battalion (1919)
The Lost Missile (1958)
The Lucifer Complex (1978)
The Lucky One (2012)#
The Lucky Ones (2008)#
The Marines Are Here (1938)
The McConnell Story (1955)
The Men (1950)
The Messenger (2009)#
The Mountain Road (1960)
The Mummy (2017)#
The Navy Comes Through (1942)
The Navy Way (1944)
The Net (1995)
The Next Karate Kid (1994)

The November Men (1993)
The Outsider (1961)
The Package (1989)
The Perez Family (1995)
The Perfect Furlough (1958)
The Perfect Storm (2000)
The Pigeon that Took Rome (1962)
The Private Navy of Sgt. O'Farrell (1968)
The Private War of Major Benson (1955)
The Proud and the Profane (1956)
The Rack (1956)
The Right Stuff (1983)
The Rocketeer (1991)
The Russians are Coming, the Russians are Coming (1966)
The Sad Sack (1957)
The Search (1948)
The Seas Beneath (1931)
The Shepherd (2008)#
The Silence Of The Lambs (1991)
The Singing Marine (1937)
The Sky's the Limit (1943)
The Sound of Music (1965)
The Spirit of St Louis (1957)
The Spirit of West Point (1947)
The Starfighters (1964)
The Story of Dr. Wassell (1944)
The Story of GI Joe (1945)
The Sullivans (1944)
The Swarm (1978)
The Tanks are Coming (1951)
The Thousand Plane Raid (1969)
The Treehouse of the August Moon (1956)
The Tuskegee Airmen (1995)
The Ultimate Solution Of Grace Quigley (1984)
The Unbeliever (1918)
The Unknown Soldier (1926)
The Visiting (2007)#
The Wackiest Ship in the Army (1960)
The War Loves (1962)

The West Point Story (1950)
The Wild Blue Yonder (1951)
The Wings of Eagles (1957)
The Young Lions (1958)
Them! (1954)
They Went That-a-Way and That-a-Way (1978)
They were Expendable (1945)
Thirteen Days (2001)
Thirty Days over Tokyo (1944)
Thirty Seconds Over Tokyo (1944)
This is the Army (1943)
This Man's Navy (1945)
Three Brave Men (1957)
Three Day Pass (1968)
Three Stripes in the Sun (1955)
Three Wishes (1995)
Thunder Afloat (1939)
Thunder Birds (1942)
Thunderball (1965)
Thunderbirds (1952)
Thundering Jets (1958)
Till the End of Time (1946)
Time Limit (1957)
To Hell and Back (1955)
To the Shores of Hell (1965)
To The Shores Of Tripoli (1942)
Tobruk (1967)
Tokyo Joe (1949)
Tomorrow Never Dies (1997)
Top Gun (1986)
Top Sergeant (1942)
Top Sergeant Mulligan (1941)
Tora! Tora! Tora! (1970)
Torpedo Alley (1952)
Torpedo Run (1958)
Touchdown Army (1938)
Toward the Unknown (1956)
Towering Inferno (1974)
Toy Soldiers (1991)
Transformers (2007)#
Transformers Dark Of The Moon (2009)#
Transformers: Revenge Of The Fallen (2011)#

Transformers: The Last Knight (2017)#
Tropic Thunder (2008)#
True Lies (1994)
Tugger (2005)#
Turkey Shoot (2014)#
Twelve O'Clock High (1949)
Twister (1996)
Twister's Revenge (1988)
U-Boat Prisoner (1944)
Unaccompanied Minors (2006)#
Unbroken (2014)#
Under Seige (1992)
Underwater Warrior (1958)
United 93 (2006)#
Unsung Heroes (1978)
Up Front (1951)
Up Periscope (1959)
USS Indianapolis: Men of Courage (2016)#
Verboten! (1959)
Via Wireless (1915)
Waiting For The Light (1990)
Wake Island (1942)
Walk In The Sun (1945)
War Dogs (1942)
War for the Planet of the Apes (2017)#
War of The Worlds (1952)
War of The Worlds (2005)#
Warrior (2011)#
We Were Soldiers (2002)
West Point (1928)
West Point of the Air (1935)

West Point Widow (1941)
We're in the Navy Now (1926)
We've Never Been Licked (1943)
What Am I Bid? (1967)
What Price Glory (1926)
What Price Glory (1952)
When Willie Comes Marching Home (1950)
Whiskey Tango Foxtrot (2016)#
Who'll Stop the Rain (1978)
Why America Will Win (1918)
Why Sailors Go Wrong (1928)
Wild America (1997)
Windjammer (1958)
Windtalkers (2002)
Wing And A Prayer (1944)
Winged Victory (1944)
Wings (1927)
Wings for the Eagle (1942)
Wings Of Eagles (1957)
Wings of the Navy (1939)
Wings over Honolulu (1937)
Wings over the Pacific (1943)
Winslow of the Navy (1942)
Womanhood, the Glory of the Nation (1917)
Women of all Nations (1931)
WWZ (2013)#
X-15 (1961)
You Came Along (1945)
You're in the Army Now (1941)
You're in the Navy Now (1951)

Appendix B.
DOD sponsored TV – All time (1133 items) (977 items between 2004 and 2017; 156 pre-2004 marked by *)

1 vs. 100

1,000 Men And A Baby*

10 Things you Didn't Know

10 Years of Terror

10.5 The Apocalypse

100 Women, 100 Years

101 Foods That Changed History

101 Foods That Changed the World

101 Gadgets that Changed the World

101 Weapons that Changed the World

10th Mountain Division

12 O'Clock High*

2056

21st Century Warrior

24

30 for 30

3rd Degree*

442

4th and Long

65th Anniversary of the Atomic Age

700 Club

7th Heaven*

82nd Airborne in Afghanistan

A Beautiful Resistance

A Bright Shining Lie*

A Call to Arms

A Company of Soldiers

A Conception Story

A Fight for the Troops

A Football Life – The Forward Pass

A Grateful Nation

A Hero's Welcome

A Rockport Christmas*

A Soldier's Gift

A Soldier's Long Journey Home

A Time To Triumph*

A Tour of the Inferno: Revisiting Platoon*

A War That Never Ends – Day of Discovery

Above And Beyond

Acceptable Levels

Adapting to Extreme Weather

Aerial America

Afghan Dreams

Afghanistan: 10 Years On

Afghanistan: The Surge

Aftermath*

Air Crash Investigation

Air Warriors

Airpower Vietnam, The Real Top Gun*

AirShow

Al Qaida

Alaska Mega Machine

Alcoa Premiere*

Alex Reid: The Fight For His Life

Alien Sharks: Close Encounters

All The Unsung Heroes*

All-Star Salute To Our Troops*

Almost Sunrise

Alpha Dogs

Altered Course

Alternative History

Amazing Race America

America Post 9/11

America Revealed

America United: In Support of Our Troops

America, You're Too Young To Die*

America: The Price of Peace

America: The Story of Us

American Axe

American Birthright

American Chopper

American Couples

American Experience

American Federale

American Giving Awards

American Gladiators

American Heroes

American Idol

American Lives

American Ninja Challenge

American Ninja Warrior

American Ride

American Rifleman

American Soldier

American Truckers

American Valor*
American Warriors
America's Got Talent
America's Most Secret
America's Most Wanted
America's Next Top Model
An Officer and a Movie
Anatomy of a Stryker
Ancient Aliens
Ancient Superweapons
Animal Planet (Virus Hunters)
Apache War Machine
Aquaman
Arlington
Arlington National Cemetery
Army Elite
Army Wives
Army Wives of Alaska
Army/Navy Game
Army/Navy Pregame Show.
Army's Drill Sgt. Of the Year Competition
Around the World
Around the World in 60 minutes
Artificial Reefs
Asteroid
Attack of the Show
Auction Hunters
Automotivation Garage
Avalon*
Aviators
AWOL
Babies: Special Delivery
Back From Iraq

Baggage Battles
Baghdad ER
Baker Boys: Inside the Surge
Ball Up
Bama Belles
Band of Brides
Band of Brothers: One Year in Iraq with the 101st Airborne
Bang for the Buck
Barrett Firearms
Barrett: A .50 Caliber Family
Bataan
Bathroom Crashers
Battle for Marjah
Battle Gear
Battle Lab
Battle of Verdun and General Phillippe Petain
Battle Xross
Battlefield Detectives .- Big Hole
Battlefield Diaries
Battlefield O.R.
Battlefield Priests
Battleground
Baywatch*
Bear in the House
Behind the Scenes
BeLIEve
Best of the Best
Best Ranger 2006
Best Ranger Competition
Best Ranger: The World's Toughest Competition
Best Warrior Competition
BET Awards

Beverly Hills, 90210*
Beyond Scared Straight
Beyond the Border
Beyond The Diamond
Beyond the Glory
Beyond the Lightswitch
Beyond Tomorrow
Big Bang
Big Food
Big Kitchens
Big Picture
Big Smo
Bigger, Higher, Faster
Biggest Loser
Bill Mauldin
Billy Graham Special
Biography
Black Ops Garage
Black Wings
Bletchley Park: Code-Breaking's Forgotten Genius
Blood Road
Blood We Shed
Blood, Sweat, and Code
Bob Dole – A Great American
Bob Hoover Salute
Bomb Hunters
Bomb Patrol
Bomber's Dream
Bombshell: The Hedy Lamarr Story
Bones
Boneyard
Boneyard 2
Bonnie Hunt Show
Border Wars

Born Fighting Documentary

Bound for Glory

Brad Meltzer's Decoded

Brats*

Brave New World with Stephen Hawking

Bravo Company

Breakfast, Lunch and Dinner

Breaking the Maya Code

Breakthrough with Tony Robbins

Bridging the Gap

Bridging Urban America

Bringing Home The Fallen

British versus American Army

Britney Spears Live from Las Vegas*

Brothers at War

Brush of Honor

Building the Bionic Body

Building Wild

Built to Shred

Buying Alaska

C-Span – America: The Price of Peace

Cake Boss

California Connected

California's Gold

Camp Hope: Children of 9.11

Camp Leatherneck

Candy Queen

Canine Soldiers

Cantore Stories

Captain Skyhawk*

Capture of Al Zarqawi

Capture of Hussein

Capturing the Universe

Car Science

Carbon Nation

Career Day

Catch 21

Celebrities in Uniform

Celebrity Boot Camp*

Celebrity Sweat

Chain of Adventure

Change of Heart

Chaplains

Cheers*

Chicago

Chicago Hope*

Chips, The War Dog*

Chopped

Citizen Soldiers

City Gridiron

Class 186: Making of a Marine Officer

Class 186: The Making of a Marine Officer

Close Comabat: First to Fight

CMT in Iraq

CMT Outlaws

CMT's Next Superstar

Coach Carter

Coast Guard Alaska

Code 3*

Cold Case

College Hill

Columbo*

Comanche

Combat Camera

Combat Hospital

Combat Medic Challenge

Combat Tech

Coming Home

Command And Control

Commander In Chief

Commanders and Coaches

Common Threads: Stories from the Quilt*

Concert for Valor

Cookie Commandos

Cool School

Counter-Insurgency

Counting Cars

Country Music Association (CMA)

Country Christmas Special

Country Music Awards

Covert Action*

Craig Morton: Salute to Our Troops

Crash Course: US History

Crash Landing: The Rescue Of Flight 232*

Crisis

Criss Angel Mindfreak

CRL

CrossFit Workout of the Day

Crusade in the Pacific*

Cupcake Wars

Curiosity: The Questions of Life

Custer's Last Stand

D-Day Laid Bare

Daily Planet – JLENS System Test

Dale Con Ganas

Dancing with the Stars

Dangerous Encounters

Daughters Of The Dust*

Dave Does

David Letterman Show

Daytime Emmy's

Deadly Depths

Deal Or No Deal

Dear Santa

Death Row Stories

Declassified

Decoded

Deep Dive

Deep Encounter*

Defectors

Defending America

Design Star

Designing Women*

Diary of Facebook

Dickens in America

DietTribe

Digging the Great Escape

Dinner Impossible

Dirtwater Dynasty*

Dirty Bomb

Dirty Dozen*

Dirty Jobs

Disaster At Silo 7*

Discovery Channel

Canada: Mega World

Dispatches: America's

Serial Killers

Dixie Divas

Do We Really Need the

Moon?

Docere Palace.

Dog First Aid

Dog X

Dogfights

Don't Forget the Lyrics

Down the Aisle in Style

Drill Sergeant in the

House

Drill Sergeant School

Drug Wars-Columbia*

Ducks Unlimited

Dust Off

Ears, Open. Eyeballs,

Click.

Earth – The Operators'

Manual

Earth: The Climate Wars

Earth: The Power of the

Planet

Eisenhower: A Place in

History*

Ellen

Embrace Your Design

Emeril Live

Emeril's Green Planet

Engaged and Enlisted

Engaged and Underage

Engineering Alaska

Enlisted

Enola Gay*

Enough Already! with

Peter Walsh

ER

Escape From Alcatraz

Espionage

ESPN Boxing Telecast

ESPN Fight Night

ESPN Game Day

ESPN Sports Center

ESPN Veteran's Day Live

Broadcast

ESPN: Outdoors Visit to

Afghanistan

Everwood

Everyday Things

Exercise Tiger

Exercising the Real:

Immersion

Extraordinary Acts of

Courage

Extraordinary Dogs

Extreme Chef

Extreme Engineering:

Really Big Things

Extreme Laboratories

Extreme Makeover

Extreme Makeover: Home

Edition

Extreme Makeover:

Weight Loss Edition

Eyewitness War

F-15 First Family of

Fighters

Fabulous Cakes

Face Behind The File

Facing

Fact or Faked: Paranormal

Files

Faith of my Fathers

Faking It

Family Flight*

Family Of Spies*

Fantasy Huddle

Fathom

FBI's Ten Most Wanted

Female Engagement Team

Female Veterans on the

Long Journey Home

Fight for Freedom

Fighting Season: Soldier

Story

Fightzone Present: Pure

Combat

Final Report: Mogadishu

Finder Of Lost Loves*
Fireball of Tutankhamen
Fireball Run
First Command
First in Battle: The Black Panthers of World War II
First Take
First Take Salutes America's Heroes
Fishing Behind the Lines
Fix It Finish It
Flight 93
Flip My Food with Chef Jeff
Fly Away Home*
Fly Fishing Top-2-Bottom
Flying Misfits*
Follow the Honey
Food Court War
Forensic Files
Forgotten Flag Raisers
Forgotten Planet
Fort Knox
Fort Lee Culinary Competition
Fort Monmouth: Unexpected History
Freedom: More Than Just a Word
From Combat to The Classroom
From Earth To The Moon*
Frontline
Frontline Battle Machines
Frontline Medicine
Fuerzas Comando 2011
Fuerzas Comando 2012
Fully Charged

Future Fight
Future Tech
Future Weapons
Galileo Magazine
Gene Simmons Family Jewels
Generals of the North and South
Generation Next
George To The Rescue
George Washington*
German engineering in WWII
Gettysburg
Ghost Hunters
Ghost Lab
GI Factory
GI Hollywood
Glory Hounds
Go Back Where You Came From
Going Home
Golden Gate*
Good Morning America
Grateful Nation
Great American Railroad Journeys
Great Planes
Greatest Ever
Grey Berets
Grey's Anatomy
Gun Gurus
GunnyTime with R. Lee Ermey
Guys Choice Awards
Haiti One
Halfway Home
Hardcore Heroes: John Stapp

Harry Hopkins: A Biography*
Hart To Hart*
Have Cake, Will Travel
Haven
Hawaii Five-0 (reboot)
Hawaii Five-O (original)*
Hawaii Undiscovered
HawthoRNe
Heaven and Hell*
Heavy Metal Taskforce
Hell Below
Hellfire Missile
Hell's Kitchen
Heroes Of Desert Storm*
High Ground
Highway to Heaven*
Hire Heroes
Hiring America
Hiroshima*
History and Future of Nuclear Power
History Center
History Detectives
History Of Alaska
History of Explosives
History of Interrogation
History of Religion
History of the 75th Ranger Regiment
History of the National Guard
History Rocks
History vs Hollywood*
Hitler's GI Death Camp
Holiday Facts & Fun: Veterans Day
Home & Family
Home Free

Home Front
Home Front: Texas in WWII
Home Improvement*
Homecoming
Homecoming Salute
Homefront
Homeland
Hometown Hero Challenge
Honor's War
Horizon
Hornet's Nest
Hot 20 Countdown
House Hunters
House Hunters International
How Do I Look?
How Do They Do It
How the States Got Their Shapes
How Things Work
How to Look Good Naked
How to Stay Young
How We Invented the World
Hungry Men at Work
Hunt for Osama Bin Laden
Hunt in Corsicana
Hunt Masters
Hurricane Hunters
Hurricanes*
I Forgive You
I Fought For You
I Spy
Ice Bound
Ice Road Truckers
Illegal immigration

Impossible Routes
In Dogs We Trust
In Love And War*
In The Line Of Duty*
Indiana Reserve Soldiers in Iraq
Ink Masters
Inside Afghanistan
Inside Combat Rescue
Inside Marine Special Operations
Inside Operations
Inside the Afghanistan War
Inside the White House*
Inside West Coast Customs
Inspector Mom
Insurgency
International Sniper Competition
Intersection
Intersections
Invasion
Iraq battles
Iron Chef
Iron Chef America
Ironclads
Island Soldiers
Iwo Jima: From Combat to Comrades
I'm Alive
I'm Alive: Ambushed
James May at the Edge of Space
James May on the Moon
Jay Leno's Garage
Jay Leno's Tonight Show
Jeopardy!

Jeremy Nelson Watershed
Jeremy's Egg*
Jesse James in Iraq
Jesse James is a Dead Man
JFK Plaza
Jim Zumbo Outdoors
Jimi Hendrix, the Nashville Years
John Basilone: The Legacy of A Hero
Journey to Normal
Judge Hatchett
Jump Rope
K-9 Pride
Kansas City S.W.A.T
Kathy Griffin: My Life on the D-List
Kevin Hill
Kicking and Screaming
Killing Lincoln-Inside the Conspirator
Kissimmee Basin Documentary
Known Universe
Korea: Remembering The Forgotten War*
Korengal
LASIK: The Right Stuff
Last Party 2000*
Law and Order: Los Angeles
LBJ*
Legacy of Patriotism and Valor
Let's Ask America
Life After People

Life And Times Of World Famous Test Pilot Bob Hoover

Life Flight

Life is Great

Life of Dogs

Lingo

Lions of Babylon

Live Fire

Living in La La Land

Loan Survivors

Lock and Load

Long Lost Family

Longhorn Army Ammunition Plant

Looking for America

Looking for Love

Lost

Louie

Louisiana Maneuvers

lraq Wars

lraq: Frontline ER

Luxury Unveiled

Made

MadLab

Magic Man

Magnum PI*

Mail Call

Major Dad*

Major League Soccer

Make Peace or Die

Makers: Women In War

Making of the Band

Making Stuff

Making Things Smarter

Man vs. Food

Man vs. Wild

Man, Moment, Machine

Manhunt

Margaret Bourke-White*

Marine Battlehercs

Marine K-9

Marines in the South Pacific

Marines: First to Fight

Married to the Army – Alaska

Martha Stewart Show

Mary Surratt

Massive Nature

Master Chef

Medal of Honor

Medical investigation

Medium

Memorial Day Show

Memories of 1970-1991*

Men of Honor

Mending Fences

Mental Valor

Meteorite Men

MEU

Microkillers

Mighty Planes

Mighty Ships

Mile High Militia

Military Chef

Military Heroes

Military History of Arizona and Arizonans

Military Medicine

Military Miracles

Military of the Future

Military Top Tens

Military Women

Military Working Dogs

Military's Toughest Jobs

Milton Friedman

Mind Zone: Therapists Behind the Front Lines

Minute To Win It

Miracle Landing*

Miss America Pageant

Miss America Pageant Parade

Mission Impossible*

Modern Marvels

Modern Sniper

Mojave Viper

Monk

Monster Garage

Montel Williams Show

Montgomery Gentry concert.

Monument Guys

Monumental Mysteries

Most Shocking Love Stories

Motor Trend

Moving the Heaviest Metal

MTV News

MTV True Life

MTV's Coming Home

My Country, My Country

My Life

My Live on the D-List

My Mother: Ethel Kennedy

Mysteries at the Museum

Mythbusters

N.A.S. Emerald Point*

Naked Science

Nashville

Nashville Cupcakes

Natural Disasters

Navy Log*

Nazi Collaborators

NCIS

NCIS - Investigation

NCIS: LA

Need to Know

New Family Feud*

New Year's Eve

Newark Riots

Newlyweds: Nick and Jessica

Nic Mom

Night Fire

No Greater Love

None More American

North America

North Shore

North to the Future

Nova

Now

Nowhere Safe

Nuclear Race

Numbers

NYPD Blues

Obese

Occupation Dreamland

Off Limits

On Target

On the Road with Austin & Santino

One Day, Three Ways

One Man Army

One Nation Under Ground

One Night on Earth

One Step Beyond

One Tree Hill

Only in America

Only in America with Larry the Cable Guy

Op Center*

Operation El Dorado Canyon*

Operation Flintlock

Operation Hardwood

Operation Homecoming

Operation Hope

Operation Infrastructure

Operation Viking Hammer

Oprah Winfrey Show

Oprah: Where Are They Now

Oprah's Favourite Things

Orange County Choppers

Osborne Family Variety Show

Our House*

Our Vietnam Generation

Outfitter

Outrageous Foods

Outside the Wire: Through the Eyes of a Soldier

Over There

Overcoming Obstacles- Treating Your Diabetes

Overkill

Owner's Manual

P.O.W.--Americans In Enemy Hands: WWII, Korea, And Vietnam*

Pain Management

Pancho Barnes*

Parris Island: We Make Marines

Party Planner with David Tutera

Patrol Base Jaker

Penn and Teller's Secrets of the Universe

Pennsylvania National Guard PSA

Pensacola Wings Of Gold*

Perfect Crime

PGA Reach

Photography During Wartime

Picatinny Arsenal

Pioneers in Skirts

Pioneers of Television

Pit Bulls and Parolees

Piñon Canyon Maneuver Site

Plane Spotting

Planes of War

Polka Kings

Powerblock

Praise

Preserve, Protect, and Defend

Presidential Leadership

Price for Peace

Prison Break

Private Chefs

Private Contentment*

Profiles in Caring

Project Blue Coral

Pro's Versus Joes

PTSD documentary

Puller: Adventures Of The Last American Hero*

Pulp Fiction: The Golden Age of Storytelling

Punch List Olympics

Purple Heart

Purple Heart Stories

Quantum Leap*

Queen Latifah

Race Against Winter*
Rachel Ray
Raging Planet*
Raiders
Rain*
Raw War
Real Heroes
Real NCIS
Reality Revealed: Boot Camp
Realtree Roadtrips
Rebuilding the Connection with Canadians
Recon Challenge
Red White and New
Regenerative Medicine
Regenesis
Reporting Under Fire
Requiem
Rescue
Restaurant Impossible
Resting Place*
RESTREPO
Return Of The Six-Million-Dollar Man And The Bionic Woman*
Return to Iwo Jima
Reunion*
Revolutionary War
Richard Hammond's Crash Course
Richard Hammond's Miracles of Nature
Richard Hammond's Invisible Worlds
Richard Reeves on the Kennedy Presidency

Riddles in Stone: The Secret Architecture of Washington, D.C.
Road Crew
Robby Gordon and the Troops
Robert Kennedy And His Times*
Robots: AI and the Future of a Mechanical Species
Robowars
Rockin' the Corps: An American Thank You
Route 66 – Along The Mother Road
Sabrina the Teenage Witch*
Sabu: The Elephant Boy*
Sandhurst Games
Save Our History
Saving Heroes
Saving Jessica Lynch*
Saving Private K-9
Say Yes to the Dress
Sayonara, Daddy-san
Sci Fi Science: Physics of the Impossible – Holodeck
Science of Star Wars
SEAL Dog
Search & Restore
Seconds To Disaster
Secret Access
Secret History: The Roswell Incident*
Secret Iraq
Secret Pakistan
Secrets Of The Arsenal
See Jane Win
Separate But Equal*

Set for Life
Shok Valley
Shoot Out
Shoot the Hero
Shooting USA
Shooting War*
Shoulder to Shoulder
Showdown
Simon And Simon*
Sleeper Cell
Small Town Boy
Sniper School: Only in America
Sniper: Bulletproof
Sniper: Deadliest Mission
Sniper: Inside the Crosshairs
Sniper: The Unseen Warrior
Snoop Dogg's Father Hood
So You Think You Can Dance
Soldier Girl*
Somebody's Gotta Do It
Sons of Guns
Souvenirs
Space Command
Space Flight
Space Junk
Space*
Spotlight on Women in Helicopter Aviation
Spring Training with the Troops
Star Wars Technology
Star-Spangled Children
Stargate SG-1*
Stargate Universe

213

Stargate: Atlantis
Stargate: Continuum
Stargazing Live
Stars Earn Stripes
State of Affairs
Steve Canyon*
Steve Harvey Show
Storm Stories
Strictest parents
Strike Fighters
Strike Group
Strip The Cosmos
Summer Colony
Super Planes
Superbowl Fox Sports
Supercarrier*
SuperNanny
Supervolcano
Surprise Homecoming
Surviving Disaster
Surviving Families
Helping Others
Surviving the Cut
Survivor
Swamp Loggers
Sworn to Secrecy: Secrets
of Warriors*
Tactical Arms
Taking Chance
Tale of Two Systems
Tangier: The Disappearing
Island
Tank Battalion
TapouT
Teen Idol
Telephone Time*
Temps Present
Terminal
Test Pilot School

Test Pilot*
Texas Country Reporter
Thank You for Your
Service
The 26th Story
The Achievement of
Governor William L. Guy
The Adventures Of Mark
And Brian*
The Adventures of Young
Indiana Jones
The Amazing Race
The American Dream
Contest*
The ANG, America's
Hidden Strength*
The Arsenal
The B.R.A.T Patrol*
The Bachelor
The Big Break
The Biggest Loser
The Birth of Modern
Football
The Brady Bunch*
The Butch Factor
The Call to Serve
The Caregivers
The Chew
The Choir
The Colbert Report
The Complete History of
US Wars
The Court-Martial Of
Jackie Robinson*
The Daily Planet; Army
Green Round
The Day After Disaster
The Deadliest Weapon:
The War against IEDs

The Devil's Brigade
The Doctors
The Dog Whisperer
The Draft
The Drew Carey Show*
The Ed Sullivan Show*
The Eddie Keating Story*
The Ellen DeGeneres
Show
The Entertainer
The Eve of War
The Fighting Season
The Final Report
The Fitzgeralds And The
Kennedys*
The Ford Story*
The Generals
The Great Air Race Of
1924*
The Great Christmas Light
Fight
The Great Escape*
The Great Food Truck
Race
The Hiijacking Of The
Achille Lauro*
The Homefront
The Hornet's Nest
The Hunt for Eagle One
The Jackie Bushman
Show
The Jeff Dunham Show
The Jimmy Dooliitle
Saga*
The Kamen Code
The Last Days Of Patton*
The Last Days of World
War II
The Last Official Act*

The Last Ship
The Late Night Show with
Jay Leno
The Lieutenant*
The List
The Longoria Affair
The Lost Valentine
The Magic of Flight*
The Martha Stewart Show
The Material World
The Mighty Mississippi
The Mississippi*
The New Hollywood
Squares*
The Night Shift
The O.C.
The Pacific War
The Pentagon
The Planets*
The Practice*
The Price is Right
The Raid
The Raising of America
The Reagan Years*
The Restorers
The River
The Road Home
The Rule of Law: West
Virginia's Military Police
in Iraq
The Sandbox
The Science of
Decomposition
The Secret Government*
The Secret History of 9/11
The Secret Life of
Machines
The Singing Bee
The Surge

The Suze Orman Show
The Talk
The Tennesseans
The True Story of Black
Hawk Down
The Tuskegee Airmen*
The Twilight Zone*
The Universe
The Unknown Soldier*
The View
The Voice
The Volcano that Stopped
Britain
The Wackiest Ship in the
Army*
The War After
The West Wing
The Western Front
The Wonder Years*
The World of Jenks
The X-Factor
The Years
The Young & the Restless
The Young Marines
Things That Move
Things to Do Before You
Die
This One's For You!
Threads
Three Secrets*
Three Wishes
Through the Wormhole:
Are there more than two
sexes?
Tiger Cruise
To Heal A Nation*
To Save A Life
To Those Behind The
Wall*

Today Show
Togetherness
Top 10
Top Chef
Top Chef: Masters
Top Engineer
Top Gear
Top Gear USA
Top Secret Science
Top Ten
Top Trumps
Total Divas
Touched By An Angel*
Toughest Jobs
Tour of Duty
Tournament of Roses
Parade
Trading Spaces
Transformation
Transistorized!*
Treasure Hunters
Treme
Tribeca Stories*
Triggers
Troop Star
Truck-U
True Life Textaholic
Truth Actually
Tunnel
Twentieth Century
Battlefields
Two Guys Garage
Tyra Banks Show
UFC Fight for the Troops
UFC Iraq tour
UFO Files: Deep Sea
UFOs
UFO: Enigma of the
Skies*

UFO: Exclusive*
UFOs Past, Present and
Future*
Ultimate Dogfighting*
Ultimate Factories
Ultimate Factory
Ultimate Fishing
Experience
Ultimate Warfare
Ultimate Weapon
Ultimate Weapons
Una Vida Via
Under the Skin: Stories
Behind the Ink
Undercover Boss
University
Unlikely Animal Friends
Unnatural Selection
Unsung Heroes
Untold Stories of the ER
Vampire Diaries
Veep
Vegas Stripped
Vestige Of Honor*
Veteran of The Game
VH1 Concert For The
Troops
VH1 Divas Salute The
Troops
Vice Guide to Everything
VICE on HBO
Victory at Sea*
Vietnam in HD
Virus*
Voice Awards

Voyages of Discovery:
Hanging by a Thread
Wake Up Call
Walking with the
Wounded
Walt Disney's Wonderful
World of Color*
War And Remembrance*
War Factory
War Heroes
War Stories with Oliver
North
War Wounds
Warbots
Warrior POV
Warriors to Lourdes
Wartorn: 1861-2010
Washington the Warrior
Way of the Warriors
Weather Geeks
Weird Warfare
Weird, True and Freaky
West Point
What Happened on the
Moon?*
What History Forgot
What Not To Wear
What's In Your Pocket
Wheel of Fortune
When Hell Was In
Session*
When the Levees Broke
While You Were Out
Who Do You Think You
Are?

Who Let the Dogs Out
Whose Wedding Is It
Anyway?
Why Me*
Wild Blue*
Wild Planet: North
America
Wild West Alaska
Wild, Wild, West: Deserts
Win the War: Alpha to
Zulu
Woman Abroad
Women at War
Women of Honor
Women Of Valor*
Women, War and Peace
World Without America
Worlds Apart
World's Strangest
World's Top Five
World's Toughest Driving
Test
WWE Tribute to the
Troops
WWII: The War
Chronicles*
X-Machines
Xtractor
Years Of Living
Dangerously
You Deserve It
Your Momma Wears
Combat Boots*

Appendix C
CIA, OSS, & FBI-supported products 1939-2016

OSS supported films

O.S.S. (1946)
Cloak and Dagger (1946)
13 Rue Madeleine (1946)

CIA supported/influenced films

The Caddy (1953)
Sangaree (1953)
Flight to Tangier (1953)
Houdini (1953)
Money from Home (1953)
Arrowhead (1953)
Elephant Walk (1954)
Secret of the Incas (1954)
The Naked Jungle (1954)
Animal Farm (1954)
Men of the Fighting Lady (1954)
Strategic Air Command (1955)
1984 (1956)
The Quiet American (1958)
Thunderball (1965)
Scorpio (1973)
Telefon (1977)
Patriot Games (1992)
Mission: Impossible (1996)
Enemy of the State (1998)
Spy Game (2001)
The Bourne Identity (2001)
The Sum of All Fears (2002)
Bad Company (2002)
The Recruit (2003)
Meet the Fockers (2004)
The Interpreter (2005)
Mission: Impossible III (2006)
The Good Shepherd (2006)
Charlie Wilson's War (2007)
Race to Witch Mountain (2009)
Salt (2010)
Argo (2012)

Zero Dark Thirty (2012)
Dying of the Light (2014)
Mission: Impossible - Rogue Nation (2015)
13 Hours (2016)

CIA supported TV

24
Air America
Air America: The CIA's Secret Airline
Alias
CIA Secrets
Covert Action
Covert Affairs
Game of Pawns
Extraordinary Fidelity
Greatest Intelligence Agency
Homeland
Inside the CIA
In the Company of Spies
JAG
Spies Above Us
Stories of the CIA
Sworn to Secrecy: Secrets of War
The Agency
The Path to 9-11
The Secret War on Terror
Top Chef
Top Secret Missions of the CIA

Ex-CIA supported films

Three Days of the Condor (1975)
The Man with One Red Shoe (1985)
Sneakers (1992)
Syriana (2005)
Rendition (2007)
The Kite Runner (2007)
Bruno (2009)
Red (2010)
Fair Game (2010)
Hanna (2011)
Kill the Messenger (2014)
The Interview (2014)
Spy (2015)

Ex-CIA supported TV

Argo: Inside Story
Berlin Station
Blackhat
Burn Notice
Car Bomb
Person of Interest
State of Affairs
The Americans
The Assets
The Blacklist
The Cult of the Suicide Bomber
Berlin Station

FBI supported films

Confessions of a Nazi Spy (1939)
House on 42nd Street (1945)
The FBI Story (1959)
The Silence of the Lambs (1991)
Toy Soldiers (1991)
In the Line of Fire (1993)
Catch Me If You Can (2002)
The Kingdom (2007)
Shooter (2007)
Breach (2007)
Public Enemies (2009)
Fast and Furious (2009)
The Town (2010)
Knight and Day (2010)
Ironmen (2010)
Dear Mr Gacy (2010)
J. Edgar (2011)
Mission: Impossible: Ghost Protocol (2011)
Man of Steel (2013)
The Wolf of Wall Street (2013)
Patriots Day (2016)
War Dogs (2016)

FBI supported TV/documentaries

Alien Encounters from New Tomorrowland
America's Most Wanted
Criminal Minds
CSI
Inside Deep Throat
Numb3rs
The Closer
The FBI Files
The Secret History of 9/11
Without a Trace

Appendix D – Document Samples

These samples are representative of the over 4,000 pages of documents we obtained from the DOD via FOIA requests.

DEPARTMENT OF THE AIR FORCE
SECRETARY OF THE AIR FORCE OFFICE OF PUBLIC AFFAIRS

U.S. DEPARTMENT OF DEFENSE
MOTION PICTURE AND TELEVISION
PRODUCTION ASSISTANCE AGREEMENT
(Feature Film "Tomorrow Never Dies"-U.S. Air Force-1997)

The United States Department of Defense (hereinafter referred to as "DoD"), acting on behalf of the United States of America, hereby agrees with Metro-Goldwyn-Mayer, Inc. and EON Productions Limited and Eon Studios, 29-33 Frogmore, Park Street (postal address P.O. Box 007, St. Albans, AL2 2UA) UNITED KINGDOM, (hereinafter referred to as "the production company"), subject to the provisions herein, for the assistance itemized in Attachment 1, to be rendered in conjunction with the production of the feature film known at this time as "Tomorrow Never Dies," aka "Bond-18."

Production Assistance Agreement between the Pentagon and the makers of Tomorrow Never Dies.

2. DoD approved military assistance as in the best interest of the DoD, based on the Feb 19, 1997 version of the script and subsequent changes to scenes 248B, 248C and 248D which were faxed to the project officer by the production company 26 March 1997. The production company must obtain, in advance, concurrence from DoD for any subsequent changes to the military depictions made to either the picture or the sound portions of the production before it is exhibited to the public. The production company agrees to advise the DoD Project Officer of these changes, including those that may be made during post-production.

A clause in the agreement highlighting how military support was dependent on changes to the script.

05/11/2010   **TRANSFORMERS III (TF3)**   Mr (b) (6)
(b) (6)   visited Bay Films on 9 MAR 10 and read the Transformers III script. Monday, 22 MAR 10 representatives from all the Services, along with Mr (b)(6) from DoD, met to discuss script notes and revisions. On 23 MAR 10, all Service representatives met with the director, producer, and writer of the film to discuss the possibility of further changes Michael Bay was very receptive to our notes and expressed his desire for us to "help (him) make it better." As you know, TF2 was the biggest blockbuster of 2009 (Avatar's revenue's split '09 and '10) and the TF3 script is showing this "episode" will be no different. It will give us the opportunity to showcase the bravery and values of our Soldiers and the excellent technology of today's Army to a global audience, in an apolitical blockbuster. Proposed shooting locations include Chicago and Washington DC. Filming began 11 May 10 at Edwards AFB, CA. On 15 JUN the Production Company completed 10 days of filming in Long Beach, CA. The scenes included an Apache, 2-Blackhawks, a Chinook, 2-Gray Eagle UAVs, a Palletized Loading System (PLS) and an Army Fire Truck. Coordinating with PM Stryker for vehicles in Chicago, 16-24 JUL 10. Update: TF3 has requested 25 military extras for the weekend in Chicago. The schedule has been in a bit of turmoil due to weather issues. Coordinating for interior Mortar Stryker Vehicle shots in the Detroit area in SEP 10.

Entry in US Army ELO reports on their influence on the Transformers III script during the pre-production phase and the large scale support during filming.

"NCIS" – CBS: LA PAO was asked to review the script for Episode #133, "Dead Reckoning," and no changes were found in the scripts. Reviewed Episode #134 "Toxic" with significant storyline changes requested by DoD. Storyline involves military personnel making bio-weapons illegally. **DoD currently in discussion with NCIS concerning this issue.**

Entry in USMC ELO report on an episode of NCIS that was rewritten to change the central storyline where military personnel make illegal bio-weapons.

"Combat Outpost: Afghanistan" AKA "Afghanistan: The Surge" – PBS: Hodierne Productions LLC produced a character-driven documentary about Marines serving in Afghanistan. The two-hour film focused on Marines and corpsmen from 2nd Platoon, A Co., 2/1. The producer was embedded during the company's 7-month deployment to Helmand province. LA PA reviewed rough cut on 9 April and had major concerns with both the message behind the film and multiple OPSEC violations. Overall intent behind the movie seemed to be a condemnation of policy and of the USMC's mission in Afghanistan. The overall tone was failure and hopelessness despite the efforts of the Marines and Navy corpsmen. **LA PA is re-engaging Production Company to discuss rough cut corrections.**

Entry in USMC ELO report on PBS documentary Afghanistan: The Surge, which was recut at the Pentagon's request to alter the negative tone regarding the war in Afghanistan.

DoD Notes on Hawaii 5-0 Pilot Episode (1-13-10)

1. We like your idea of giving McGarrett a military background for both his character and the possibilities for further military involvement in future episodes. We want to make sure you want his background to include being a SEAL, because the Navy will want to let the SEAL leadership know about it.

2. We understand that you're willing to reset the opening scene from South Korea to some other locale. We'd like to avoid annoying our allies or alienating neutrals. Can the location either be identified (on-screen) as a fictional country, an obscure regional area ("A CLASSIFIED LOCATION IN SE ASIA"), or avoided altogether?

3. We understand that the bad guys in the opening assault scene are not foreign military and therefore their equipment need not be specifically Chinese, etc.

4. You agreed that the Army portrayal in this scene can be made more capable and lethal. We think the best approach would be for you to get together with the Army to work out the details of a revised attack and defense. I have attached a list of the Military Service offices for your information.

Section from US Army script notes on the pilot episode of the rebooted Hawaii Five-O.

-----Original Message-----
From: Strub, Philip Mr OSD PA (b) (6)
Sent: Monday, June 04, 2012 7:04 AM
To: Newell, Rob D CIV CHINFO, OI-G; Nye, Edward T COL USSOCOM HQ; Fenick,
William R CAPT USSOCOM NAVSOC; (b) (6)   Hawes, Kenneth A CIV
(US)
Subject: Joint Lone Survivor notes

All,

Here's my compilation of our comments during last week's teleconference
call, plus a scan of the "goat herder discussion" from the book. Sometimes
when I'm doing these I include sample dialogue because it's simpler than
explaining what needs to be said -- the filmmakers can rewrite it to suit
their needs. But in this case I was hesitant to rewrite what Luttrell
believes was said to the best of his memory, so I opted for the explanation
rather than suggested dialogue. Don't know if this was the better choice or
not.

No pride of authorship here, I welcome comments, corrections, additions, and
other suggestions.

There's some kind of meeting taking place at Film 44 on June 12 or 13, with
Pete, Sara, Harry Humphries, Louis Freedman, Bob, and Chad, with me maybe
being able to call in. Neither Bob nor I understand what the purpose of the
meeting is, but I'm assured that it's not to discuss the script. The
filmmakers are aware that we discussed the script and that notes will be
forthcoming very soon. I expect that we will have a face-to-face discussion
with Pete on our notes, but don't know when.

Bob, I don't have Chad's email address for some reason.

Best,

Phil

Email from Phil Strub to Navy Public Affairs on rewriting the 'goat herder scene' in Lone Survivor, even though it meant telling a very different version of events to that in Marcus Luttrell's book.

The production company filmed for several days at Kirtland AFB, because of positive, if short AF portrayal, which was edited out of the final version. The script portrayed a U.S. Army transport brake failure, resulting in it hitting a group of Afghani shoppers in Kabul, killing and injuring them. This was changed to an NGO vehicle. Considerable Marine Corps portrayal, though the Marine Corps only provided on-set uniform and other technical advice.

The primary motivation in providing support was the very last act, in which the Tina Fe character visits the home of a young Marine who had suffered the loss of both legs in combat. His character is the complete opposite of the stereotypical "wounded warrior," as he and young family are doing quite well, and sets the reporter in pursuit of a new, positive life style.

Entry in DOD database on Whiskey Tango Foxtrot detailing script changes and the Pentagon's motives for supporting the film.

████ I'm very apprehensive about sending these notes to you. For one thing, they're incomplete, ████ won't have ████ input until later, perhaps as early as today (Monday). But the main reason for my hesitancy is that in the past we've usually been able to offer suggestions within the context of existing plot and characters. These, however, are pretty radical. I hope they don't have the effect of aggravating everyone, because we certainly aren't trying to intrude on the creative process. It's just that I see no other practical, straightforward way of communicating our concerns.

████

DoD "Hulk" Notes of Sunday, Feb 3.

Overall: The primary purpose of these notes is civilianize the desert lab and the direct action against the Hulk, leaving only one actual deadly military strike, against the Absorbing Man at the end. All the other military operations would be nonlethal and other unconventional attempts to contain, distract, or subdue the Hulk, or to provide reconnaissance information regarding him. There are also some technical suggestions.

Pg 1, Sc 1 and elsewhere, INT. DESERT BASE: This would be a commercial entity (Talbot's later "Atheon"?), as a company under contract to the Defense Advanced Research Projects Agency – even though there wasn't one per se in 1965. If the physical look of the place is military, it would be good to make it clear that it's no longer an active military installation, using signage and/or superimposed titles to make the distinction.

Pg 1, Sc 2: To keep General Ross as an active-duty general in the present day, he'd have to be younger and more junior in 1965, probably a major. Technically, after 30 years of commissioned service, officers face mandatory retirement, though there have been exceptions (Admiral Rickover, the submariner, for one). As a young major, Ross could be an important program manager in an emerging mission area – unconventional defenses. In this encounter with Banner, then, he'd be with his civilian "employees," perhaps, his "I" and "I've" would be "We" and "We've," emphasizing the nature of the relationship between program manager and contractor.

Would Talbot be here, too? As a lieutenant or captain? We would prefer that Talbot left the military and assumed Ross's role as director of the lab in the present day. We would like Ross to be at a distance organizationally from the lab, and unaware of all that's going on there. This is so that he does not give orders that would exceed his military authority and also so that he is credible as a general officer now in charge of overall unconventional defenses for the entire DoD.

Excerpt from USMC script notes on Hulk outlining the 'radical' changes the DOD requested to settings, characters and storylines to demilitarise the desert base where dangerous experiments accidentally create the Hulk.

Indices

Film Index

226

General Index

227

Endnotes

1   Donald Baruch's formal title was Special Assistant to the Assistant Secretary of Defense for Public Affairs for Entertainment Media. Phil Strub is now known as the Director of Entertainment Media or simply the DOD's Hollywood Liaison.

2   Reports from the Pentagon's ELOs continually reference these preview screenings and sometimes mention Strub and others making further suggestions or requesting 'corrections' at this stage, e.g. the USMC entries on *Lock n Load*, August 14th 2009, on *Afghanistan: The Surge*, July 9th 2012 and on *101 Weapons That Changed the World*, March 28th 2012, and US Army entries on *Fox Sports Spring Training with the Troops*, 19th March 2013 and *A Hero's Welcome*, 15th October 2014. Sometimes these late changes can have a substantial effect on the finished production. On *Afghanistan: The Surge* the USMC reports say they, 'reviewed rough cut on 9 April and had major concerns with both the message behind the film and multiple OPSEC violations. Overall intent behind the movie seemed to be a condemnation of policy and of the USMC's mission in Afghanistan. The overall tone was failure and hopelessness despite the efforts of the Marines and Navy corpsmen. LA PA is re-engaging Production Company to discuss rough cut corrections.'

3   Suid (2002), *Guts and Glory*, p. 686. Also see emails from Georgetown University library staff to Alford, 8th December 2011.

4   Matthew Alford (2016), The Political Impact of the Department of Defense on Hollywood Cinema, *Quarterly Journal of Film and Video*, 30th January.

5   Phil Strub's Internet Movie Database (IMDB) page credits him on around 50 films but his predecessor Don Baruch is not referenced on IMDB at all, despite spending 40 years in the job. The Pentagon has multiple pages on IMDB but between them they list several dozen films and another 200 or so episodes of TV series. The IMDB entries omit numerous projects that the military did support, and the pages also contradict one another, for example the 2014 version of *Godzilla* is on Strub's page but not on the DOD's and the 1998 *Godzilla* isn't on either. It's not realistic to expect IMDB to be comprehensive and nor are we suggesting that the DOD has a particular policy on this data base, but as IMDB is the standard web source for listings, the omissions are significantly misleading. The appendix to Lawrence Suid's book *Guts and Glory* (2002) lists about 200 films on which the DOD cooperated. His 2005 book *Stars and Stripes on the Silver Screen* brings his total up to around 575 – missing an estimated hundred or so pre-2004 films but still a really impressive piece of work. See Suid, Lawrence H. (2002) *Guts and Glory: The Making of the American Military Image in Film*, Kentucky UP, Second Edition

and Suid, Lawrence and Haverstick, Delores (2005) *Stars and Stripes on the Silver Screen: A Comprehensive Guide to Portrayals of American Military on Film*, Oxford: Scarecrow Books.

6   USMC (2008) ELO report, June 20th. These diary-like reports were obtained via FOIA requests to the different branches of the DOD, though so far the Navy ELO has refused to release any of their documents. If they did, this would likely significantly expand the number of productions, especially TV programmes, that we can confirm the DOD supported. For copies of these reports see spyculture.com.

7   US Army (2010), ELO report, August 26th to September 1st.

8   US Army (2010), ELO report entry on conference call with McCann Worldwide, April 14th.

9   US Army (2010), ELO report, February 6th.

10   See Mirrlees, Tanner (2017), Transforming *Transformers* into Militainment: Interrogating the DoD-Hollywood Complex, *American Journal of Economics & Sociology*, 76: pp. 405–434.

11   Laura Bennett (2012), The Pentagon's Man in Hollywood: I'm a Eunuch, *New Republic*, December 21st.

12   Iran-Contra is the name for a major scandal in which the US covertly sold weapons to Iran while it was subject to an arms embargo during the Iran-Iraq war. Some of the money made from these sales was diverted to fund the Contras – a right-wing terrorist organisation in Nicaragua who were fighting the left wing Sandinistas with CIA assistance. The under-the-table sales to Iran were also designed as sweeteners to encourage the Iranian government to help with the release of several US hostages. See Lawrence E Walsh's (1998) *Firewall: The Iran-Contra Conspiracy and Cover-up (*W. W. Norton & Company) and the government's own *Report of the Congressional Committees Investigating the Iran/Contra Affair* (1987), here: https://assets.documentcloud.org/documents/2702436/Iran-Contra-report.pdf.

13   US Department of Defense (DOD) Inspector General (1993), *Tailhook 91: Events At The 35th Annual Tailhook Symposium* (February).

14   Elsewhere, David Robb cites a screenplay called *The Smoldering Sea*, which the DOD rejected on the grounds that it "shows the Navy in a very objectionable light." Another was a film based on the book by Clay Blair, which painted a flattering picture of the Navy Admiral Hyman Rickover but which Rickover himself opposed because he would not have full control over its production. See: Alford, Matthew (2016), The Political Impact of the Department of Defense on Hollywood Cinema, *Quarterly Journal of Film and Video*, 30th January. See also: McElwee, Sean (2013), "Man Of Steel" Review: You Wouldn't Get a Chance to See It If the Pentagon Didn't Like It, June 23rd, https://mic.com/articles/48091/man–of–steel–review–you–wouldn–t–get–a–chance–to–see–it–if–the–pentagon–didn–t–like–it#.WiUspLnJ6

15   Video clips here indicate Suid's remarkable view that recruitment is 'not intentional' when the DOD helps make movies:

https://www.youtube.com/watch?v=IMHUj9eGXsA and
https://www.youtube.com/watch?v=_69UayH4Y7s. Here is the independent
military adviser Dale Dye claiming that, when it comes to movies, DOD
politicisation is 'inadvertent' and 'not intentional' and how the military is
'willing to call it warts and all': www.youtube.com/watch?v=RU4KI6q1uhQ.
16   Tully, Francis (1967), Memo to Director of Security Review, March
24th, para. 1.
17   Tully, Francis (1967), Memo to Director of Security Review, March
24th, *Green Berets* folder (Fort Worth, Government in Hollywood Special
Collection, Gwendolyn P. Tandy Film Library, Texas Christian University).
18   Tully, Francis (1967), Memo to Director of Security Review, March
24th, *Green Berets* folder (Fort Worth, Government in Hollywood Special
Collection, Gwendolyn P. Tandy Film Library, Texas Christian University).
19   Wayne, Michael (1968), Letter to Donald Baruch, February 22nd
(David Robb's collection).
20   Suid, Lawrence (2002), *Guts & Glory* p. 248
21   Strub, Phil (1995), Email to Mr. Tom Pevsner, Exec Producer of
Goldeneye at Eon Productions, January 20th.
22   Robb, David (2004), *Operation Hollywood: How the Pentagon Shapes
and Censors the Movies*, Amherst, MA: Prometheus Books, pp. 29-32. In the
same scene the agent also says, 'We have no interest in seeing World War III,
unless we start it'. Tellingly, the Pentagon had no objection to this line. Nor did
they object to M's line in *Goldeneye*: 'Unlike the American government we
prefer not to get our bad news from CNN'.
23   Strub, Phil (2014), Email to Matthew Alford, November 7th.
24   Suid, Lawrence and Haverstick, Delores (2005) *Stars and Stripes on
the Silver Screen*, Oxford: Scarecrow Press, pp. 337-340
25   See Sledge, Eugene (1981) *With the Old Breed: At Peleliu and
Okinawa*, New York: Oxford UP. Sledge describes in detail how a Marine rips
the teeth out of a paralysed but still breathing Japanese soldier: 'The Marine
cursed him and with a slash cut his cheeks open to each ear' (p. 287).
26   Robb, *Operation Hollywood*, pp. 59-67.
27   DOD database, entry on *Tears of the Sun*. This (incomplete) database
on Pentagon support to the entertainment industry was obtained via FOIA
requests, initially in extracts and then a complete copy. For a copy of the
database see spyculture.com.
28   Beginning in 1996, indigenous, environmental, and human rights
groups brought a series of cases against Royal Dutch Shell and its Nigerian head
Brian Anderson, for crimes in Nigeria, including summary execution, crimes
against humanity, torture, inhumane treatment and arbitrary arrest and detention.
The US District Court for the Southern District of New York set a trial date for
June 2009 and, just a few days before it was to begin, Shell agreed to an out-of-
court settlement of US$15.5 million to victims' families. The company denied

any liability for the deaths, stating that the payment was part of a reconciliation process.

29   Vancheri, Barbara (2003), Fuqua hopes 'Tears of the Sun' isn't lost in war propaganda, March 9th, p. G-5, archived here: http://old.post-gazette.com/movies/20030309fuqua0309fnp3.asp Fuqua's book was Peress, Gilles (1995) *The Silence – Rwanda*, Scalo.

30   Tarabay, James (2014), Hollywood and the Pentagon: A relationship of mutual exploitation, *Al Jazeera*, July 29th.

31   Ibid.

32   The DOD had so many problems with the story in *Apocalypse Now* that they refused all requests for assistance, including when the producers asked President Jimmy Carter to intervene. The DOD's database says, 'Coppola came into Pentagon with script... wanted help. Since script called for "termination" of one officer by another Army always refused to consider assistance. Despite subsequent efforts, DOD did not answer telegram to President Carter which marked end of communications on film'. As a result *Apocalypse Now* was made on location in the Philippines without DOD support, where it was beset by endless problems including storms destroying the sets and star Martin Sheen suffering a major heart attack. As Coppola himself said, 'It was the largest, most expensive military film that was made without any cooperation from the government.' See Appelo, Tim (2014), Telluride: Francis Ford Coppola Spills 'Apocalypse Now' Secrets on 35th Anniversary, *Hollywood Reporter*, 30th August, www.hollywoodreporter.com/news/telluride-francis-ford-coppola-spills-729281

33   Breznican, Anthony (2008), 'Tropic Thunder' stars take Marine base by storm, *USA Today*, August 4th.

34   Cohen, Etan, Stiller, Ben and Theroux, Justin (2006), Draft Script for *Tropic Thunder*, May 9th.

35   DOD database, entry on *Forrest Gump*.

36   USMC (2009), ELO report, February 20th. See also *NCIS* season 6 episode 21, 'Toxic', broadcast April 7th 2009.

37   US Army (2010), Script notes on pilot episode of *Hawaii Five-0*, January 13th. See also *Hawaii Five-0* episode 'Pilot', broadcast September 20th 2010. For copies of all script notes cited in this book see spyculture.com.

38   DOD database, entry on *If I Could Turn Back Time*.

39   Forbes, Daniel (2000), 'Prime-time propaganda: How the White House secretly hooked network TV on its anti-drug message', *Salon*, 13 January, archive.salon.com/news/feature/2000/01/13/drugs.

40   Macaffrey opposed Congressional efforts to extend the campaign to underage drinking.

41   McCoy, Alfred W (2003), *The Politics of Heroin. CIA Complicity in the Global Drug Trade*, Chicago Review Press.

42   For extensive and excellent discussion, see Graham, Robbie (2016), *Silver Screen Saucers*, White Crow Books. In 1953, the CIA-sponsored

Robertson Panel was a group of leading scientists assembled for the task of reviewing the USAF's files on Unidentified Flying Objects (UFOs). The Panel concluded that UFOs did not pose a direct threat to national security but nevertheless recommended the USAF begin a "debunking" campaign employing the talents of psychiatrists, astronomers, and celebrities, with the goal of demystifying UFO reports. Its formal recommendation was that, 'The national security agencies take immediate steps to strip the Unidentified Flying Objects of the special status they have been given and the aura of mystery they have unfortunately acquired.' The panel further stated that this should 'be accomplished by mass media such as television [and] motion pictures...' and specifically advocating the involvement of Walt Disney.

The extent to which the Robertson Panel's recommendations were implemented is not entirely clear. Nevertheless, the mentality of the Panel was reflected during the 1950s, as where the USAF literally cut the microphone as Marine Corps naval aviator Donald Keyhoe broke from the agreed script on a live CBS documentary, *UFO: Enigma of the Skies* (1958), just as he was saying that UFOs were run by intelligent forces.

The *Steve Canyon* TV series (1958-1959) was similarly made with the full cooperation of the USAF. The USAF took objection to one episode called 'Project UFO', in which Colonel Canyon enthusiastically investigated a spate of flying saucer sightings. By the time the USAF had finished with the script, the UFO sightings were attributed to a combination of hoax-induced hysteria and misidentified weather balloons. Producer, John Ellis, of the Milton Caniff Estate (which owns *Steve Canyon*) told Robbie Graham, 'Every single page got re-written, and re-written, and re-written...' and David Haft, the show's producer, said the USAF's reaction when he submitted the first script draft for official approval was 'Oh, oh, oh, oh! No, no, no, no!' Despite the heavy rewrites, the USAF insisted that the episode not be aired at all and it was only through a last act of defiance on the part of the show's producers toward the end of its run in 1959 that the episode was screened at all.

Even as late as 1966 the Robertson panel wielded a demonstrable influence over the CBS TV broadcast of UFOs: Friend, Foe, or Fantasy? – an anti-UFO documentary narrated by Walter Cronkite. In a personal letter addressed to former Robertson Panel Secretary, panel member Frederick C. Durant, Dr. Thornton Page confided to having 'helped organize the documentary around the Robertson Panel conclusions,' even though this was thirteen years after the panel had disbanded and despite the fact that he was personally sympathetic to the existence of flying saucers.

The military's motives for such a heavy-handed approach to the representation of UFOs are unclear. Regardless, it's important that the government has been able to exercise such serious control over controversial content throughout the 1950s and beyond.

43   Suid, Lawrence and Robb, David (2005) "Review", *Film and History*, Vol 35.1, pp. 75-77.

44   Bennett, The Pentagon's Man in Hollywood: I'm a Eunuch.

45   Suid and Haaverstick (2005), p. 49.

46   See CIA website: https://www.cia.gov/offices-of-cia/public-affairs/entertainment-industry-liaison

47   Vice have published several major articles on the CIA's role in Hollywood but they almost exclusively focus on *Zero Dark Thirty*. Likewise Nick Shou's 2016 book *Spooked: How the CIA Manipulates the Media and Hoodwinks Hollywood* (Hot Books) is a good introduction but offers only a cursory examination of the topic.

48   For example, Brandon said in a 2001 interview that he rejected requests for assistance from the producers of *24*, *Spy Game* and *The Bourne Identity*, saying that *Bourne* was 'so awful that I tossed it in the burn bag after page 25'. However he listed all three of these productions on his website and even appeared in a featurette on the Special Edition DVD of *The Bourne Identity* praising the film in glowing terms. The latter two films in the original Bourne trilogy both include original footage of Langley which was either filmed with the Agency's permission or provided to the filmmakers by their ELO. On *24* Brandon later contradicted his claim to have turned down their request, saying 'Yes, we weren't involved at first because they didn't ask. Now they have and I've been out to their offices and the set so we're doing more to help them out.' See Patterson, John (2001), The Caring, Sharing CIA, *The Guardian*, October 5th and Williams, Andrew (2009), Chase Brandon, *Metro*, October 27th.

49   This is most apparent in *Animal Farm* where in the original book the farm animals realise that the pigs (the Soviets) and the humans (the capitalists) are working together, and that there is no distinction to be made between them and thus that the revolution has failed. In the CIA-assisted film version the humans do not appear and the pigs are simply shown to be corrupt and behaving like humans, sparking another attempted revolution by the rest of the farm. See Leab, Daniel J.(2007), *Orwell Subverted: The CIA and the Filming of Animal Farm*, Pennsylvania State UP, and Saunders, Frances Stonor (1999) *Who Paid the Piper? The CIA and the Cultural Cold War*, London: Granta Books.

50   Hunt, Howard (2007), *American Spy: My Secret History in the CIA, Watergate and Beyond*, John Wiley & Sons, p. 50.

51   See Eldridge, David (2000), 'Dear Owen': The CIA, Luigi Luraschi and Hollywood, 1953, *Historical Journal of Film, Radio and Television*, Vol. 20, No. 2. See also Saunders, Francis (1999) *The Cultural Cold War: The CIA and the World of Arts and Letters*. In her books Saunders documented how the CIA used the Congress for Cultural Freedom and numerous contacts within the Museum of Modern Art, to help promote abstract expressionism to contrast and subvert the socialist realism favoured in the USSR. They considered that abstract, emotive notions of freedom were a suitable counter to socialist artworks grounded in economic realities. Saunders saw this, the Orwell adaptations, the Luraschi letters and other propaganda programmes as part of a

cohesive CIA strategy to weaponise both high culture and popular culture against the Soviet Union.

52   Luigi Luraschi letters to 'Owen', C. D. Jackson Records, Box 5, file folder "Movies", Eisenhower Presidential Library. For copies of these letters see spyculture.com.

53   On *Houdini* and *Legend of the Incas* see Luraschi letter to 'Owen', February 6th 1953, On *Strategic Air Command* see Luraschi letter to 'Owen', February 14th 1953.

54   May, Lary (2000), *The Big Tomorrow: Hollywood and the Politics of the American Way*, Chicago University Press, pp. 203-4.

55   FitzGerald, Michael Ray (2016), 'Adjuncts of Government': Darryl F. Zanuck and 20th Century-Fox in Service to the Executive Branch, 1935-1971, *Historical Journal of Film, Radio and Television*, 36:3, pp. 373-391.

56   Quoted in Francis Stonor Saunders, *The Cultural Cold War*, p.244.

57   FitzGerald, Michael Ray 'Adjuncts of Government': Darryl F. Zanuck and 20th Century-Fox in Service to the Executive Branch, 1935–1971 Michael Ray FitzGerald Pages 373-391

58   Eldridge (2000), 'Dear Owen'.

59   See, for example, letters to Allen Dulles from Eric Johnston and letters to Eric Johnston from Allen Dulles available through the CREST archive.

60   Eldridge (2000), 'Dear Owen'.

61   The National Security Act of 1947, July 26th 1947, Public Law 253, 80th Congress; Chapter 343, 1st Session; S. 758.

62   National Security Council (1948), NSC 10/2, National Security Council Directive on Office of Special Projects, June 18th.

63   Nashel, Johnathan (2005), *Lansdale's Cold War*, Massachusetts UP, pp. 164–172.

64   Willmetts, Simon (2016) *In Secrecy's Shadow: The OSS and CIA in Hollywood Cinema, 1941-1979*, Edinburgh UP.

65   Letter from Edward Lansdale to Joseph Mankiewicz, 17th March 1956 in Nashel, *Lansdale's Cold War*, p. 165.

66   Nashel, *Lansdale's Cold War*, p. 166; Willmetts, *In Secrecy's Shadow*, p. 150.

67   CIA (1953), Meeting in Pentagon on 29 September 1953, October 1st, CREST reference CIA–RDP80R01731R001300220008–0.

68   Willmetts, *In Secrecy's Shadow*, p. 32.

69   Willmetts, *In Secrecy's Shadow*, p. 57-68.

70   Willmetts, *In Secrecy's Shadow*, chapter 2.

71   OSS (1943), The Motion Picture as a Weapon of Psychological Warfare, declassified January 14th 2004, for a copy see www.spyculture.com/docs/US/OSS-motionpicturesasweapons.pdf.

72   Willmetts, *In Secrecy's Shadow*, p. 127.

[73] CIA (1951), Memo re: Forthcoming Movie by Paramount Apparently Involving the Name of CIA, January 1st, CREST reference CIA-RDP58-00597A000100070144-7.

[74] CIA (1956), Memo for DCI re: Project OSS TV Series, November 1st, CREST reference CIA–RDP80R01731R001100160085–4.

[75] Moran, Christopher (2013) Ian Fleming and the Public Profile of the CIA, *Journal of Cold War Studies*, Volume 15, Issue 1, Winter.

[76] On the screening of *Goldfinger*, see CIA (1964), Memorandum for the Record from Marshall S Carter, September 5th, in the CREST archive or on spyculture.com. Following up on media reports and articles on the CIA's website about their use of skyhooks in the 1960s, Secker sought to find out where the *Thunderball* producers acquired the plane and skyhook used at the end of the film. He found confirmation that it was registered to CIA front company Intermountain Aviation in *The Aircraft of Air America* by Dr Joe F. Leeker. Three years before it appeared in *Thunderball* the plane was used in a CIA operation to drop off and then pick up a small team of agents exploring an abandoned Soviet base in the Arctic.

[77] Willmetts, *In Secrecy's Shadow*, p. 132.

[78] CIA (1951), Letter from Walter Bedell Smith to Eugene B Rodney, August 1st, CREST reference CIA–RDP80R01731R001300130077–4.

[79] Willmetts (2016) *Quiet Americans*, p. 6.

[80] CIA (1952), Daily Staff Meeting, January 3rd, CREST reference CIA–RDP80B01676R002300080010–0; Willmetts, *In Secrecy's Shadow*, p. 128.

[81] CIA (1975), Memo for Angus Thuermer re: Questions from a PFIAB member re: "Scorpio", January 26th, CREST reference CIA-RDPBB-M365R000300210001-3 and CIA (1975), Memo for CMDR Olmer, PFIAB staff, re: Mr Cherne's questions about re the motion picture, "Scorpio", January 1st, CREST reference CIA-RDP80M01133A001100090061-1.

[82] Willmetts, *In Secrecy's Shadow*, p. 234.

[83] CIA (1973), Extracts from Pictorial Services Branch Daily Diary, March 20th 1973, CREST reference CIA-RDP88-01365R000300210008-6.

[84] Rizzo was speaking at the Mitchell Hamline School of Law in a presentation called *A Strange Bond: CIA and the Cinema* (2007) DVD. St. Paul, MN: William Mitchell College of Law.

[85] High Jinks Around the CIA, Boston Record-America, June 22nd 1972, CREST reference CIA-RDP88-O1365R000300210012-1.

[86] JFK Assassination System record number 104–10119–10305, CIA documents re: Movie or TV series on CIA based on books by St. John. February 27th 1974. This story was originally broken by Jim Lesar in AARC Quarterly, Fall 1995–Winter 1996, article titled Valenti/Helms Plan For CIA Television Show.

[87] CIA (1984), The Man with One Red Shoe, August 27th, CREST reference CIA–RDP88–01070R000201350011–7.

88   Butterfield, Fox (1987), WASHINGTON TALK; Contra Connection: Stalking Film Rights, New York Times, January 29th.

89   Gozstola, Kevin (2016), Interview with Nick Schou, www.shadowproof.com, June 30th.

90   *A Strange Bond: CIA and the Cinema* (2007). In the year following that movie, Navy recruitment figures saw a spike of 16,000, and enlistment for naval aviators jumped 500%. Richard D. Parker in his article The Armed Forces Needs Another Top Gun in *US Naval Institute Proceedings*, December 2005, Vol. 131 Issue 12, p. 58.

91   Chase Brandon's website is no longer available but some pages are accessible through the internet's "wayback machine" and some are screen-grabbed on spyculture.com.

92   CIA Press Release (1999), 'CIA Hosts Screening of In the Company of Spies', 14th October, https://www.cia.gov/news–information/press–releases–statements/press–release–archive–1999/pr101499.html.

93   Jenkins, Tricia (2009), Get Smart: A Look at the Current Relationship between Hollywood and the CIA, *Historical Journal of Radio, Film and Television*, Vol. 29, No. 2, p. 232.

94   Jenkins, Tricia and Alford, Matthew (2012), Intelligence Activity in Hollywood: Remembering the 'Agency' in CIA, *Scope* https://www.nottingham.ac.uk/scope/documents/2012/june-2012/jenkins.pdf. For the "terrorists watch TV too" comment, see Jenkins (2016), *The CIA in Hollywood*, p. 94.

95   Jenkins, Tricia (2009) Get Smart: A Look at the Current Relationship between Hollywood and the CIA, *Historical Journal of Film, Radio and Television* Vol. 29 , Iss. 2.

96   Michael Frost Beckner, personal interview with Tricia Jenkins, 2nd Dec. 2009 (transcript supplied to Matthew Alford). For further details, see: Jenkins (2016), *The CIA in Hollywood*, pp. 66-70.

97   Jenkins, Tricia and Alford, Matthew (2012)

98   Jenkins (2016) *The CIA in Hollywood*, p. 82. Jenkins' assessment is 'the CIA's entertainment liaison functioned as a type of ghost writer for *The Recruit* and his role far exceeded the one that even an aggressive studio executive or producer would play in the development of the film' (p. 87).

99   Kelbaugh, Paul (2008), Email to Matthew Alford, 6th August.

100   Anon. (2008), Telephone interview with Robbie Graham, 28th July.

101   *Top Chef* season 7 episode 10 'Covert Cuisine', broadcast August 18th 2010.

102   CIA (2011), email from Public Affairs Officer Marie E Harf re: Meeting with Hollywood screenwriter tomorrow, June 30th, 1:31 p.m. released under FOIA to Judicial Watch.

103   CIA (2012), Memo recording conference calls with Mark Boal, undated, released under FOIA to *Gawker*.

104   Ibid.

105   CIA (2012), Memo summarising conference calls with Mark Boal. Chen, Adrian (2013), Newly Declassified Memo Shows CIA Shaped *Zero Dark Thirty's* Narrative," *Gawker*, 6th May.

106   Mayer, Jane (2014), The Unidentified Queen of Torture, *New Yorker*, December 18th.

107   CIA (2012), Statement to Employees from Acting Director Michael Morell: "Zero Dark Thirty", December 21st.

108   The remarks came from an interview with Brandon in David S. McCarthy's unpublished PhD thesis, p. 267-8. We have seen McCarthy's forthcoming book *The Selling of the CIA: Politics, Public Relations, and the Culture of Secrecy, 1974-2014*, which is similarly oustanding.

109   Pautz, Michelle C. (2015), Argo and Zero Dark Thirty: Film, Government, and Audiences, *Political Science and Politics*, Volume 48, Issue 1 January 2015, pp. 120-128.

110   Dilanian, Ken (2014), *Hollywood figures spied for CIA, book asserts*, *LA Times*, January 10th.

111   Bierly, Mandy (2009), Mike Myers visits the CIA. Naturally, Entertainment Weekly, May 12th; Bart, Peter and Fleming, Michael (2009); Strangest PR Call of the Year: The CIA, Variety, December 19th; CIA (2000), Superman Visits Headquarters, What's News at CIA, October 10th, CREST reference 0001243420; CIA (1997), Headlines: Patrick Stewart Visits CIA, What's News at CIA, December 24th, CREST reference 0001243294; CIA (1998), Headlines: Mr Smith goes to CIA, What's News at CIA, January 3rd, CREST reference 0001243421; CIA (1996), Dan Ackroyd Developing Television Series on CIA, What's News at CIA, September 4th, CREST reference 0001243427; Brandon, Chase (undated), Lights... Camera... Action!, What's News at CIA issue 538, CREST reference 0001243289; DVD feature The Making of Enemy of the State; DVD feature Mission: Spies Among Us for *Mission: Impossible*; CIA (1991) Internal memo from Joe DeTrani to Robert Gates, November 12th re Patriot Games; Wiebe, Sheldon (2010), Covert Affairs: Spy Piper Perabo Talks Up Entertaining Espionage Series!, Hollywood Insider, July 12th; CIA (2010), OPA email re: VIP Hollywood Guest – Claire Danes, sent by George Little, December 17th; See also: Making of features The CIA and Hollywood Connection and A Discussion With the Cast of Argo, *Argo* blu-ray (for Bryan Cranston and Affleck the second time).

112   Winer, Stuart (2013), Hollywood producer Arnon Milchan reveals past as secret agent, *Times of Israel*, November 25th. FBI Counterintelligence telegram from Los Angeles Field Office re: MILCO and Heli Trading, June 17th 2002.

113   CIA, (2012), Office of the Inspector General, Report No. 2012–0013–AS, CIA Processes for Engaging With the Entertainment Industry, pp. 1–5. See spyculture.com/docs/US/CIA-OIG-Engaging-with-Entertainment-Industry.pdf.

114   Ibid.

115   The comments are made by *Salt* director Philip Noyce on the DVD commentary.

116   See, for example, Thomas, June (2013), A Conversation With *The Americans* Showrunners Joe Weisberg and Joel Fields, Slate.com, January 31st.

117   Johnston, Rich (2016), Any Comic Tom King Writes Involving The CIA Has To Be Vetted, bleedingcool.com, March 26th.

118   Brandon, Chase (2012), Coast to Coast radio, July 12th.

119   See, for example: Ceplair, Larry and Englund, Steven (2003), *The Inquisition in Hollywood: Politics in the Film Community*, 1930-60, Chicago: Illinois UP.

120   The Bureau currently runs a Public Affairs Unit, with an annual budget of around $1.5 million. Efforts have been made between Fox and the FBI to develop a series centring on an Iraq war veteran who is appointed as the Fed's new anti–terrorism head. In 2007 FBI public affairs specialist Betsy Glick said that the previous year alone they had assisted 649 projects, likely mostly books. See Bond, Paul (2007) Federal pens: FBI seminar hosts H'wood scribes, *Hollywood Reports*, January 11th.

121   FBI memo to Cartha D. DeLoach re Movie Based On Pocketboot Entitled Goldfinger by Ian Fleming, January 23rd 1964, in Ian Fleming's FBI file. See spyculture.com.

122   See the four part series of articles, Robb, David (2008), 'Special Report: J. Edgar Hoover's Hollywood Obsessions Revealed', *Hollywood Today*, 27th February, www.hollywoodtoday.net/2008/02/27/special–report–j–edgar–hoover's–hollywood–obsessions–revealed.

123   Charles J. Maland (1991) *Chaplin and American Culture: The Evolution of a Star Image*, Princeton UP.

124   Davis, James Kirkpatrick (1992) *Spying on America: The FBIs Domestic Counterintelligence Program*, New York: Praeger, p. 120–1.

125   Hershberger, Mary (2004) "Peace Work, War Myths: Jane Fonda and the antiwar movement", *Peace and Change* Vol 29 no. 3 and 4, July, pp. 556-7.

126   Ibid, pp. 557-8.

127   Ibid, p. 567.

128   Ibid, p. 554.

129   Hockstader, Lee (2003) "A Film Back from the Blacklist," *Washington Post* https://www.washingtonpost.com/archive/lifestyle/2003/03/03/a-film-back-from-the-blacklist/740399a3-9ca7-4d20-9887-36832e9df5a8/.

130   Thompson, Neal (1998), NSA goes to the movies, *Baltimore Sun*, February 15th. See also internal NSA emails on *Enemy of the State* obtained under FOIA by Andrew Kaczynski (the emails dispute that the former NSA employee who consulted on *Enemy of the State* was 'offered up' but not that the script was changed at their behest). Both Secker and Tricia Jenkins discovered that the CIA also helped to produce *Enemy of the State* with Will Smith and the main creative crew being invited to Langley to see surveillance technologies which were then portrayed in the film.

131   CIA (2012), CIA Processes for Engaging With the Entertainment Industry, p. 3–4.

132   CIA (2013), Office of the Inspector General, Report of Investigation, Potential Ethics Violations Involving Film Producers, 16th September, Exhibit C.

133   Fretts, Bruce (2015), Alex Gansa on 'Homeland' and Responding to Real–Life Terrorism, *New York Times*, December 14th.

134   CIA (2010), OPA email re: VIP Hollywood Guest – Claire Danes, sent by George Little December 17th. See spyculture.com.

135   S.133 – Intelligence Authorization Act for Fiscal Year 2017, Section 308. 'Annual report.—Each report required by subsection (b)(2)(B) shall include the following: (1) A description of the nature and duration of each engagement included in the review. (A) The cost incurred by the United States Government for each such engagement. (B) A description of the benefits to the United States Government for each such engagement. (C) A determination of whether any information was declassified, and whether any classified information was improperly disclosed, or each such engagement. (D) A description of the work produced through each such engagement.'

136   Devine, Miranda (2010), Hit by the Leftie Sledgehammer, *Sydney Morning Herald*, 2nd January, p. 7.

137   Atzmon, Gilad (2009), Avatar and Humanism in Hollywood, *Pacific Free Press*, 30th December *www.pacificfreepress.com/.../5286–avatar–and–humanism–in–hollywood.html*.

138   See, for example, Medved, Michael (2009), '*Avatar* Offers Stunning Style, Inane Substance', December 23rd, www.townhall.com/blog/g/6e844544–e105–4cc2–89ce–0e90a341d1a0.

139   Leader, Michael (2009), Avatar: producer Jon Landau interview, *Den of Geek*, 17th December, www.denofgeek.com/movies/383132/avatar_producer_jon_landau_interview.html.

140   Ibid.

141   Thottam, Jyoti (2010), Echoes of *Avatar*: Is a Tribe in India the Real–Life Na'vi?, *Time*, 13th February. www.time.com/time/world/article/0,8599,1964063,00.html#ixzz0ij205PqG. Also Survival International, email correspondence with author, 18th March 2010.

142   Survival International (2012), Email to Matthew Alford, 28th June.

143   Baar, Aaron (2009) McDonald's Ties Avatar To Big Mac Promo, *Marketing Daily*, 10th December, www.mediapost.com/publications/?fa=Articles.showArticle&art_aid=118900.

144   *Fox Business* (2009), James Cameron the Impact of *Avatar*, 18th December video.foxbusiness.com/v/3953732/james–cameron–the–impact–of–avatar/?playlist_id=87066.

145   US Marine Corps (2009), ELO report, May 1st.

146   US Marine Corps (2010), ELO report, February 12th.

241

147 US Army (2011), ELO report, 18th July.
148 Bowden, Mark (2002), *Black Hawk Down*, New York: Corgi Books, pp. 54–7.
149 Ibid., p. 42.
150 Ibid., pp. 49–50.
151 Ibid., p. 116.
152 Ibid., pp. 110–14; 143–4.
153 Ibid., pp. 72, 77.
154 Ibid., p. 115.
155 Ibid., p. 319.
156 Ibid., p. 476.
157 Waal, Alex de (1998), US War Crimes in Somalia, *New Left Review*, Issue 230, July–August www.newleftreview.org.ezp2.bath.ac.uk/?view=1962.
158 Lancaster, John (1992) For Marine Corps, Somalia Operation Offers New Esprit; Mission Could Generate "Good News" As Service Confronts Shrinking Budgets, *Washington Post*, December 6th, p. A34.
159 Nelan, Bruce W. (1992), Taking on the Thugs, *Time Magazine*, December 14th, p. 29; Lancaster (1992), For Marine Corps, Somalia Operation Offers New Esprit, p. A34.
160 Fineman, Mark (1993), The Oil Factor in Somalia, *LA Times*, January 18th www.netnomad.com/fineman.html.
161 Bowden, Mark (2002), *Black Hawk Down*, p. 110.
162 Schmitt, Eric (1993), Somali War Casualties May Be 10,000, *New York Times*, December 8th, p. A14.
163 *BBC News Online* (2002), Warlord Thumbs Down for Somalia Film, January 29th www.news.bbc.co.uk/1/hi/world/africa/1789170.stm.
164 Gray, Geoffrey (2002), Activists Protest No. 1 Movie: "Black Hawk" Damned, February 6th–12th, www.banadir.com/damned.shtml.
165 Ibid.
166 The DVD commentary reveals the film–makers considered adding a caption to this effect.
167 Robb (2004), *Operation Hollywood*, p. 91.
168 Ibid., p. 93.
169 Ibid., p. 228.
170 Bowden (2002), *Black Hawk Down*, p. 119.
171 Ibid.
172 *The Essence of Combat: Making Black Hawk Down* (2002) www.imdb.com/title/tt0367710/.
173 Kozaryn, Linda D. (2002), 'Army Declares "Black Hawk Down" "Authentic"', *Department of Defence News* www.defenselink.mil/news/newsarticle.aspx?id=43855.
174 Johnston, David (2003), 'Charlie Wilson's War': Arming the Mujahedeen, May 25th.

175   Ressner, Jeffrey (2007), Political Movies Can Tweak the Truth, *Politico.com*, December 19th, www.politico.com/news/stories/1207/7477.html.

176   Crile, George (2007), *Charlie Wilson's War*, Atlantic Books, p. 212.

177   Edmund McWilliams (2009), Email to Matthew Alford, 11th December.

178   Rozen, Laura (2007), Hollywood and the CIA: The Spook Stays in the Picture, *Mother Jones* www.motherjones.com/politics/2007/12/hollywood–and–cia–spook–stays–picture.

179   Sorkin, Aaron (2005), Draft script for *Charlie Wilsons War*, pp. 55–57.

180   Ibid., p. 138

181   Ressner, Jeffrey (2007), 'Political Movies Can Tweak the Truth', *Politico*, December 19th.

182   *Le Nouvel Observateur* (1998), 'The CIA's Intervention in Afghanistan: Interview with Zbigniew Brezezinski', January 15th–21st, transcript at www.globalresearch.ca/articles/BRZ110A.html.

183   Sorkin (2005), p. 132–3; Sorkin, Aaron (2006), Draft script for *Charlie Wilson's War*, pp. 124–5.

184   *Investors Business Daily* (2007), Reagan's War, Not Charlie Wilsons, Issues and Insights, Editorials, 26 December, p. A10. The editorial thought that the film should have congratulated Republicans for the Afghan campaign, namely Reagan, Under–Secretary of Defense Fred Ikle, CIA Director William Casey and Senator Gordon Humphrey.

185   Jenkins, Trisha (2009), How the Central Intelligence Agency works with Hollywood, *Media Culture and Society*, p. 492.

186   DOD database, entry on *Contact*.

187   Goldenberg, Michael (1995), Draft screenplay of *Contact*, September 8th, pp. 45-46.

188   Ibid., p. 64.

189   Ibid., p. 56.

190   Suid (2002), p. 588.

191   Devlin, Dean, DVD commentary for *Independence Day*.

192   Robb (2004), *Operation Hollywood*, pp. 67-70.

193   Emmerich, Roland, DVD commentary for *Independence Day*.

194   Lilley, Kevin (2016), Celebs join soldiers for 'Independence Day: Resurgence' screening, *Army Times*, June 22nd.

195   DOD database, entry on *Whiskey Tango Foxtrot*.

196   Power, Samantha (2001), Bystanders to Genocide, *The Atlantic*, September www.theatlantic.com/doc/200109/power–genocide.

197   Taylor, Charles (2004), Eyes Wide Shut, *Salon.com*, 22nd December, www.salon.com/entertainment/movies/review/2004/12/22/hotel_rwanda.

198   Gourevitch, Philip G. (1999), *We Wish to Inform You that Tomorrow we will be Killed with our Families*, London: Picador. The book was funded by the United States Institute for Peace, which was established by Congress. See

www.usip.org/resources/we–wish–inform–you–tomorrow–we–will–be–killed–
our–families–stories–rwanda.
199	French, Howard (2004), *A Continent for the Taking*, New York: Knopf,
p.243.
200	Taylor, Phil (2005), Hotel Rwanda: No room for the truth, *Taylor
Report*, January 17ᵗʰ, www.taylor–report.com/articles/index.php?id=11. See
also Dr. Barrie Collins (2014) *Rwanda 1994: The Myth of the Akazu Genocide*,
Palgrave.
201	McGreal, Chris (2006), French judge accuses Rwandan president of
assassination, *The Guardian*, 22 November,
www.guardian.co.uk/world/2006/nov/22/france.rwanda; Fergal Keane (2006),
Will we ever learn the truth about this genocide?, *The Independent*, 22nd
November, www.independent.co.uk/opinion/commentators/fergal–keane–will–
we–ever–learn–the–truth–about–this–genocide–425257.html.
202	Simon Robinson and Vivienne Walt (2006), 'The Deadliest War in the
World', *Time*, May 28th,
www.time.com/time/magazine/article/0,9171,1198921,00.html; International
Rescue Committee (2006), '*The Lancet* Publishes IRC Mortality Study from DR
Congo; 3.9 Million Have Died: 38,000 Die per Month', January
www.theirc.org/news/page–27819067.html.
203	Da Silva, Steven (2007), 'Revisiting the "Rwanda Genocide"', *Center
for Research on Globalization*, June 1st,
www.globalresearch.ca/index.php?context=va&aid=5848>; Chossudovsky,
Michel (2006), 'The Geopolitics Behind the Rwanda Genocide', *Center for
Research on Globalization*, November 23rd,
www.globalresearch.ca/index.php?context=viewArticle&code=20061123&articl
eId=3958.
204	Rusesabagina, Paul and Zoellner, Tom (2006), *An Ordinary Man: An
Autobiography*, New York: Viking Adult, p. 199.
*205	Taylor Report*, 'Letter protests Kagame visit to England', December
2nd, www.taylor–report.com/articles/index.ph p?id=28.
206	Taylor (2004), Eyes Wide Shut.
207	Mitchell, Houston (2013), Dennis Rodman says FBI wants to use him
as an informant, *LA Times*, April 16th.
208	Grow, Kory (2014), Dennis Rodman's North Korea Visit Inspires
Comedy Movie 'Diplomats', *Rolling Stone*, February 24ᵗʰ.
209	Ryall, Julian (2014), North Korea 'threatens war' over Hollywood Kim
Jong-un comedy film, *The Telegraph*, June 26th.
210	Secker has made repeated FOIA requests to the FBI for files on their
investigation of the Sony Pictures hack. The response has always been that no
such documents exist. His most recent was submitted February 2nd 2017,
reference number 1367519-000.
211	Seal, Mark (2015), An Exclusive Look at Sony's Hacking Saga, *Vanity
Fair*, February 4th.

212   Klein, Rich (2014), "The Interview" really does subvert North Korea's regime, *Washington Post*, December 24th.

213   Emails between Marisa Liston and Keath Weaver Re, The Interview / Set Visit Recap. Sony emails, available via https://wikileaks.org/sony/emails/emailid/106084.

214   Itzkoff, Dave (2014), James Franco and Seth Rogen talk about *The Interview*, *New York Times*. December 16th

215   Shaw, Tony and Jenkins, Tricia (2017) An Act of War? The Interview Affair, the Sony Hack, and the Hollywood–Washington Power Nexus Today, *Journal of American Studies*, 1-27.

216   Itzkoff, James Franco and Seth Rogen talk about *The Interview*.

217   Agence France-Presse (2015), Balloon activist sends 'thousands of copies' of *The Interview* to North Korea, April 8th.

218   Email from Bruce Bennett to Michael Lynton, Sony emails, available here: https://wikileaks.org/sony/emails/emailid/128396. The official was Daniel Russel, Assistant Secretary of State for East Asian and Pacific Affairs.

219   Brody, Richard (2014), How "The Interview" Handled the Assassination of Kim Jong-Un, *The New Yorker*, December 18th.

220   Eells, Josh (2014), Seth Rogen's 'Interview': Inside the Film North Korea Really Doesn't Want You to See, Rolling Stone, December 17th.

221   USMC (2002), script notes for *The Hulk*, February 3rd.

222   Ibid.

223   James G. Lewis; James G. Lewis on Smokey Bear in Vietnam. *Enviro Hist Durh N C* 2006; 11 (3): 598-603. doi: 10.1093/envhis/11.3.598

224   Pentagon email (sender and recipient redacted), February 4th 2002, in USMC folder on *The Hulk*

225   Respectively, Franklin, Garth (2008), Iron Man, May 2nd, www.darkhorizons.com/reviews/423/Iron–Man; *Chicago Sun Times* (2008), Downey steels the show as irrepressible "Iron Man"; Comic fans won't be only satisfied customers, May 1st, p. 33; Rickey, Carrie (2008), Superhero Genre Welded into a New Form, *Philadelphia Inquirer*, May 2nd, p. W8; Bradshaw, Peter (2008), 'Scrap metal: Robert Downey Jr's Iron Man is a cheerfully unpretentious addition to the superhero pantheon. Unfortunately, it's also rather disposable', *Guardian*, May 2nd, 'Film and Music' section, p. 7; Partridge, Des (2008), 'Hardcore hero', *Daily Telegraph* (Australia), May 1st, p. 43.

226   Miles, Donna (2007), Edwards team stars in 'Iron Man' superhero movie, *American Forces Press Service*, May 2nd.

227   Draft screenplay for *Iron Man* by Alfred Gough and Miles Millar, Revisions by David Hayter, October 21st 2004, pp. 17 and 23. Secker discovered this early draft online when looking into why the film was in development for several years and still didn't have a finished screenplay when they started shooting.

228   Ibid,, pp. 89–90.

229   Quigley, Samantha L (2015), To Tap Into the Military's Arsenal, Hollywood Needs the Pentagon's Blessing, *On Patrol*, December 16th.

230   Draft screenplay for *Iron Man*, p. 90.

231   DOD–Hollywood collaboration database entry on *Iron Man 2*.

232   USMC (2010), ELO report, May 14th.

233   US Army (2011), ELO report, April 4th.

234   US Army (2010), ELO report, December 28th.

235   Ackerman, Spencer (2012), Pentagon Quit The Avengers Because of its 'Unreality'.

236   Bell, Chris (2013), White House Down: how Roland Emmerich was snubbed by the Pentagon, *The Telegraph*, September 12th.

237   Strub, Phil (2012), Interview on *The Kojo Nnamdi Show*, July 19th.

238   Megan Jacobs (2008), 'Connecting through *The Kingdom, The Jerusalem Post*, January 20th.

239   Ibid.

240   Ibid.

241   *ABC News*, (2007), Saudi Arabia under Hollywood spotlight, September 27th, www.abc.net.au/news/stories/2007/09/27/2044754.htm.

242   Shaheen, Jack G. (2008), *Guilty: Hollywood's verdict on Arabs after 9/11*, Olive Branch Press, pp. 128–131.

243   Cieply, Michael (2007), 'The Kingdom Gambles That Entertainment Can Trump Politics, *New York Times*, June 19th.

244   *Danieleagan.com* (2006), Interview: Peter Berg on *The Kingdom*. danieleagan.wordpress.com/2007/09/07/interview–peter–berg–on–the–kingdom/ January.

245   Paul Fischer (2007), Berg On New Terrorism Thriller, *Film Monthly*, September 5th, www.filmmonthly.com/Profiles/Articles/PeterBergKingdom/PeterBergKingdom .html.

246   Ibid.

247   *Danieleagan.com* (2006), Interview: Peter Berg on *The Kingdom*. danieleagan.wordpress.com/2007/09/07/interview–peter–berg–on–the–kingdom/ January.

248   *Lone Survivor*, Marcus Luttrell and Patrick Robinson, p.119.

249   How Accurate is Lone Survivor?, Michael and Eric Cummings, Slate.com, January 10th 2014.

250   *Lone Survivor* Production Notes, Universal Pictures.

251   Strub, Phil (2012), email re: Joint Lone Survivor Notes, July 4th 2012.

252   DOD (2012), script notes on *Lone Survivor*, June 3rd.

253   Phil Strub (2012), email re: revised Lone Survivor script, July 18th.

254   US Army (2012), ELO report, November 13th.

255   US Army (2012), ELO report, October 31st.

256   US Army (2014), ELO report, June 12th.

257   US Army (2011), ELO report, 8th–14th February.

258   Kurie, Brendan (2016), Q&A: An exclusive interview with screenwriter of 'Patriots Day', southcoasttoday.com, December 16th.

259   Studio Briefing (2000), 'Yemen Calls for Boycott of *Rules of Engagement*', April 21st imdb.com/news/sb/2000–04–21#film4.

260   CAIR Media Release (2000), Rules of Engagement Stereotypes Muslims', April 11th.

261   DVD Commentary: *Rules of Engagement.*

262   Quotes from USMC (2000) script notes on Rules of Engagement.

[263] USMC (2000) script notes on Rules of Engagement.

264   Klawans, Stuart (2000). 'Semper Fi, But Why?', *The Nation*, May 1st www.thenation.com/docprint.mhtml?i=20000501&s=klawans.

265   Fisk, Robert (2005), *The Great War for Civilisation – The Conquest of the Middle East*, London: Fourth Estate, pp. 318–29.

266   James, Caryn (1991), A Warmer, Fuzzier Arnold, *New York Times*, 14 July, p. H9.

267   French, Sean (1996), *The Terminator*, London: BFI Modern Classics and University of California Press, pp. 37–9.

268   The Pentagon (2001), 'Nuclear Posture Review [Excerpts]', Submitted to Congress on 31 December 2001, 8 January 2002 www.globalsecurity.org/wmd/library/policy/DOD/npr.htm.

269   DOD database, entry on *Terminator: Salvation.*

270   Staff Sgt. Matthew Bates (2009), 'US Air Force, Kirtland provides Airmen, location for "Terminator Salvation"', 6 April, US Air Force website www.af.mil/news/story.asp?id=123139441.

271   Hoscik, Martin (2009), 'Terminator Salvation: Crew interview', Seeit.co.uk, 3 June www.seenit.co.uk/terminator–salvation–crew–interview/063517/.

272   Robb, (2004), *Operation Hollywood*, pp. 18–19.

273   Schlesinger Jr, Arthur (1965), *A Thousand Days: John F. Kennedy in the White House*, New York: Black Dog & Leventhal Publishers Inc.

274   Sorensen, Theodore C. (1965), *Kennedy*, New York: Harper & Row.

275   Morley, Morris (1987) *Imperial State and Revolution*, Cambridge, UK and New York: Cambridge University Press.

276   CIA Memorandum of 12 November 1962, cited by Gleijeses, Piero (2002), *Conflicting Missions: Havana, Washington, and Africa, 1959–76*, Chapel Hill: North Carolina University Press, p. 16.

277   White, Mark J. (2001), *The Kennedys and Cuba: The Declassified Documentary History*, revised edn, Chicago, IL: Ivan R. Dee Publishers.

278   Ibid., p. 71.

279   Ibid.

280   Garthoff, Raymond L. (1987), *Reflections on the Cuban Missile Crisis*, Washington, DC: Brookings Institution, p. 5.

281   Ibid., pp. 77–9, 108–109.

282   Gleijeses (2002), *Conflicting Missions*, p. 25.

283   Robb (2004), *Operation Hollywood*, p. 56.
284   Lloyd, Marion (2002), 'Soviets Close to Using A–Bomb in 1962, Forum is Told', *Boston Globe*, 13 October.
285   Haymann, David (2001) *A Woman named Jackie*, p. 796-319; 648.
286   White, Mark (2011) The Cinematic Kennedy: Thirteen Days and the Burnishing of an Image, in Iwan Morgan (2011) *Presidents in the Movies: American History and Politics on Screen*, Palgrave: Macmillan, p 144-5.
287   White in Morgan (2011), p. 146.
288   Hewitt, Chris (2006), Is it too soon for a film about 9/11? we ask, *Empire*, July, p. 100.
289   Ibid., p. 98.
290   *Federal News Service* (2005), 'Remarks by George W. Bush in a Conversation on Social Security (as released by the White House, Athena Performing Arts Center, Greece Athena Middle and High School, Rochester, New York', May 24th.
291   DOD (2005), Production Assistance Agreement for *United 93*.
292   Kermode, Mark (2006), Chaos and cock–up always trump conspiracy, *Guardian*, April 9th.
293   Air Force (2005) ELO report, October 31st.
294   Air Force (2005) ELO report, November 7th.
295   Air Force (2005) ELO report, December 16th.
296   Air Force (2006) ELO report, March 24th.
297   Lim, Dennis (2006) A Flight to Remember, *Village Voice*, April 18th.
298   Air Force (2006) ELO report, May 12th.
299   *Associated Press Worldstream* (2006), Bush watches "United 93" movie with relatives of those killed in hijacking.
300   *Associated Press Worldstream* (2006), Bush invites "United 93" families for White House screening of the Oliver Stone film.
301   *United 93: The Families and the Film* (2006) www.imdb.com/title/tt0899176.
302   Borger, Julian (2004), The Best Perk in the White House, *Guardian*, June 4th www.guardian.co.uk/film/2004/jun/04/1.
303   ABC News Online (2006), Bush likens "War on Terror" to WWIII, June 5th www.abc.net.au/news/newsitems/200605/s1632213.html.
304   Chossudovsky, Michel (2007), 'Slip of the tongue? Rumsfeld admits that "Flight 93" was shot down', video footage and transcripts, *Global Research*, 12 May www.globalresearch.ca/index.php?context=va&aid=5626.
305   DVD commentary.
306   *Film Review* (2006), Is it too Soon?, No. 671, Summer, p. 59.
307   *Daily News* (Los Angeles, CA) (1998), Levinson's Double Irony; Wag the Dog, Sphere, Two Wildly Different Filmmaking Experiences, February 13th, www.highbeam.com/doc/1G1–83810954.html.

308   Ahmed, Nafeez (2006), *The London Bombings: An Independent Inquiry*, Duckworth, 2005; Srebrenica: A 'Safe' Area, *Netherlands Institute of War Documentation*, 2002.

309   DVD commentary for *Wag the Dog*

310   *Gawker* (2013), Read the CIA's Hilarious Parody of Tom Clancy's Most Famous Book, February 10th.

311   The Hunt for Red October, *Empire*, March 1990.

312   *LA Times* (1992), MOVIES : Mr. Nice Guy Dives Back Into Action : Harrison Ford returns to the genre that made him a star. In 'Patriot Games,' he inherits the role of the CIA agent from Alec Baldwin, but the production is in trouble with author Tom Clancy, March 22nd.

313   CIA (1991) internal memo from Joe DeTrani to Robert Gates, November 12th.

314   *LA Times* (1992), Paramount to Reshoot 'Patriot Games' Ending: Movies: Studio to change climactic boat scene after test audiences complained about film's ambiguous finale, April 30th.

315   *LA Times* (1992) MOVIES : Mr. Nice Guy Dives Back Into Action, March 22nd.

316   The Spectator (2013), Will Boston still fund the Real IRA?, April 27th.

317   *The Guardian* (2003), Revealed: Five British spies inside IRA, 18th May.

318   Belfast Telegraph (2011), Half of all top IRA men 'worked for security services', December 21st.

319   Zhekova, Olga (2011), Strange Bedfellows: Cooperation between the Pentagon and Hollywood, Lehigh University, Theses and Dissertations, Paper 1328.

320   Robb (2004) *Operation Hollywood*, p. 35.

321   Ibid., p. 37.

322   Ballvé, Teo (2009), Mr. President: Don't Make Colombia Another Afghanistan, *The Progressive*, 9 August www.progressive.org/mpballve080909.html.

323   Amnesty International (1995), *Annual Report for Colombia* < www.amnestyusa.org/annualreport.php?id=A94484565573F40980256A0F005B B4CB&c=COL%20amnesty%201995.

324   Santiago, Daniel (1993), *The Harvest of Justice: The Church of El Salvador Ten Years after Romero*, New York: Paulist Press, p. 12.

325   Jake Hamilton interview with Ben Affleck and Tony Mendez, https://www.youtube.com/watch?v=WW6Woa87ePQ.

326   Hearing of the Senate Armed Services Committee, April 8th 2003.

327   *NY Times* (2002), When Hollywood's Big Guns Come Right From the Source, June 10th.

328   Hamburg, Eric (ed.) (1995), *Nixon: An Oliver Stone Film*, London: Bloomsbury, p. 90.

329   *Federal News Service* (1992), 'Hearing of the Legislation and National Security Subcommittee of the House Government Operations Committee Subject: H.J Res 454, Assassination Materials Disclosure Act of 1992 Chaired by Representative John Conyers (D–MI)', Capitol Hill Hearing, May 15th.

330   Thomas, Cal (2006), 'World Trade Center' is a world class movie, July 20th townhall.com/columnists/CalThomas/2006/07/20/world_trade_center_is_a_world_class_movie.

331   Halbfinger, David M. (2006), 'Odd bedfellows align to market film about 9/11', *New York Times*, July 27th, p. A1

332   The film does not mention Afghanistan or al–Qaeda, which leaves it open to the interpretation that Iraq was responsible for 9/11.

333   Rich, Ruby B. (2007), 'Out of the Rubble', *Sight and Sound*, June 27th www.bfi.org.uk/sightandsound/feature/49320.

334   Friend, Tad (2001), 'Oliver Stone's Chaos Theory', *The New Yorker*, October 22nd, p. 25.

335   Wolf, Jaime (1997), 'Stoning Oliver; Director a target whatever he films', *Plain Dealer* (Cleveland, OH), October 5th, p. 11.

336   Wolf, Jaime (1997), Oliver Stone Doesn't Want to Start an Argument, *New York Times*, September 21st, p. F54.

337   Ibid.

338   Ibid.

339   Friend (2001), 'Oliver Stone's Chaos Theory'.

340   Said, S.F. (2003), 'Shooting Castro', *Daily Telegraph*, September 23rd www.telegraph.co.uk/culture/film/3603193/Shooting–Castro.html.

341   Galloway, Stephan (2016) Oliver Stone Reveals Clandestine Meetings With Edward Snowden, NSA Worries, *Hollywood Reporter*, March 8th, www.hollywoodreporter.com/news/oliver-stone-reveals-clandestine-meetings-873770.

342   Ibid.

343   Ibid.

344   Galloway, Stephan (2016) Oliver Stone on Edward Snowden: "America Is Fed Bullshit and We Buy It" (Q&A), The Hollywood Reporter, September 7th, www.hollywoodreporter.com/news/oliver-stone-edward-snowden-america-925611.

345   Elizabeth Gordon, Salvador: Too Hot for US Distribs, The Film Journal vol 89 issues 1-6, p. 36

346   Marshall, Kingsley (2011), Oliver Stone's Improbable W., in Iwan W. Morgan (2011), p 180.

347   www.independent.co.uk/arts-entertainment/films/news/oliver-stone-writers-guild-awards-speech-donald-trump-a7590041.html.

348   Verhoeven, Director's Cut DVD commentary for *Robocop*.

349   DOD database, entry on *Robocop*.

350   Davison, Director's Cut DVD commentary for *Robocop*.

351   Verhoeven, DVD commentary for *Total Recall*.

352   Schwarzenegger, DVD feature *Imagining Total Recall*.

353   Verhoeven, *Imagining Total Recall*.

354   *Entertainment Weekly* (1990), The 101 Most Powerful People in Entertainment, Entertainment Weekly, November 2nd.

355   US Army (2012) ELO report, February 22nd to 28th.

356   DOD database, entry on *Whiskey Tango Foxtrot*.

357   Paul Verhoeven, *The Close Up*, podcast of the Film Society Lincoln Center, March 2nd 2017. Verhoeven gave a pair of very candid and funny interviews to introduce screenings of *Robocop* and *Starship Troopers*.

358   Ebert, Roger (1997), *Starship Troopers*, November 7th, rogerebert.com.

359   Maslin, Janet (1997), CRITIC'S NOTEBOOK; Invading Theaters: Bugs, Drugs And Thugs, New York Times, November 27th; Rosenberg, Scott (1997), Melrose vs. the monsters, Salon, November 7th.

360   Marsh, Calum (2013), *Starship Troopers*: One of the Most Misunderstood Movies Ever, The Atlantic, November 7th - 'But you can feel the conversation beginning to shift; it rightfully has come to be appreciated by some as an unsung masterpiece. Coming in at number 20 on *Slant Magazine*'s list of the 100 best films of the 1990s last year (a poll in which, full disclosure, I was among the voting critics), the site's Phil Coldiron described it as "one of the greatest of all anti-imperialist films," a parody of Hollywood form whose superficial "badness" is central to its critique. It fared well in *The A.V. Club's* '90s poll, too, appearing in the top 50, where it was praised as a "gonzo satire destined, even *designed*, to be misunderstood."'

361   Tobias, Scott (2010), Starship Troopers, AV Club, June 10th.

362   Paul Verhoeven, *The Close Up*.

363   Ibid.

364   The majors were so keen on Pentagon support that when their Hollywood liaison Phil Strub found his job under threat as part of an 'overall downsizing' of Department of Defence spending, production executives were up in arms and Jack Valenti wrote to Defence Secretary William Cohen to campaign, successfully, for Strub to remain in post. Two years later, and possibly to show their gratitude, the Pentagon spent $295,000 hosting a star-studded dinner in Valenti's honour, where he received the first ever Citizen Patriot Award. At the ceremony Cohen said, 'Valenti has been an avid proponent of the men and women in uniform, and has used his influence to perpetuate the positive image of the military both on and off screen.' Similarly, the Writers Guild of America, which claims to fight for the creative rights of its members, has never complained about Pentagon interference and David Robb found that one of its presidents, Charles Holland, was a former Army officer and writer for *JAG* who wholeheartedly endorsed Pentagon involvement.

365   Ebert, Roger (2006), I Knew I Would Lose Friends Over This Film, *Sunday Telegraph*, January 1st, 'News Review and Comment' section, pp. 14–15.

366   Reich, Walter (2006) Something's Missing in Spielberg's Munich, *Washington Post*, January 1st.

367   *The Age* (2006), Spielberg donates $US1m to Israeli relief August 10th, http://www.theage.com.au/news/people/spielberg-directs-aid-to-israel/2006/08/10/1154803000553.html

368   Cockburn, Andrew and Cockburn, Leslie (1992), *Dangerous Liaison: The Inside Story of the US–Israeli Covert Relationship*, New York: Harper Perennial; Cockburn, Leslie (1987), *Out of Control: The Story of the Reagan Administration's Secret War in Nicaragua, the Illegal Arms Pipeline, and the Contra Drug Connection*, New York: Atlantic Monthly Press; Cockburn, Andrew (2007), *Rumsfeld: An American Disaster*, London: Verso.

369   Roger Stahl argues that this theme has intensified as the weapon's-eye-view has become more prominent in public culture. The figure of the drone pilot is archetypal in this regard. Stahl, Roger. Through the Crosshairs: The Weaponized Eye in Public Culture. Newark: Rutgers UP (2017). *Good Kill* (2014), *Eye in the Sky* (2015) are the main ones. *Zero Dark Thirty* (2012) and *Homeland* (S4E1, 2014) do not feature the drone pilot per se but the basic character looking through the drone sight is the same. Empathetic but subject to forces beyond (usually) her control. should say that ZDT and Homeland set the tone as officially supported productions. The other two, including the sleeper Drones (2013), are independent and supposedly "critical" but reproduce the same themes.

370   Lyman, Rick (2000) Media Talk: Changes at Fox Studio End Pax Hollywood, *New York Times*, June 26th; *Hollywood Reporter* (2011) Media Bigwigs Wish Rupert Murdoch a Happy 80th Birthday, 11th March.

371   Ross, Steven J. (2011) *Hollywood Left and Right: How Movie Stars Shaped American Politics*, Oxford UP, p. 349

372   Brière, Elaine (2014), email to Matthew Alford, 17th February.

373   Ibid.

374   Segrave, Kerry (2004) *Product Placement in Hollywood Films: A History*, McFarland and Company p. 180.

375   Goettler, Ronald L. and Leslie, Phillip (2005) Cofinancing to Manage Risk in the Motion Picture Industry, *Journal of Economics & Management Strategy*, Volume 14, Issue 2, June 2005, pp. 231–261.

376   Lehu, Jean-Marc (2007) *Branded Entertainment: Product Placement & Brand Strategy in the Entertainment Business*, Kogan Page.

377   Bignell, Paul and Dunne, Lauren (2013), Superman is already a $170m brand superhero as *Man of Steel* tops the product placement charts, *Independent*, 10th June, http://www.independent.co.uk/arts-entertainment/films/news/superman-is-already-a-170m-brand-superhero-as-

man-of-steel-tops-the-product-placement-charts-8651215.html (19th September 2014).

378   According to Owner of Weapons Specialists Utd Rick Washburn the Desert Eagle 'owes almost everything' about its success to being placed in the movies. Washburn explains: 'Here's a gun that has very little practical usage. It's too big and heavy. There's not much of a market for handgun hunting'. See Hornaday, Ann (1999) *Hamilton Spectator* (Ontario, Canada) January 23rd Weekend, p. W9.

379   Commercial and marketing concerns continue to compromise the creative freedom of film-makers. While writing and casting *Doctor Strange* (2016) Marvel changed the character of The Ancient One from a Tibetan man to a Celtic woman, and cast British actress Tilda Swanton in the part. Screenwriter C. Robert Cargill explained that this was about appealing to the Chinese government and film market, saying, 'If you acknowledge that Tibet is a place and that he's Tibetan, you risk alienating one billion people, and risk the Chinese government going, "Hey, you know one of the biggest film-watching countries in the world? We're not going to show your movie because you decided to get political"'. Other aspects of the film also seem to have been aimed at the increasingly lucrative Chinese audience, including a major set piece set in Hong Kong, the product placement of Chinese smartphones and the fact that *Doctor Strange* debuted in China. As a result *Doctor Strange* took over $100 million in China alone, the highest of any foreign market.

        This decision was widely criticised on the grounds that they could have changed the character in other ways, for example making him Chinese and casting a Chinese actor. Director Scott Derrickson defended the change as being in favour of diversity, saying, 'I think diversity is the responsibility of directors and producers. In this case, the stereotype of [the Ancient One] had to be undone. I wanted it to be a woman, a middle-aged woman. Every iteration of that script played by an Asian woman felt like a "Dragon Lady". I'm very sensitive to the history of "Dragon Lady" representation and Anna May Wong films. I moved away from that. Who's the magical, mystical, woman with secrets that could work in this role? I thought Tilda Swinton.' Likewise writer Jon Spaihts echoed this, saying, 'We were looking for opportunities to have not only ethnic diversity, but to have gender diversity in the film'. See: Yee, Lawrence (2016), 'Doctor Strange' Cast Addresses Whitewashing Controversy at Film's World Premiere, *Variety*, October 21st. Similarly, *Iron Man III* has Chinese doctors save Iron Man, *Independence Day: Resurgence* has China and the US team up to fight the aliens. See also: www.today.com/video/china-s-influence-on-hollywood-is-growing-changing-the-films-you-see-883181123530

380   Bart, Peter (2001) The monster that ate hollywood, April, PBS Frontline, www.pbs.org/wgbh/pages/frontline/shows/hollywood/

381   Lancaster, David (2005) Product Placement in Hollywood Films: A History (review), *Film and History: An Interdisciplinary Journal of Film and Television Studies*, Volume 35, Issue 2, p. 95–96.

382   Hamad, Marwa (2016), A look back at 'Star Trek Beyond', *Dubai, Gulf News*, July 20th.

383   Elliott, Stuart (1997), 'Reebok's Suit Over *Jerry Maguire* Shows Risks of Product Placement', *New York Times*, February 7th.

384   Andrews, Marke (2005), How companies get their products onto the screen: North Shore firm negotiates with studios for placement in movies, TV shows, *The Vancouver Sun*, February 4th, 'Business BC' section, p. G1

385   *Entertainment Weekly* (1997), 'Sneaky Business', January 24th, No. 363 www.ew.com/ew/article/0,,286552,00.html.

386   Churnin, Nancy (2000), 'Tiny Titan A.E's opening shows merchandising makes kind movies', *Dallas Morning News*, June 28th.

387   Black, Lewis (2003), 'More McCanlies, Texas', *The Austin Chronicle*, September 19th, www.austinchronicle.com/gyrobase/Issue/story?oid=oid:178259.

388   Puig, Claudia (1999), Family-friendly concept crashes as "Giant Falls to Earth", *USA Today*, August 30th, 'Life' section, p. 4D.

389   York, Anthony (2001), The Product Placement Monster that E.T. spawned, *Salon.com*, April 26th, dir.salon.com/tech/feature/2001/04/26/product_placement/index.html.

390   Conlogue, Ray (2001), Why Can't Hollywood kick the habit?, *Globe and Mail* (Canada), 'Globe Review' section, February 13th, p. R1; Wetzstein, Cheryl (1990), 'Tobacco companies decide to stop smoking up the silver screen', *Washington Times*, 20 December, p. C1; Booth, Jenny (2003), "Give smoking in films an X-certificate" say doctors, *Sunday Telegraph*, July 27th, p. 8.

391   Andrew Molchan, Director of the National Association of Federally Licensed Firearms dealers, America's largest association of firearms retailers, estimates that the gun industry gets 90 per cent of its advertising through TV and movies, all for free. Magnum Research, producers of the Desert Eagle pistol has placed guns in hundreds of movies. The poster for *Last Action Hero* was changed to include a Desert Eagle gun after flagging ticket sales, though Schwarzenegger peculiarly defended himself by commenting 'I don't pick myself as a role model … I don't run around every day with a gun in my hand.' Well, true - not every day, just every movie. See Granados, Oriana de (2003), 'Selling Guns at the Box Office', *Christian Science Monitor*, October 6th, 'Opinion' section, p. 9; Hornaday, Ann (1999), 'Guns and Movies: An Uneasy Relationship', *The Star Ledger*, February 15th, p. 29. Owner of Weapons Specialists Utd Rick Washburn explained of the Desert Eagle pistol, 'Here's a gun that has very little practical useage. It's too big and heavy. There's not much of a market for handgun hunting. So I would say the success of that particular weapon owes almost everything to the movies.' See Hornaday, Ann (1999), 'Hollywood and the gun: Firearms companies get free publicity but it can blow up in their faces', *Hamilton Spectator*, January 23rd, p. W9. Up-to-date research on this matter is lacking.

392   Murphy, Tim (2013), How Hollywood Made the Gunmakers' Day, *Mother Jones*, January 10th.

393   McKay, Hollie (2014), How Hollywood helps Gunmakers sell their guns, *Fox News*, March 25th.

394   Moore, Michael (1998) *Adventures in a TV Nation*, New York: HarperCollins, p. 3.

395   Ibid, p. 10.

396   Moore, Michael (1995) TV Nation Newsletter, December 15th, Dog Eat Dog Films.

397   Moore, Michael (1997) TV Nation Newsletter January 29th.

398   Silverman, David (2007) *You Can't Air That*, New York: Syracuse UP, p. 131.

399   Rutenberg, Jim (2004), Disney Is Blocking Distribution of Film That Criticizes Bush, *New York Times*, May 5th.

400   Finke, Nikki (2004), 'When Might Turns Right – Golly GE, Why Big Media is Pro-Bush', *LA Weekly*, October 1st-7th.

401   Moore, Michael (2011) *Here Comes Trouble*, Grand Central Publishing.

402   Thompson, Anne (2008). Buyers waiting for *Che*, *Variety*, May 19th; Taubin, Amy (2008), Guerrilla Filmmaking on an Epic Scale, *Film Comment*, September-October.

22496918R00147

Printed in Great Britain
by Amazon